New ENTERPRISE A2

Teacher's Book

Jenny Dooley

Express Publishing

Published by Express Publishing

**Liberty House, Greenham Business Park, Newbury,
Berkshire RG19 6HW, United Kingdom**
Tel.: **(0044) 1635 817 363**
Fax: **(0044) 1635 817 463**
email: **inquiries@expresspublishing.co.uk**
www.expresspublishing.co.uk

© Jenny Dooley, 2018

Design and Illustration © Express Publishing, 2018

First published 2018
Third impression 2021

Made in EU

All rights reserved. No part of this publication may be reproduced, stored in a retrieval system, or transmitted in any form, or by any means, electronic, photocopying, or otherwise, without the prior written permission of the publishers.

This book is not meant to be changed in any way.

ISBN 978-1-4715-6968-5

Contents

Introduction to the Teacher		p.	5
Unit 1	Lifestyles	p.	9
Unit 2	Shop till you drop	p.	18
Unit 3	Survival stories	p.	26
Values A	Diversity	p.	34
Public Speaking Skills A		p.	35
Unit 4	Planning ahead	p.	36
Unit 5	Food, glorious food!	p.	44
Unit 6	Health	p.	52
Values B	Volunteering	p.	59
Public Speaking Skills B		p.	60
Unit 7	Stick to the rules!	p.	61
Unit 8	Landmarks	p.	69
Unit 9	Live and let live	p.	77
Values C	Good citizenship	p.	85
Public Speaking Skills C		p.	86
Unit 10	Holiday time	p.	87
Unit 11	Join in the Fun!	p.	95
Unit 12	Going online!	p.	103
Values D	Cooperation	p.	111
Public Speaking Skills D		p.	112
CLIL A	History	p.	113
CLIL B	Food Preparation & Nutrition	p.	114
CLIL C	Science	p.	115
CLIL D	Art & Design	p.	116
Student's Book Audioscripts		p.	117
Evaluations		p.	123
Workbook key		p.	142
Workbook Audioscripts		p.	157
Grammar Book key		p.	161

Introduction to the Teacher

New Enterprise A2 is a modular course for young adults and adults studying British English at CEFR Level A2. It allows flexibility of approach, which makes it suitable for classes of all kinds, including large or mixed ability classes.

New Enterprise A2 consists of twelve units. Each unit consists of three lessons plus Culture sections, Reviews & Competences. The corresponding unit in the Workbook provides the option of additional practice.

COURSE COMPONENTS

Student's Book

The **Student's Book** is the main component of the course. Each unit is based on specific themes and the topics covered are of general interest. All units follow the same basic structure (see **Elements of the Coursebook**).

Workbook

The **Workbook** is in full colour and contains units corresponding to those in the Student's Book, with practice in Vocabulary, Grammar, Everyday English & Reading. There is a Revision Section every three units for students to revise the vocabulary and grammar taught. There is also a Skills Practice section for students to get more practice in Listening, Everyday English, Reading and Writing. All the exercises in the Workbook are marked with graded level of difficulty (*, **, ***).

Teacher's Book

The **Teacher's Book** contains step-by-step lesson plans and suggestions on how to present the material. It also includes answers to the exercises in the Student's Book, the audioscripts of all the listening material, suggested speaking and writing models, and evaluation sheets as well as the answers to the exercises in the Workbook and Grammar book.

Class Audio CDs

The Class Audio CDs contain all the recorded material which accompanies the course. This includes the monologues/dialogues and texts in the Listening and Reading sections as well as the Pronunciation/Intonation sections in the Student's Book, and the material for all listening tasks in the Workbook.

IWB

The IWB contains all the material in the Student's Book, Teacher's Book, Workbook, Grammar Book and Audio CDs and aims to facilitate lessons in the classroom. It also contains grammar presentations of all the grammar structures in the Student's Book as well as **videos** closely linked to the texts in the course and activities for Ss to further practise their English and expand their knowledge, as well as **games** for students to revise the vocabulary and grammar taught.

Digibook applications

The **Digi apps** contain all the material in the Student's Book, Workbook and Grammar Book and help students monitor their progress and improve their stats which are stored so that they can be accessed at any time.

Grammar Book

The Grammar Book contains clear, simple presentations of all grammar structures that appear in the course with a variety of graded exercises.

ELEMENTS OF THE COURSEBOOK

Each unit begins with a brief overview of what will be covered in the unit.

Each unit contains the following sections:

Vocabulary

Vocabulary is introduced in a functional and meaningful context. It is practised through a variety of exercises such as picture-word association and completing set phrases in order to help students use everyday English correctly.

Reading

Each unit contains reading texts, such as: articles, blog entries, postcards, emails, etc. These allow skills such as reading for gist and reading for specific information to be systematically practised.

Grammar

The grammar items taught in each unit are first presented in context, then highlighted and clarified by means of clear, concise theory boxes. Specific exercises and activities methodically reinforce learners' understanding and mastery of each item. The Workbook contains practice on each grammar structure presented within each unit. Detailed explanations of all grammar points and exercises are in the Grammar Bank.

Listening

Learners develop their listening skills through a variety of tasks which employ the vocabulary and grammar practised in the unit in realistic contexts. This reinforces learners' understanding of the language taught in the unit.

Speaking

Controlled speaking activities have been carefully designed to allow learners' guided practice before leading them to less structured speaking activities.

Everyday English

Functional dialogues set in everyday contexts familiarise students with natural language. The dialogues are followed by language boxes to help learners practise.

Pronunciation/Intonation

Pronunciation/Intonation activities help learners to recognise the various sounds of the English language, distinguish between them and reproduce them correctly.

Writing

There are writing activities throughout the units, based on realistic types and styles of writing, such as emails, letters, blogs, postcards, stories, articles, etc. These progress from short sentences to paragraphs and finally to full texts, allowing learners to gradually build up their writing skills.

Culture

Each unit is accompanied by a *Culture* section.

In each *Culture* section, learners are provided with cultural information about aspects of English speaking countries that are thematically linked to the unit. Learners are given the chance to process the information they have learnt and compare it to the culture of their own country.

Study Skills

Brief tips, explanations and reminders, at various points throughout each unit, help learners to develop strategies which improve holistic learning skills and enable them to become autonomous learners of the English language.

Review

This section appears at the end of each unit, and reinforces students' understanding of the topics, vocabulary and structures that have been presented in the unit. A *Competences* marking scheme at the end of every Review section allows learners to evaluate their own progress and identify their strengths and weaknesses.

Values

This section aims to develop moral values learners need to have in our globalised world.

Public Speaking Skills

This section aims to help learners develop their public speaking skills, giving them guidance on how to become competent public speakers.

CLIL

The *CLIL* sections enable learners to link the themes of the units to an academic subject, thus helping them contextualise the language they have learnt by relating it to their own personal frame of reference. Lively and creative tasks stimulate learners and allow them to consolidate the language they have learnt throughout the units.

Each *CLIL* section is aimed to be taught after the corresponding Values & Public Speaking Skills sections.

Irregular Verbs

This provides students with a quick reference list for verb forms they might be unsure of at times.

SUGGESTED TEACHING TECHNIQUES

A   Presenting new vocabulary

Much of the new vocabulary in *New Enterprise A2* is presented through pictures (*see Student's Book, Unit 2, p. 16, Ex. 1*).

Further techniques that you may use to introduce new vocabulary include:

- **Miming.** Mime the word you want to introduce. For instance, to present the verb sing, pretend you are singing and ask learners to guess the meaning of the word.
- **Synonyms, opposites, paraphrasing, and giving definitions.** Examples:
  - present the word **strong** by giving a synonym: 'powerful'.
  - present the word **strong** by giving its opposite: 'weak'.
  - present the word **weekend** by paraphrasing it: 'Saturday and Sunday'.
  - present the word **famous** by giving its definition: 'very well-known (person or thing)'.
- **Example.** Use of examples places vocabulary into context and consequently makes understanding easier. For instance, introduce the words **city** and **town** by referring to a city and a town in the learners' country: 'Rome is a city, but Parma is a town.'
- **Sketching.** Draw a simple sketch of the word or words you want to explain on the board. For instance:

tall

short

- **Use of L1.** In a monolingual class, you may explain vocabulary in the learners' native language. This method, though, should be employed in moderation.
- **Use of a dictionary.** In a multilingual class, learners may refer to a bilingual dictionary.

The choice of technique depends on the type of word or expression. For example, you may find it easier to describe an action verb through miming than through a synonym or a definition.

> **Note:** ✓ sections can be treated as follows: Go through the list of words after Ss have read the text and ask Ss to explain the words using the context they appear in. Ss can give examples, mime/draw the meaning, or look up the meaning in their dictionaries.

B Choral & individual repetition

Repetition will ensure that learners are thoroughly familiar with the sound and pronunciation of the lexical items and structures being taught and confident in their ability to reproduce them.

Always ask learners to repeat chorally before you ask them to repeat individually. Repeating chorally will help learners feel confident enough to then perform the task on their own.

C Reading & Listening

You may ask learners to read and listen for a variety of purposes:

- **Reading for detail.** Ask learners to read for specific information. *(See Student's Book, Unit 1, p. 4, Ex. 3. Ss will have to read the text in order to do the task. They are looking for specific details in the text and not for general information.)*
- **Listening for detail.** Learners listen for specific information. *(See Student's Book, Unit 1, p. 8, Ex. 3)*
- **Listening and reading for gist.** Ask learners to read and/or listen to get the gist of the dialogue or text being dealt with. *(See Student's Book, Unit 2, p. 18, Ex. 1. Tell Ss that in order to complete this task successfully, they do not need to understand every single detail in the text.)*

> **Note:** ▶ VIDEO
> Main texts in the Student's Book are accompanied by videos that are included in the digi applications and the IWB. The videos can be watched after learners have read the texts. Activities that accompany the videos can be done in class or assigned as HW.

D Speaking

- Speaking activities are initially controlled, allowing for guided practice *(see Student's Book, Unit 1, p. 7, Ex. 5 where Ss use the same structures to act out exchanges.)*.
- Ss are led to free speaking activities. *(See Student's Book, Unit 1, p. 8, Ex. 4b where Ss are provided with the necessary lexical items and structures and are asked to act out their dialogues.)*

E Writing

All writing tasks in *New Enterprise A2* have been carefully designed to closely guide learners to produce a successful piece of writing. They are fully analysed in the *Skills in Action* sections in the Student's Book with model texts and exercises that aim to help learners improve their writing skills.

- Make sure that Ss understand that they are writing for a purpose. Go through the writing task so that Ss are fully aware of why they are writing and who they are writing to *(see Student's Book, Unit 3, p. 25, Ex. 10. Ss are asked to write a blog entry.)*.
- It would be well-advised to actually complete the task orally in class before assigning it as written homework. Ss will then feel more confident with producing a complete piece of writing on their own.

F Assigning homework

When assigning homework, prepare learners as well as possible in advance. This will help them avoid errors and get maximum benefit from the task.

Commonly assigned tasks include:

Copy – learners copy an assigned extract;

Dictation – learners learn the spelling of particular words without memorising the text in which they appear;

Vocabulary – learners memorise the meaning of words and phrases or use the new words in sentences of their own;

Reading Aloud – assisted by the digi apps, learners practise at home in preparation for reading aloud in class;

Writing – after thorough preparation in class, learners are asked to produce a complete piece of writing.

G Correcting learners' work

All learners make errors – it is part of the learning process. The way you deal with errors depends on what the learners are doing.

- **Oral accuracy work:**
  Correct learners on the spot, either by providing the correct answer and allowing them to repeat, or by indicating the error but allowing learners to correct it. Alternatively, indicate the error and ask other Ss to provide the answer.

- **Oral fluency work:**
  Allow learners to finish the task without interrupting, but make a note of the errors made and correct them afterwards.

Written work:

Do not over-correct; focus on errors that are directly relevant to the point of the exercise. When giving feedback, you may write the most common errors on the board and get the class to attempt to correct them.

Remember that rewarding work and praising learners is of great importance. Praise effort as well as success.

H   Class organisation

- **Open pairs**
  The class focuses its attention on two learners doing the set task together. Use this technique when you want your learners to offer an example of how a task is done (see Student's Book, Unit 1, p. 7, Ex. 5).

- **Closed pairs**
  Pairs of learners work together on a task or activity while you move around offering assistance and suggestions. Explain the task clearly before beginning closed pairwork. (See Student's Book, Unit 1, p. 8, Ex. 4b)

- **Stages of pairwork**
  - Put Ss in pairs.
  - Explain the task and set a time limit.
  - Rehearse the task in open pairs.
  - In closed pairs, get Ss to do the task.
  - Go around the class and help Ss.
  - Open pairs report back to the class.

- **Group work**
  Groups of three or more Ss work together on a task or activity. Class projects or role play are most easily done in groups. Again, give Ss a solid understanding of the task in advance.

- **Rolling questions**
  Ask Ss one after the other to ask and answer questions based on the texts.

I   Using L1 in class

Use L1 in moderation and only when necessary.

ABBREVIATIONS

Abbreviations used in the Student's and Teacher's Books.

T	Teacher	p(p).	Page(s)
S(s)	Student(s)	e.g.	For example
HW	Homework	i.e.	That is
L1	Students' native language	etc	Et cetera
		sb	Somebody
Ex(s).	Exercise(s)	sth	Something

Key to symbols used in the Student's/Teacher's Books

🎧 audio

👥 pairwork

💬 groupwork

✅ words to be explained using the context each appears in

ICT research

Study Skills suggestions to help learners become autonomous

Writing Tip suggestions to help learners develop their writing skills

THINK sections to develop Ss' critical thinking skills

Culture texts to familiarise Ss with the culture of the English-speaking countries, and develop cross-cultural awareness

VALUES sections to help Ss develop critical thinking skills & values

CLIL Sections that link the themes of the units to a subject from the core curriculum

Lifestyles 1

Topic
In this unit, Ss will explore the topics of daily routines, free-time activities, appearance & character.

1a   Reading & Vocabulary   4-5
Lesson objectives: To listen for key information, to read for specific information, to learn prepositional phrases, to talk about daily routines, to act out an interview, to write a text comparing your daily life to an astronaut's **Vocabulary:** Daily routine & free-time activities *(meet friends; play video games, tennis, cards; watch a film, the news on TV; listen to music, the radio; have dinner, a shower, coffee, a lesson, breakfast; do my homework, the washing-up, the ironing, the housework; ride a bicycle, a motorbike; wash the dishes, the car, my clothes; go shopping, ice skating, fishing, to bed; read a book, a magazine, a newspaper)*; Noun *(shaving)*; Phrasal Verb *(take over)*; Adverbs *(aboard, fortunately)*

1b   Grammar in Use   6-7
Lesson objectives: To learn/revise the present simple, the present continuous and stative verbs, to learn/revise adverbs of frequency, to learn the use of *so/neither/nor* when agreeing/disagreeing, to act out dialogues, to write an email about their holiday

1c   Skills in Action   8-9
Lesson objectives: To learn vocabulary for describing people, to listen for specific information (multiple matching), to act out a dialogue and practise everyday English for introducing people, to learn intonation in homophones, to read for specific information, to write a blog entry **Vocabulary:** Appearance *(tall/short, plump/thin, dark/pale complexion, late/early thirties, thin/full lips, long/short/straight/wavy hair, young/old, of medium height, slim/well-built, dark brown/fair hair, moustache, freckles, middle-aged, overweight, wrinkles, bald, chubby, friendly smile)*; Character *(calm, kind, jealous, lazy, reliable, careful, clever, brave, friendly)*

Culture 1   10
Lesson objectives: To listen and read for specific information, to read for specific information, to talk and write about teen life in your country and in Ireland **Vocabulary:** Phrasal verb *(hang out)*; Verb *(contact)*; Adjective *(single-parent)*; Adverb *(outdoors)*

Review 1   11
Lesson objectives: To test/consolidate vocabulary and grammar learnt throughout the unit; to practise everyday English

Go through the objectives box and tell Ss that these are the topics, skills and activities this unit will cover.

1a
Reading

1 Aim To introduce the topic through pictures and subject-related vocabulary

- Ask Ss to look at the picture and read out the questions.
- Elicit what the Milky Way is and then elicit what Ss think life can be like on a space station.

Suggested Answer Key

The Milky Way is the galaxy that contains our Solar System.
I think life on a space station can be quite difficult but exciting. I think it can be difficult to do daily tasks without gravity.

Background Information

Mission Control is a facility that manages space flights, usually from the point of launch until landing or the end of the mission.

2 Aim To listen for key information

- Explain the task and ask Ss to read the sentences.
- Play the recording. Give Ss time to choose the correct answers.
- Check Ss' answers.

Answer Key

1 music   2 projects   3 work

- Give Ss time to look up the meanings of the words in the **Check these words** box in the Word List.
- Play the video for Ss and elicit their comments.

3 Aim To read for specific information (multiple choice)

- Ask Ss to read the questions and the answer choices and then give Ss time to read the text again and choose the correct answers.
- Check Ss' answers.

Answer Key

1 A   2 C   3 A   4 C

- Then give Ss time to look up the meanings of the words in bold in the Word List or in their dictionaries and elicit definitions from Ss around the class.

1

Suggested Answer Key

mission (n): an expedition into space
towel (n): an absorbent cloth
involve (v): to have or include sth as a part
equipment (n): the necessary item or items for a purpose
spacesuit (n): a special type of clothing worn in space
break (n): a pause in work
admire (v): to like/enjoy sth

4 **Aim** To consolidate new vocabulary

- Ask Ss to read out the words in the list and then give them time to use them to complete the phrases.
- Check Ss' answers and then elicit sentences using the phrases from Ss around the class.

Answer Key

1 space	4 typical	7 science
2 daily	5 running	8 short
3 crew	6 ordinary	

Suggested Answer Key

Astronauts work on a space station.
The crew members have a daily routine.
A typical day for an astronaut includes science projects.
There is no running water on the space station.
Astronauts work in their ordinary clothes.
Astronauts have a short break for lunch.

Prepositions

5 **Aim** To practise prepositional phrases

- Explain the task and give Ss time to complete the phrases.
- Check Ss' answers and then elicit sentences using the phrases from Ss around the class.
- Ask Ss to memorise these prepositional phrases and revise them in the next lesson.

Answer Key

2 in	4 on	6 to	8 by
3 on	5 for	7 to	

Suggested Answer Key

Astronauts go on missions in space. They work on science projects on a space station in orbit around the Earth. Sometimes they go on a spacewalk. They have a short break for lunch and then they go back to work. In their free time they can listen to music or sit by the window and enjoy the amazing view.

Vocabulary

6 **Aim** To present and practise vocabulary relating to daily routines & free-time activities

- Explain/Elicit the meanings of any unknown words and explain the task.
- Do the first couple of items as examples and then give Ss time to complete the task.
- Check Ss' answers around the class.

Answer Key

1 play	5 meet	9 wash
2 ride	6 watch	10 do
3 go	7 have	
4 read	8 listen to	

7 **Aim** To practise new vocabulary and talk about daily routines and free-time activities

- Read the instructions aloud and check that Ss understand the task.
- Ask various Ss around the class to say what they do every day/weekend.
- Ask Ss to discuss their habits and everyday experiences in pairs.
- Then ask some Ss to share their answers with the class.

Suggested Answer Key

I have lunch at 1 o'clock every day. I go shopping every weekend. I don't like playing tennis. I hate washing the dishes. I don't mind washing the car. I like watching films.

8 **Aim** To consolidate new vocabulary

- Explain the task and give Ss time to complete it.
- Check Ss' answers.

Answer Key

1 crew	2 team	3 club	4 staff

Speaking & Writing

9 a) **Aim** To make notes from a text

- Write the headings on the board and help Ss to find references in the text to routine activities. Use Ss' responses to make notes under the headings and then have Ss copy the notes into their notebooks.
- Ask various Ss to use the notes to talk about a typical day in the life of an astronaut on a space station.

Suggested Answer Key

the morning: *wake up, wash, have breakfast, get messages, shave, brush teeth, start work, do science projects, check systems, sometimes go on a space walk*
the afternoon: *take a break for lunch, go back to work*
the evening: *have dinner, relax, video call families, read books, listen to music, admire the view, go to bed*

b) Aim To act out an interview based on an information in a text

- Explain the task and have Ss use their answers in Ex. 9a to help them.
- Have Ss complete the task in closed pairs.
- Walk around the class and monitor the activity and then ask some pairs to act out their interview in front of the rest of the class.

Suggested Answer Key

Interviewer: *What do you do when you get up?*
Astronaut: *I wash, have breakfast, shave, brush my teeth, get messages from Mission Control and start work.*
Interviewer: *What work do you do in space?*
Astronaut: *I do science projects, check the systems and sometimes go on a space walk.*
Interviewer: *What do you do at lunchtime?*
Astronaut: *I have a short break and then I go back to work.*
Interviewer: *What do you do in the evenings?*
Astronaut: *I have dinner and relax. I video call my family and listen to music.*

10 Aim THINK To write a text comparing two people's typical days

- Ask Ss to write a short text comparing their daily life to the daily life of an astronaut using their answers from Exs 7 and 9.
- Give Ss time to complete the task and then ask various Ss to present their text to the class.

Suggested Answer Key

Mission Control wakes astronauts on a space station up with music. My alarm clock wakes me up. An astronaut washes, has breakfast, brushes his/her teeth, gets messages from Mission Control and starts work. I have a shower and have breakfast and then go to college.
An astronaut works on science projects and checks systems, but I go to lessons. Astronauts have a short break at lunchtime, like me.
In the evenings, an astronaut has dinner and relaxes. I have dinner and relax in the evenings, too. Astronauts also listen to music in the evenings. I listen to music in the evenings and I sometimes watch TV or go online.

1b Grammar in Use

1 Aim To present/revise the present simple and the present continuous

- Present the present simple. Say: *I go to college.* Write it on the board.
- Underline *go* and explain that this verb is in the present simple. Point to a S, say: *You go to college.* Then write it on the board. Underline *go*. Point to another S, say: *He/She goes to college.* Then write it on the board. Underline *goes*. Gesture to yourself and the class, say: *We go to college.* Then write it on the board. Underline *go*. Point to a group of Ss, say: *They go to college.* Then write it on the board. Underline *go*.
- Explain that we use the present simple for habits & routines (actions we do every day), permanent states (an action we do all the time) and timetables. Explain that we form the present simple in the affirmative with personal pronoun + bare infinitive, in the negative with personal pronoun + the auxiliary verb **do** + **not** + bare infinitive, and in the interrogative with the auxiliary verb **do** + personal pronoun + bare infinitive.
- Present the present continuous.
- Explain that we form the present continuous affirmative with subject pronoun/noun + **am/is/are** + main verb + **-ing**. We form the present continuous negative with subject pronoun/noun + **am not/isn't/aren't** + main verb + **-ing**. We form the present continuous interrogative with **am/is/are** + subject pronoun/noun + main verb + **-ing** and we form short answers with **Yes/No, I am [not]/he/she/it is[n't]/we/you/they are [not]**.
- Explain that we use this tense to talk about actions which are happening now and for fixed arrangements in the near future.
- Ask Ss to read the theory.
- Then give Ss time to read the email and ask Ss to match the uses to the tenses in bold.
- Check Ss' answers and then elicit two examples of stative verbs from the email.
- As an extension ask Ss to give more examples for each use.

Answer Key

habits/routines/repeated actions = 4, 5, 6
permanent states = 7, 9
timetable = 10
action happening at the moment of speaking = 3, 11
fixed arrangements in the near future = 8
actions happening around the time of speaking = 1, 2
Stative verbs = love, like

1

2 **Aim** To practise the present simple and the present continuous

- Explain the task and give Ss time to complete it.
- Check Ss' answers.

Answer Key

1. do you do (routine)
2. likes (state)
3. Do you want (state)
4. plays (routine)
5. is raining (action happening at the moment of speaking)
6. are getting (fixed arrangement in the near future)
7. leaves (timetable)
8. are staying (action happening around the time of speaking)
9. lives (permanent state)
10. don't want (stative verb)

3 **Aim** To practise the present simple and the present continuous

- Explain the task and give Ss time to complete it.
- Check Ss' answers.
- Then elicit the tenses of the verbs 1-13 and their uses from Ss around the class.

Answer Key

1. are (present simple, permanent state)
2. am (present simple, permanent state)
3. is (present simple, permanent state)
4. do (present simple, permanent state)
5. am (present simple, permanent state)
6. are (present continuous, action happening around the time of speaking)
7. am (present continuous, action happening around the time of speaking)
8. are (present continuous, action happening around the time of speaking)
9. do (present simple, stative verb)
10. isn't (present simple, permanent state)
11. do (present simple, stative verb)
12. does (present simple, repeated action)
13. are (present simple, permanent state)

4 **Aim** To present/practise adverbs of frequency

- Ask Ss to read out the grammar box and then read the list of activities.
- Explain/Elicit the meanings of any unknown words and then ask various Ss around the class to tell the rest of the class how often they do the activities.

Suggested Answer Key

I always make my bed every day.
I rarely do the washing-up.
I never cook.
I sometimes do online shopping.
I often go to the gym.
I hardly ever do the ironing.

Speaking

5 **Aim** To practise the present simple and the present continuous

- Ask two Ss to read out the example. Ss ask and answer in pairs using the pictures and the prompts and the correct form of the present simple and present continuous following the example.
- Monitor the activity around the class and then ask some pairs to ask and answer in front of the class.

Suggested Answer Key

A: Where does Glen live?
B: He lives in Australia.
A: Is he married?
B: No, he isn't.
A: What does he do?
B: He's a mechanic.
A: What does he do at work?
B: He fixes cars.
A: What is he doing now?
B: He's playing tennis.

A: Where does Marie live?
B: She lives in France.
A: Is she married?
B: No, she isn't. She's divorced.
A: What does she do?
B: She's a doctor.
A: What does she do at work?
B: She treats sick people.
A: What is she doing now?
B: She's cutting flowers. / She's gardening.

A: Where does Hans live?
B: He lives in Germany.
A: Is he married?
B: Yes, he is.
A: What does he do?
B: He's a lawyer.
A: What does he do at work?
B: He advises people about the law.
A: What is he doing now?
B: He's fishing.

6 **Aim** To present *so/neither/nor* when agreeing-disagreeing

Present the grammar table. Check Ss' understanding by asking individual Ss to agree with the first thing you say, (e.g. "I like orange juice." – "So do I.") and agree in a negative meaning with the second thing you say *(e.g. "I don't wear glasses." – "Neither/Nor do I.")*.

7 a) Aim To practise *so/neither/nor* when agreeing/disagreeing

Give Ss two minutes to fill in the missing words. Play the recording. Ss listen and check their answers.

Answer Key

1 So
2 Neither
3 do
4 don't

b) Aim To practise *so/neither/nor* when agreeing - disagreeing

- In open pairs, then in closed pairs, Ss act out dialogues similar to the models in the S's book, using adverbs of frequency with the prompts given.
- Check Ss' performance around the class.

Suggested Answer Key

A: I always walk to college/work.
B: So do I. / Oh, really? I don't.
A: I often go to the gym in my free time.
B: I don't. I hate going to the gym.
A: I sometimes hang out with friends after college/work.
A: So do I.
A: I don't do the housework at weekends.
A: Neither/Nor do I.

8 Aim To practise the present simple and the present continuous

- Explain the task and give Ss time to complete it.
- Check Ss' answers and elicit reasons.

Answer Key

1 are you (state)
2 am (state)
3 are staying (action happening around the time of speaking)
4 visit (repeated action)
5 go (repeated action)
6 are visiting (action happening now)
7 isn't raining (action happening now)
8 is buying (action happening now)
9 am having (action happening now)
10 wants (state)
11 are going (fixed arrangement in the near future)
12 are coming (fixed arrangement in the near future)

9 Aim To write an email about their holiday

- Explain the task and give Ss time to write their email including all the points in the directions.
- Then ask various Ss to read out their emails to the class. Alternatively, assign the task as HW and have some Ss' read out their emails in the next lesson.

Suggested Answer Key

Hi John,
How are you? I am on holiday in Rome with Phoebe and Victor. We are staying at a beautiful hotel in the city centre. Every morning, we visit famous sights and then we go out to eat. The food here is amazing. Right now, we are sitting in a café. Phoebe is drinking a hot chocolate and Victor is eating cake. Tonight, we are going on a trip to the theatre. We are really looking forward to it. We are coming back on Friday.
Hope you are OK. See you soon.
Angie

1c Skills in Action

1 Aim To present vocabulary for describing people

- Ask Ss to look at the pictures and read the text under each one and give them time to choose the correct items in bold to match the people in the pictures.
- Elicit answers from Ss around the class.

Answer Key

A
1 short
2 plump
3 pale
4 early
5 full
6 long
7 wavy

B
1 young
2 height
3 slim
4 wavy
5 brown
6 moustache

C
1 in his late seventies
2 tall
3 thin
4 thin
5 wrinkles
6 bald
7 smile

Optional activity

Choose one of your classmates. The rest of the class ask questions to find out who the person is, as in the example.

S1: Is it a male?
L: Yes, he is.
S3: Has he got ...?
L: Yes, he has.
S2: Is he ...?

L: No, he isn't.
S4: Is it ...?
L: Yes, you're right. It is ...

2 **Aim** **To present vocabulary for character**

- Read aloud each of the adjectives in the left-hand column. Ss repeat, chorally and individually.
- Give Ss three minutes to match the items, then ask individual Ss to use the adjectives to make sentences about people they know well.

Answer Key

kind: always helps others
jealous: want things others have
lazy: not like hard work
reliable: do what you say you will do
careful: rarely makes mistakes
clever: learn new things quickly
brave: not be afraid of anything
friendly: like talking to people

Suggested Answer Key

Steve is very friendly. He likes talking to people.
Ann is very careful. She rarely makes mistakes.
John is very lazy. He doesn't like hard work.
Jane is very kind. She always helps others.
David can be jealous. He wants things others have.
Darren is very reliable. He always does what he says he will do.
Kim is very clever. She learns new things quickly.
Kelly is very brave. She isn't afraid of anything!

Listening

3 **Aim** **To listen for specific information (multiple matching)**

- Explain that some people believe one's favourite colour reveals one's character. Read aloud the words in the columns and explain/elicit the meaning of any unknown vocabulary.
- Play the recording. Ss listen and complete the task.
- Check Ss' answers.

Answer Key

1 E   2 D   3 A   4 B   5 C

Everyday English

4 a) **Aim** **To match dialogues to situations**

- Give Ss time to read the dialogues 1-3 and then play the recording. Ss listen and match the dialogues to the situations.
- Check Ss' answers.

Answer Key

1 c   2 b   3 a

b) **Aim** **To act out dialogues introducing people**

- Play the recording again, asking Ss to pay close attention to the speakers' intonation. Ss listen, then act out the dialogues, first in open groups of three, then in closed groups.
- Encourage Ss to reproduce the intonation of the speakers on the recording.
- Write this diagram on the board for Ss to follow.

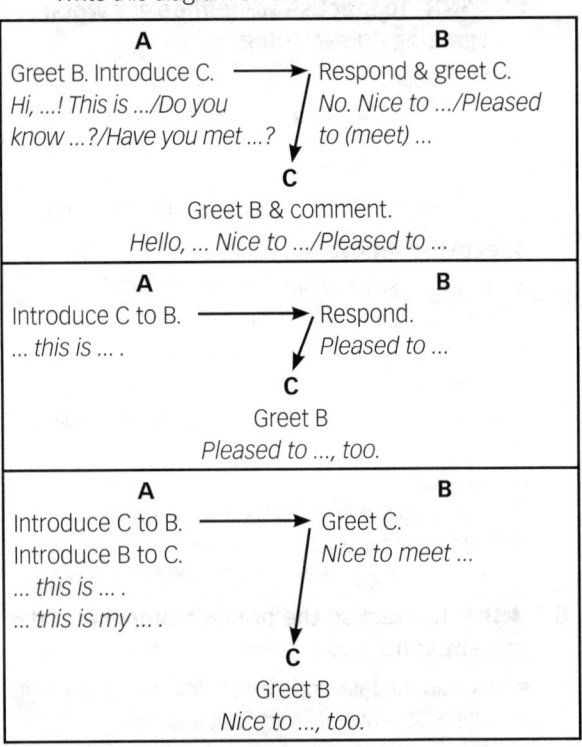

A	B
Greet B. Introduce C. →	Respond & greet C.
Hi, ...! This is .../Do you know ...?/Have you met ...?	No. Nice to .../Pleased to (meet) ...
C	
Greet B & comment.	
Hello, ... Nice to .../Pleased to ...	

A	B
Introduce C to B. →	Respond.
... this is	Pleased to ...
C	
Greet B	
Pleased to ..., too.	

A	B
Introduce C to B. →	Greet C.
Introduce B to C.	Nice to meet ...
... this is	
... this is my	
C	
Greet B	
Nice to ..., too.	

- Monitor the activity around the class and offer assistance as necessary.
- Then ask some pairs to act out their dialogues in front of the class.

Suggested Answer Key

A: Hi, James! This is Carl. Carl, do you know James?
B: No. Nice to meet you, James.
C: Hello, Carl. Nice to meet you, too.

A: Susan, this is my business partner, John Smith.
B: Pleased to meet you, Mr Smith.
C: Pleased to meet you too, Susan.

A: Grandma, this is my friend, Jane. Jane, this is my Grandma.
B: Nice to meet you, Jane.
C: Nice to meet you, too.

Pronunciation

5 **Aim** To identify homophones

- Remind Ss that, in English, words that are spelt differently may sound the same, and vice versa.
- Play the recording. Ss listen and circle the odd word out. Check Ss' answers around the class, then play the recording again. Ss listen and repeat, chorally and individually.

Answer Key

1 we're   2 she   3 hair   4 now

Reading & Writing

6 **Aim** To read for specific information

Read out the Writing Tip and then direct Ss to the text and give them time to read it and answer the question.

Answer Key

sociable – likes meeting her friends, can be talkative at times – the other person can't get a word in

7 **Aim** To identify key information; to complete a spidergram

- Ask Ss to copy and complete the spidergram in their notebooks according to the text.
- Check Ss' answers on the board.

Answer Key

comments/feelings: she makes me feel happy, she's a real friend

name: Sally

relationship: flatmate

interests: exercising, riding her bike, running

my favourite person

age: late twenties

character: sociable, talkative

appearance: pretty, slim, long straight brown hair, brown eyes, freckles

8 **Aim** To practise joining sentences describing appearance

- Explain the task and read out the example and then give Ss time to rewrite the sentences using the words in brackets.
- Check Ss' answers around the class.

Answer Key

2 He's short and plump with brown eyes.
3 She's got short, curly, dark brown hair and full lips.
4 Pam's got short, straight, fair hair and blue eyes.
5 He's tall and well-built with short, fair hair.

9 **Aim** To expand vocabulary related to people

- Explain the task and give Ss time to complete the sentences using the correct words from the list.
- Check Ss' answers.

Answer key

1 listens   3 loves   5 needs
2 supports   4 knows

10 **Aim** To write a blog entry

- Explain the task and give Ss time to copy the spidergram from Ex. 6 and complete it with information about their favourite person.
- Then give Ss time to write their blog entry using the completed spidergram and the plan to help them.
- Check Ss' answers.
- Alternatively, assign the task as HW and check Ss' answers in the next lesson.

Suggested Answer Key

comments/feelings: he makes me laugh, he's a great friend

name: Simon

relationship: best friend

interests: swimming, football

my favourite person

age: 19

character: funny, lazy

appearance: handsome, slim, short curly brown hair, brown eyes

Gail's blog

My favourite person is my best friend, Simon. He's studying to be a lawyer and I really admire him.
Simon is 19 and he's very handsome. He's slim with short curly brown hair and brown eyes. He's got a great smile.
Simon is funny and can make anyone laugh. He's a bit lazy at times, though, and he doesn't like hard work, but he's a great person.
In his free time, Simon loves swimming and playing football. He's a great team player.
Simon makes a difference in my life because he always makes me laugh. He's a great friend. Who's your favourite person?

1

Values

Ss try to explain the quotation in their mother tongue. If Ss have difficulty, explain the quotation. Ask Ss to memorise this quotation and check in the next lesson.

The quotation means we should form good habits when we are young so we can grow into good people.

Culture 1

Listening & Reading

1 **Aim** To read for specific information
- Ask Ss to read the text quickly.
- Elicit two things that are the same in Ss' country.

Suggested Answer Key

Teens in my country like watching films. They also love playing sports.

2 **Aim** To recall information from a text

Play the recording and elicit answers from Ss around the class.

Suggested Answer Key

Irish teens are similar to many teens. Traditional Irish families are big. Irish teens love playing sports such as football and hockey. They also play traditional sports and they like going to festivals.

3 **Aim** To read for specific information
- Ask Ss to read the sentences 1-5 and then read the text again and mark them accordingly.
- Check Ss' answers.

Answer Key

1 DS   2 T   3 F   4 F   5 T

- Give Ss time to look up the meanings of the words in bold in the Word List or in their dictionaries.
- Elicit definitions from Ss around the class.

Suggested Answer Key

band (n) = a music group
traditional (adj) = passed down from generation to generation
different (adj) = separate

- Give Ss time to look up the meanings of the words in the **Check these words** box in the Word List.
- Play the video for Ss and elicit their comments.

Speaking & Writing

4 **Aim** THINK To compare teen life in Ireland with teen life in your country
- Explain the task and give Ss time to think of comparisons between teen life in Ireland and in their country and write a few sentences.
- Ask various Ss around the class to read out their sentences.

Suggested Answer Key

Teenagers in Ireland like playing video games, shopping, watching films and hanging out with friends and teens in my country like doing those things too.
Traditional families in Ireland are bigger than traditional families in my country.
Teens in Ireland like playing sports and going to festivals and teens in my country like doing that too.

Review 1

Vocabulary

1 **Aim** To practise vocabulary for daily routines and free-time activities
- Explain the task.
- Give Ss time to complete it.
- Check Ss' answers.

Answer Key

1 C   3 D   5 J   7 I   9 B
2 G   4 A   6 H   8 E   10 F

2 **Aim** To practise vocabulary from the unit
- Explain the task.
- Give Ss time to complete it.
- Check Ss' answers.

Answer Key

1 chubby   4 full   7 build
2 reliable   5 dark   8 late
3 pale   6 bald

Grammar

3 **Aim** To practise *so/neither/nor*
- Explain the task.
- Give Ss time to complete it.
- Check Ss' answers.

Answer Key

1 So   3 do
2 Neither   4 don't

4 **Aim** **To practise the present simple and the present continuous**

- Explain the task.
- Give Ss time to complete it.
- Check Ss' answers.

Answer Key

1 Is she going, is visiting
2 Do you know, is watching
3 Do they live, are staying
4 is studying, start
5 washes, hates
6 has, is

Everyday English

5 **Aim** **To match exchanges**

- Explain the task.
- Give Ss time to complete it.
- Check Ss' answers.

Answer Key

1 D   3 A   5 B
2 C   4 E

Competences

Ask Ss to assess their own performance in the unit by ticking the items according to how competent they feel for each of the listed activities.

Optional activity

Ask Ss to prepare in groups a T/F quiz based on the information in the unit. Groups swap papers and do the quiz.
e.g.
　1　*Astronauts can't have showers in space. (T)*
　2　*There is running water in space. (F)*
　3　*Astronauts always wear spacesuits inside the space station. (F) etc.*

2 Shop till you drop

Topic
In this unit, Ss will explore the topics of shops and shopping, clothes, patterns and materials.

2a Reading & Vocabulary	12-13

Lesson objectives: To act out dialogues. To listen for specific information, to read for key information, to present Harrods, to design a department store
Vocabulary: Shops & services (*antique shop, baker's, bank, bookshop, butcher's, chemist's, department store, florist's, greengrocer's, grocer's, hair & beauty salon, jeweller's, newsagent's, post office, supermarket, travel agent's*); Nouns (*entrance, fire brigade, blanket, opportunity*); Phrases (*delivery service, official supplier, the sales*)

2b Grammar in Use	14-15

Lesson objectives: To learn/revise the past simple and *used to*, to learn/revise order of adjectives, to learn/revise comparisons

2c Skills in Action	16-17

Lesson objectives: To learn vocabulary for clothes – patterns & materials, to listen for specific information (multiple choice), to act out a dialogue and practise everyday English for describing lost property, to learn the pronunciation of silent letters, to read for gist, to write an email about a weekend break
Vocabulary: Clothes – patterns & materials (*patterned nylon tights, striped woollen cardigan, spotted silk scarf, checked cotton shirt, plain linen trousers, floral denim skirt, plain leather jacket*)

Culture 2	18

Lesson objectives: To listen and read for gist, to read for key information, to talk about Borough Market, to write about an old market in your country
Vocabulary: Noun (*storyteller, bank, produce, waste, producer*); Adverb (*beyond*); Adverb (*outdoors*); Phrase (*living history*)

Review 2	19

Lesson objectives: To test/consolidate vocabulary and grammar learnt throughout the unit; to practise everyday English

Go through the objectives box and tell Ss that these are the topics, skills and activities this unit will cover.

2a
Reading

1 **Aim** **To introduce vocabulary related to shops & services**

- Read aloud the name of each place. Ss repeat, chorally and/or individually. Explain/Elicit their meaning in Ss' mother tongue, or by asking for examples describing what you can buy at each place. Ss identify each shop shown in the pictures.
- Ask questions about each one.

e.g. Picture A
T: Where is the woman's shopping?
S1: In a shopping trolley.
T: What is she doing?
S2: She's putting something into it.
T: What can you see behind the woman?
S3: Shelves of food.
T: What kind of shop is this?
S4: I think it's a supermarket.

Answer Key

A supermarket	D chemist's
B greengrocer's	E travel agent's
C butcher's	F florist's

2 a) **Aim** **To practise vocabulary related to shops & services**

- Read aloud the list of items. Ss repeat, chorally and/or individually.
- Explain/Elicit the meaning of any unknown vocabulary. Give Ss time to complete the task.
- Check Ss' answers around the class.

Suggested Answer Key

*You can buy apples at a greengrocer's and a supermarket.
You can buy a plane ticket at a travel agent's.
You can buy old clocks at an antique shop.
You can buy a book at a bookshop and a newsagent's.
You can buy a comb at a supermarket and a hair & beauty salon.
You can buy a pair of trousers at a department store.
You can buy a diamond ring at a jeweller's.
You can buy flowers at a florist's and a supermarket.
You can buy an armchair at an antique shop.
You can buy grapes at a greengrocer's and a supermarket.
You can buy a bottle of perfume at a chemist's, a department store and a hair & beauty salon.
You can buy lamb chops at a butcher's.
You can buy a leather suitcase at a department store.*

You can buy stamps at a post office.
You can buy a woollen skirt at a department store.
You can buy a leather jacket at a department store.
You can buy a bouquet of roses at a florist's.
You can buy a magazine at a newsagent's and a supermarket.
You can buy sugar at a supermarket.
You can buy a gold necklace at a jeweller's.
You can buy a loaf of bread at a baker's and a supermarket.
You can buy medicine at a chemist's and a supermarket.

- Elicit suggestions of other items which can be bought at each of the places listed in Ex. 1.

Ss' own answers

b) Aim To match activities to services

- Read the task aloud. Give Ss time to complete it.
- Check Ss' answers around the class.

Answer Key

1 *You can book tickets at a travel agent's.*
2 *You can post a letter at a post office.*
3 *You can have a haircut at a hair and beauty salon.*
4 *You can send flowers at a florist's.*

Optional activity

Play in pairs or in teams. Say a sentence using words from Ex. 2a. The other person or team guesses where you are.
e.g. A: *Can I have some grapes, please?*
      B: *At the greengrocers's./At the supermarket.*

3 Aim To act out dialogues asking for things & responding

- In open pairs, then in closed pairs, Ss act out dialogues similar to the model in the S's book, using the prompts given.
- Check Ss' performance around the class.

Suggested Answer Key

A: *Could I have some green apples, please?*
B: *Certainly. How many would you like?*

A: *I'd like 12 chicken sausages, please.*
B: *I'm afraid we haven't got any left, but how about some beef sausages?*

A: *I'd like some cough medicine, please.*
B: *Yes, of course.*

A: *Have you got grapes?*
B: *Yes, of course.*

A: *Do you happen to have any red roses?*
B: *Sorry, no, but we've got these lovely pink ones.*

Reading

4 Aim To read for specific information

- Ask Ss to read the statements and guess which ones are true about Harrods.
- Then play the recording for Ss to listen and read and check.
- Check Ss' answers.

Answer Key

1 F   2 T   3 F   4 F   5 T

- Give Ss time to look up the meanings of the words in the **Check these words** box in the Word List.
- Play the video for Ss and elicit their comments.

5 Aim To consolidate new vocabulary

- Read the headings aloud, and point out that Ss should read the text again quickly to understand the gist of each paragraph.
- Give Ss time to read the text silently and fill in the headings next to the correct paragraphs. Check Ss' answers.
- Then elicit explanations for the word in bold.

Answer Key

A Location & Reputation
B History of the Store
C Departments & Services
D The Sales
E Recommendation

Suggested Answer Key

take over (phr v): *to take control of sth*
in addition to (phr): *as well as*
employ (v): *to give work to sb and pay them*
ordinary (adj): *plain, normal*
customer (n): *sb who buys sth from a shop/business*
hand out (phr v): *to distribute*
miss (v): *to fail to do sth*

6 Aim THINK To consolidate information in a text

- Read out the question and give Ss time to consider their answers.
- Elicit answers from Ss around the class.

Suggested Answer Key

Harrods is a popular tourist attraction because it is the most famous department store in the world. It is a landmark in London. Also, people like to see the famous doormen and get a famous Harrods green bag.

7 **Aim** To consolidate new vocabulary

- Explain/Elicit the meanings of any unknown words and explain the task.
- Give Ss time to complete the task.
- Check Ss' answers around the class.

Answer Key

1 security	3 hot	5 fire
2 delivery	4 tourist	6 January

Speaking

8 **Aim** To consolidate & present information in a text

Ask Ss to look at the headings in Ex. 5 again and then ask various Ss to use them to present Harrods to the class.

Suggested Answer Key

Harrods is a famous department store in Knightsbridge in London. In 1849, it was a small grocer's shop but it soon added more goods and a delivery service. It has got 300 departments and 4,000 staff including security guards and its own fire brigade.
The busiest time of the year is December and January. On the first day of the sales 300,000 people visit the store. For visitors to London Harrods is a must!

9 **Aim** To design a department store

- Divide the class into small groups and give Ss time to design their own department store including all the points mentioned.
- Then ask various groups to present their store to the class.
- Alternatively, assign the task as HW.

Suggested Answer Key

Babylon is a department store in Manhattan, New York. Its motto is 'Whatever you Want' and it sells anything and everything. It has 500 departments and it is open 24 hours a day, 363 days a year. It only closes on Christmas Day and New Year's Day.

2b Grammar in Use

1 **Aim** To present/revise the past simple and *used to*

- Present the past simple. Say: *I worked hard yesterday.* Write it on the board.
- Underline *worked* and explain that this verb is in the past simple. Point to a S, say: *You worked hard yesterday.* Then write it on the board. Underline *worked*. Point to another S, say: *He/She worked hard yesterday.* Then write it on the board. Underline *worked*. Gesture to yourself and the class, say: *We worked hard yesterday.* Then write it on the board. Underline *worked*. Point to a group of Ss, say: *They worked hard yesterday.* Then write it on the board. Underline *worked*.
- Explain that we use the past simple for past habits & states which don't exist anymore and an action that happened at a specific time in the past. Explain that we form the past simple in the affirmative with personal pronoun + past participle, in the negative with personal pronoun + **didn't/did not** + bare infinitive, and in the interrogative with **Did** + personal pronoun + bare infinitive.
- Present **used to**. Explain that we use **used to/ didn't use to** + bare infinitive for past habits & states which don't exist anymore.
- Ask Ss to read the theory.
- Then give Ss time to read the article and find examples.
- Then elicit the spelling rules for regular verbs in the past simple.

Answer Key

Examples: didn't use to have, had, bought, sold, was shouted, tried, didn't go, used to go

Most verbs take **-ed** to form their past simple form. Verbs ending in **-e** add **-d**. Verbs ending in consonant + **-y** lose **-y** and take **-ied**. Verbs ending in a vowel + **-y** add **-ed**). Verbs ending in a vowel + **l, p, k, b**, etc. double the consonant and add **-ed**.

2 **Aim** To identify irregular forms – to identify spelling rules for regular verbs in the past

- Explain the task and give Ss time to complete it.
- Check Ss' answers.

Answer Key

1 a	3 b	5 i	7 g	9 h	11 d
2 c	4 e	6 l	8 k	10 j	12 f

Irregular verbs: was/were, sang, bought, went, wrote, had, learnt, ate.

3 **Aim** To practise the past simple

- Explain the task and give Ss time to complete it.
- Check Ss' answers.

Answer Key

1 Did you get, travelled, came, had, bought
2 Did you go, got, met, forgot
3 Was the high street, were, owned

4 **Aim** To practise the past simple interrogative & short answers

- Ask Ss to ask and answer questions in closed pairs following the example and using the prompts.
- Monitor the activity around the class and then ask some Ss to ask and answer in front of the class.

Suggested Answer Key

A: Did you upload videos last night?
B: No, I didn't. I watched TV.

A: Did you go shopping last weekend?
B: Yes, I did.

A: Did you text a friend yesterday?
B: Yes, I did.

A: Did you eat pizza yesterday morning?
B: No, I didn't. I ate cereal.

5 a) **Aim** To practise *used to*

- Give Ss time to complete the task.
- Check Ss' answers around the class.

Answer Key

1 used to cost
2 didn't use to be
3 used to be
4 didn't use to drive
5 used to go
6 didn't use to buy
7 used to grow

b) **Aim** To practise *used to* using personal examples

Ask various Ss around the class to tell the rest of the class about what their grandparents used to/ didn't use to do when they were young.

Ss' own answers

6 **Aim** To present order of adjectives

- Read out the theory box and explain that opinion adjectives go before fact adjectives. Explain that fact adjectives follow a specific order when there are two or more of them.
- Ask Ss to make a note of the order of adjectives in their notebooks for future reference.
- Explain the task and go through the example.
- Give Ss time to complete the task and then check Ss' answers.

Answer Key

2 cotton 3 large 1 grey 2
3 heavy 1 metal 3 black 2
4 silk 3 blue 1 Japanese 2

7 **Aim** To describe objects and practise order of adjectives

- Read aloud the words labelling the objects, and check that Ss have understood their meaning correctly.
- Help individual Ss to describe a few of the objects. Ss continue the task in closed pairs.
- Alternatively, the task may be set as a written exercise.
- Check Ss' performance around the class.

Suggested Answer Key

It's a beautiful gold ring with small diamonds in it.
It's a big red ball with large white spots on it.
It's a large red travel bag with a side pocket, a long black strap and a zip.

- As an extension ask Ss to bring photos of various objects and describe them to the class.

8 a) **Aim** To present/revise the comparative and superlative

- Explain that we use the comparative/superlative to compare two or more people or things.
- Explain that comparatives show that sb/sth has more of the quality than sth/sb else and superlatives show that sb/sth has the most of a quality in a group.
- Explain that with one-syllable adjectives, we add *-(e)r* to form the comparative and *-(e)st* to form the superlative. With one-syllable adjectives ending in a vowel + constant we double the consonant. With two-syllable adjectives we form the comparative with more + adjective and the superlative with most + adjective. For two-syllable adjectives ending in a consonant *+y*, we replace *-y* with *-i* and add *-er/est*.
- Explain that there are irregular adjectives which do not follow these rules e.g. *good-better-the best*.
- Ask Ss to read the theory box and explain any points Ss are unsure of.

b) **Aim** To revise/practise the comparative/ superlative

- Direct Ss' attention to the table and give Ss time to complete it.
- Then elicit how we form the comparative and superlative forms of adjectives.
- Then elicit examples from the text on p.14.

Answer Key

Adjective	Comparative	Superlative
big	bigger than	the biggest
short	shorter than	the shortest
dry	drier than	the driest
large	larger than	the largest
expensive	more expensive than	the most expensive

With one-syllable adjectives, we add *-(e)r* to form the comparative and *-(e)st* to form the superlative.
With one-syllable adjectives ending in a vowel + constant we double the consonant.
With two-syllable adjectives we form the comparative with *more + adjective* and the superlative with *most + adjective*. For two-syllable adjectives ending in a consonant *+y*, we replace *-y* with *-i* and add *-er/est*. Irregular adjectives do not follow these rules.
Examples from text: *the most crowded and noisiest, lower*

9 **Aim** To practise the comparative/superlative
- Explain the task.
- Give Ss time to complete the task.
- Check Ss' answers.

Answer Key

1 largest
2 more
3 oldest
4 convenient
5 less
6 cheapest
7 better
8 worst
9 warm, lighter
10 most beautiful

10 **Aim** To practise the comparative/superlative

Explain the task. Give Ss time to complete it and then check Ss' answers.

Answer Key

Hillside Market is more convenient than Green Market, but Holland Market is the most convenient of all.
Green Market is more crowded than Holland Market, but Hillside Market is the most crowded of all.
Holland Market is larger than Green Market, but Hillside Market is the largest of all.

Optional activity

Ask Ss to compare various members in their family. Ss can use these adjectives: *tall, short, old, young, thin, long, kind, careful, reliable, friendly*.

2c Skills in Action
Vocabulary

1 **Aim** To present vocabulary for describing clothes – patterns & materials
- Ask Ss to look at the pictures and read the description of each item.
- Play the recording. Ss listen and repeat chorally and/or individually.
- Then ask Ss to write the headings in their notebooks and list the bold words under each one.
- Check Ss' answers on the board.

Answer Key

materials: *nylon, woollen, cotton, silk, linen, denim, leather*
patterns: *patterned, striped, checked, spotted, plain, floral*

2 **Aim** To describe clothes
- Ask Ss to write a short description of what a classmate is wearing including some of the words from Ex.1 including three mistakes.
- Then ask Ss to swap their descriptions with a partner and correct the mistakes.
- Ask some Ss to read out the corrected descriptions to the class.

Suggested Answer Key

Jane is wearing a ~~plain~~ floral shirt and a pair of ~~striped~~ denim jeans with a ~~leather~~ cotton jacket.

Listening

3 **Aim** To predict content; to listen for specific information (multiple choice)
- Ask Ss to look at the pictures and describe the pictures in as much detail as possible (e.g. floral denim pair of trousers, etc) then ask Ss to read the questions.
- Then explain/elicit the meaning of any unknown vocabulary.
- Play the recording. Ss listen and complete the task. Check Ss' answers. You can play the recording with pauses for Ss to check their answers.

Answer Key

1 B 2 C 3 A

Everyday English

4 a) **Aim** To predict the content of a dialogue
Ask Ss to read the first exchange in the dialogue and elicit their guesses as to what the problem is.

Suggested Answer Key

I think the problem is that the customer lost their bag.

b) Aim To listen for specific information

- Ask Ss to look at the pictures and elicit what each one shows provide any relevant vocabulary as necessary.
- Play the recording. Ss listen and find out which items were in the bag.
- Check Ss' answers.

Answer Key

purse, a pair of red woollen gloves, sunglasses

5 Aim To act out dialogues

- Explain the task and ask Ss to act out similar dialogues to the ones in Ex. 4b in pairs using the prompts.
- Write this diagram on the board for Ss to follow.

A	B
Welcome B and offer help. *Welcome to ... How can I ...?*	Explain about lost item. *I was in here ... and I think I left .*
Ask for description. *What does it ...?*	Give description. *It's ... with ... .*
Ask about contents. *What it's got ...?*	List contents. *My/A/Some ... and my ...*
Ask about time and place item was lost. *Where and when ...?*	Give details. *It was ...*
Comment and present item *I think you're in luck. Is this ...?*	Agree and thank A. *Oh, yes! Thank you!*

- Monitor the activity around the class and offer assistance as necessary.
- Then ask some pairs to act out their dialogues in front of the class.

Suggested Answer Key

A: Welcome to Brampton's. How can I help you?
B: I was shopping here yesterday, and I think I left my wallet in one of your fitting rooms.
A: What does it look like?
B: It's a brown leather wallet.
A: What's it got in it?
B: Some money, some photos and my driving licence.
A: Where and when did you lose it exactly?
B: It was in the fitting room at the end. It was just before closing time.

A: I think you're in luck. Is this it?
B: Oh, yes. Thank you very much!

Pronunciation

6 Aim To identify silent letters

- Remind Ss that, in English, some words have letters in them that are silent and are not pronounced.
- Play the recording. Ss listen and underline the silent letters. Check Ss' answers around the class, then play the recording again. Ss listen and repeat, chorally and individually.

Answer Key

| know | listen | write | comb |
| talk | autumn | design | honest |

Reading & Writing

7 Aim To read for gist

- Ask Ss to read the descriptions 1-3 and then read the text and match them to the paragraphs.
- Check Ss' answers.

Answer Key

1 c   2 b   3 a

> **Background Information**
>
> **Paris** is the capital city of France, a country in Western Europe.

8 Aim To practise using adjectives

- Read out the **Writing Tip** and then ask Ss to read the paragraph and replace the adjectives in bold with others from the email.
- Check Ss' answers around the class.

Suggested Answer Key

good – amazing
big – huge
good – fantastic
bad – exhausting
small – tiny

9 Aim To practise recommending

- Explain the task and give Ss time to complete the sentences using the correct words from the list.
- Check Ss' answers.

Answer key

1 recommend   3 like
2 miss   4 worth

2

Writing

10 **Aim** To brainstorm for ideas

- Explain the task and give Ss time to copy the spidergram and complete it with information about the shops in their capital city.
- Check Ss' answers on the board.

Suggested Answer Key

- **name of city:** Brussels
- **when you visited:** last week

weekend break

- **recommendation:** if you like shopping you should definitely visit Brussels
- **Shops & what you bought:** antique shops in the Sablon District; Inno Brussels department store; Leonidas – pralines; F. Rubbrecht – lace

11 **Aim** To write an email

- Give Ss time to write their email using the completed spidergram and the plan to help them.
- Check Ss' answers.
- Alternatively, assign the task as HW and check Ss' answers in the next lesson.

Suggested Answer Key

Hi Pat,
Hope you're well. I got back from Brussels last week. It was amazing! It's a shopper's paradise!
There were some fantastic little antique shops in the Sablon District. Inno Brussels, on Rue Neuve, is a huge department store. I spent hours looking at the clothes and jewellery there. It was fun but exhausting. I also visited Leonidas, on Boterstraat, and bought some of the most delicious pralines in the world. I also discovered F. Rubbrecht in the Grand-Place. They had beautiful lace there and I bought some for my mum.
If you like shopping you should definitely visit Brussels.
Bye for now,
Connie

Values

Ss try to explain the saying in their mother tongue. If Ss have difficulty, explain the saying. Ask Ss to memorise this quotation and check in the next lesson.
The saying means that small coins can soon add up to larger amounts of money. This suggests that if you are careful with small amounts of money it will soon amount to a lot of money.

Culture 2

Listening & Reading

1 **Aim** To introduce the topic and predict the content of the text; to listen and read for gist

- Ask Ss to look at the title and the quotation as well as the pictures and elicit what Ss think they will learn about Borough Market.
- Play the recording. Ss listen and read and find out.

Suggested Answer Key

I think I will learn about where Borough Market is and what it sells as well as its history.

2 **Aim** To read for specific information

- Ask Ss to read the sentences 1-4 and then read the text again and complete them accordingly.
- Check Ss' answers.

Answer Key

1 1000
2 the River Thames
3 restaurants
4 beyond

- Then give Ss time to look up the meanings of the words in bold in the Word List or in their dictionaries.
- Elicit definitions from Ss around the class.

Suggested Answer Key

location (n): the place where sth is
produce (n): natural products (e.g. fruit)
organised (adj): planned
beyond (adv): outside an area

- Give Ss time to look up the meanings of the words in the **Check these words** box in the Word List.
- Play the video for Ss and elicit their comments.

Speaking & Writing

3 **Aim** **THINK** To develop critical thinking skills

- Give Ss time to consider what makes a market popular and whether Borough Market has any of these features.
- Elicit answers from Ss around the class.

Suggested Answer Key

I think a market is popular if it has got good quality products and it is in a place that is easy to get to. Borough Market is in a good location and it has good quality products.

4 **Aim** THINK ICT **To develop research skills; to write a short text about a historic market in your country**

- Explain the task and give Ss time to collect information about an old or historic market in their country and write a short text.
- Remind Ss to include information covering all the points mentioned.
- Then ask various Ss to read their text to the class.
- Alternatively, assign the task as HW and ask Ss to read out their texts in the next lesson.

Suggested Answer Key

The Grand Bazaar in Istanbul is the most famous market in Turkey and the biggest and oldest covered market in the world. Dating back to 1461, it has got over 3,000 shops on 61 streets, as well as fountains, wells, mosques, gates, cafés and restaurants. It has a wide range of traditional goods for sale such as tea, sweets and pottery as well as gifts and souvenirs.

Review 2

Vocabulary

1 **Aim** **To practise vocabulary from the unit**
- Explain the task.
- Give Ss time to complete it.
- Check Ss' answers.

Answer Key

1 designed   3 took   5 employed
2 looked   4 handed

2 **Aim** **To practise vocabulary from the unit**
- Explain the task.
- Give Ss time to complete it.
- Check Ss' answers.

Answer Key

1 scarf   3 comb   5 magazine
2 linen   4 leather 6 tights

Grammar

3 **Aim** **To practise the past simple**
- Explain the task.
- Give Ss time to complete it.
- Check Ss' answers.

Answer Key

1 bought   4 studied
2 got   5 didn't take
3 Did he travel

4 **Aim** **To practise the past simple**
- Explain the task.
- Give Ss time to complete it.
- Check Ss' answers.

Answer Key

1 Did you go to college on Wednesday?
2 Gemma used to have longer hair.
3 Ken's uncle didn't use to work as a doorman.
4 We met for coffee yesterday.

5 **Aim** **To practise order of adjectives**
- Explain the task.
- Give Ss time to complete it.
- Check Ss' answers.

Answer Key

1 lovely, leather, Italian   4 expensive, old, gold
2 small, round, red   5 short, heavy, wooden
3 long, striped, woollen

6 **Aim** **To practise comparatives/superlatives**
- Explain the task.
- Give Ss time to complete it.
- Check Ss' answers.

Answer Key

1 bigger than, the biggest
2 expensive, the most expensive
3 older than, old
4 the tastiest, tasty

Everyday English

7 **Aim** **To match exchanges**
- Explain the task.
- Give Ss time to complete it.
- Check Ss' answers.

Answer Key

1 B   2 D   3 E   4 A   5 C

Competences

Ask Ss to assess their own performance in the unit by ticking the items according to how competent they feel for each of the listed activities.

Optional activity

Ask Ss to find photos of people/fashion models in magazines/online and prepare a poster, then describe each person's clothes as in a fashion show.

3 Survival stories

Topic
In this unit, Ss will explore the topics of weather phenomena, feelings and sounds.

3a Reading & Vocabulary	20-21

Lesson objectives: To listen and read for gist, to read for specific information (multiple choice), to summarise sb's story, to write a blog entry
Vocabulary: Weather phenomena (*blizzard, tornado, tsunami, hurricane, lightning, flood*); Nouns (*engine, mast, stump, satellite phone, signal, deck*); Verbs (*drop, snap*); Phrasal verb (*roll over*); Adjective (*relieved*); Phrase (*on board*)

3b Grammar in Use	22-23

Lesson objectives: To learn/revise the past continuous and *while/when*

3c Skills in Action	24-25

Lesson objectives: To learn vocabulary for feelings & sounds, to listen for specific information (multiple matching), to act out a dialogue and practise everyday English for giving a witness report, to learn the pronunciation of stressed words, to read for gist, to write a story
Vocabulary: Feelings & sounds (*thrilled, anxious, sad, puzzled, amazed, angry, proud, frightened, rain falling, wind howling, dog barking, brakes screeching, siren wailing, clock ticking, knocking on the door*)

Culture 3	26

Lesson objectives: To listen and read for gist, to read for key information, to talk about an imaginary experience, to write about a historic event in your country
Vocabulary: Noun (*Antarctica, tent, lifeboat, land*); Verbs (*melt, camp, sink, survive*); Phrasal verbs (*break up, set out*); Adjective (*crazy*); Phrase (*be trapped*)

Review 3	27

Lesson objectives: To test/consolidate vocabulary and grammar learnt throughout the unit; to practise everyday English

Go through the objectives box and tell Ss that these are the topics, skills and activities this unit will cover.

3a

Vocabulary

1 **Aim** To introduce subject-related vocabulary
- Play the recording with pauses for Ss to repeat chorally and/or individually.
- Check Ss' pronunciation and intonation.
- Elicit which of the weather phenomena are common in Ss' country.

Ss' own answers

2 **Aim** To present/practise vocabulary relating to weather
- Explain the task and give Ss time to choose the correct words for the sentences.
- Have Ss check their answers in their dictionaries.

Answer Key
1 coming   3 shining
2 raining   4 blowing, pouring

Reading

3 **Aim** To listen and read for gist
- Give Ss time to read the background information and then elicit their guesses as to what happened.
- Play the recording. Ss listen and read to find out.

Suggested Answer Key
I think Abby got into some trouble on her trip.

4 **Aim** To read for specific information (multiple choice)
- Ask Ss to read the questions and answer choices. Elicit what they expect to read in the blog entries.
- Give Ss time to read the text and then choose their answers.
- Check Ss' answers.

Answer Key
1 C   2 B   3 C   4 C

- Give Ss time to look up the meanings of the words in the **Check these words** box in the Word List.
- Play the video for Ss and elicit their comments.

5 **Aim** **THINK** To develop critical thinking skills
Give Ss time to consider their answers to the question and then ask various Ss around the class to tell the rest of the class giving reasons.

Suggested Answer Key

I don't think her age had anything to do with it. What happened to her could have happened to anyone. She just had bad luck.

6 **Aim** **To consolidate new vocabulary**
- Give Ss time to complete the sentences with the words in the list.
- Check Ss' answers.

Suggested Answer Key

1 dry   3 satellite   5 giant
2 stormy   4 fishing

7 **Aim** **To form adverbs from adjectives**
- Go through the theory with Ss.
- Explain/Elicit the meanings of any unknown words and explain the task.
- Give Ss time to complete the task.
- Check Ss' answers around the class.

Answer Key

brightly   luckily   heavily
hard   suddenly

8 **Aim** **To order events**
- Ask Ss to read the prompts and then put them in order according to the events in the text.
- Check Ss' answers.

Suggested Answer Key

A 3   C 1   E 5   G 9   I 8
B 7   D 4   F 2   H 6

Speaking

9 **Aim** **To summarise a story**

Ask various Ss around the class to summarise the story using their answers to Ex. 8.

Suggested Answer Key

Abby sailed in the Indian Ocean. She went to check the engine when a giant wave hit the boat. The mast snapped and her phone broke. Abby sent a radio signal. Later she saw a plane and then a French fishing boat picked her up. After, she travelled to Reunion Island. Her brother took her home from there.

Writing

10 **Aim** **To write a blog entry**
- Explain the task and give Ss time to write a blog entry from the point of view of a rescue worker on the plane that spotted Abby's boat.
- Tell Ss to include all the points listed.
- Ask various Ss to read out their blog entry to the class.

Suggested Answer Key

11th June 2010

I was on a rescue mission over the Indian Ocean. We had received a radio signal from a boat and we were looking for it. We spotted the boat and it was in a bad condition. The mast was broken and it was just sitting in the water, not moving. There was a young girl on the deck of the boat and we were able to let her know by radio that we would send a boat to rescue her. She seemed very happy. We contacted the closest boat in the area, a French fishing boat, and sent it to her location to pick her up. We were relieved she was safe.

Background Information

The **Indian Ocean** is the third largest ocean in the world. It is bounded by Asia, Africa, Australia and Antarctica.

The **Kerguelen Islands** are a group of islands in the southern Indian Ocean. People also call them the Desolation Islands because they are among the most isolated places on Earth.

Reunion Island is a small island east of Madagascar in the Indian Ocean.

3b Grammar in Use

1 **Aim** **To present/revise the past continuous**
- Present the past continuous. Say: *I was working yesterday at 5 o'clock in the afternoon.* Write it on the board.
- Underline *was working* and explain that this verb is in the past continuous. Point to a S, say: *He/She was working yesterday at 5 o'clock in the afternoon.* Then write it on the board. Underline *was working*. Gesture to yourself and the class, say: *We were working yesterday.* Then write it on the board. Underline *were working*. Point to a group of Ss, say: *Were they working at 5 o'clock yesterday? They weren't working at 5 o'clock yesterday in the afternoon.* Then write it on the board. Underline *Were they working, weren't working*.
- Explain that we use the past continuous for an action that was in progress at a specific time in the past. Explain that we form the past continuous in the affirmative with personal pronoun/name + *was/were* + verb *-ing*, in the negative with personal

27

pronoun/name + ***wasn't/weren't*** + verb *-ing*, and in the interrogative with ***Was/Were*** + personal pronoun/name + verb *-ing*.
- Go through the theory table with Ss.
- Then elicit how we form the past continuous.

Answer Key

We form the past continuous with personal pronoun/name + ***was/were*** + verb ***-ing*** (affirmative), personal pronoun/name + ***wasn't/weren't*** + verb ***-ing*** (negative) and ***was/were*** + personal pronoun/name + verb ***-ing*** (interrogative).

2 Aim To identify past continuous usage
- Explain the task and give Ss time to read the news report and complete it.
- Check Ss' answers.

Answer Key

were having → b) background information in a story
were skiing → d) action in progress at a stated time in the past
was falling, were blowing → a) two or more actions happening at the same time in the past
was searching → c) action interrupted by another shorter action in the past

Background Information

Tignes is an area in southeastern France in the Savoie region. It is best known as a ski resort.

3 Aim To practise the past continuous (affirmative)
- Explain the task and give Ss time to complete it.
- Check Ss' answers.

Answer Key

1 were shopping   3 was driving home
2 was cooking dinner   4 was chatting online

Speaking

4 Aim To practise the past continuous affirmative with personal examples
- Ask Ss to talk in closed pairs following the example and using the prompts.
- Monitor the activity around the class and then ask some Ss to tell the class.

Suggested Answer Key

At 8:30 am last Monday, I was driving to college. At the same time last Sunday, I was sleeping.
At 11 am last Monday, I was sitting in a lecture. At the same time last Sunday, I was running in the park.
At 3:30 pm last Monday, I was studying in the library. At the same time last Sunday, I was watching a film.
At 7 pm last Monday, I was cooking dinner. At the same time last Sunday, I was hanging out with friends.

5 Aim To present/practise *while/when* with the past simple/past continuous
- Go through the theory box with Ss and explain that we use *while* with the past continuous and *when* with the past simple.
- Give Ss time to complete the task.
- Check Ss' answers around the class.

Answer Key

1 while   3 while   5 when
2 when   4 while

6 Aim To practise the past continuous (negative)
- Explain the task and read out the example. Go through the images and elicit what each person was doing.
- Then give Ss time to complete the task and check Ss answers.

Answer Key

2 Ann wasn't eating an apple. She was cutting the grass.
3 Sue wasn't watering the flowers. She was eating an apple.
4 Jane and Mary weren't cutting the grass. They were watering the flowers.
5 Bob wasn't painting the door. He was playing with the dog.

7 Aim To practise the past continuous (interrogative)
- Explain the task and ask two Ss to read out the example.
- Then give Ss time to complete the task in closed pairs.
- Monitor the activity around the class and then ask some pairs to ask and answer in front of the class.

Suggested Answer Key

A: What were you doing at 10:30 last Saturday morning?
B: I was shopping with my friend.
A: What were you doing at 3:30 yesterday afternoon?
B: I was walking home.
A: What were you doing at this time last Wednesday?
B: I was studying.
A: What were you doing at 10 o'clock last Sunday night?
B: I was watching a film.

8 Aim To practise the past continuous (interrogative)

- Explain the task and read out the example.
- Then give Ss time to complete the task and check Ss answers.

Answer Key

2 Was Paula flying to New York yesterday morning? No, she wasn't. She was having a meeting.
3 Were Mark and Terry watching TV on Sunday afternoon? No, they weren't. They were chatting online.
4 Were you working yesterday afternoon. No, I wasn't. I was studying at the library.

Extra activity

Find out what your partner was doing yesterday evening at 6 o'clock. You can ask five questions using the past continuous.

e.g. A: Were you having football practice?
B: No, I wasn't. etc

9 Aim To distinguish between the past simple and the past continuous

- Explain the task and give Ss time to complete it.
- Check Ss' answers around the class.

Answer Key

1 walked (actions that happened immediately one after the other)
2 was sleeping (action in progress at a stated time in the past)
3 were climbing (an action in progress interrupted by another action in the past)
4 didn't go (action happened at specific time)
5 started (past action that interrupted a past action in progress)
6 was watching (two past actions happening at the same time)

10 a) Aim To practise the past simple and past continuous

- Give Ss time to complete the task in closed pairs.
- Check Ss' answers around the class.

Answer Key

1 were hanging
2 was falling
3 was
4 was travelling
5 entered
6 was wearing
7 was carrying
8 sat
9 opened
10 took
11 gave

b) Aim THINK To continue a story; to practise creative writing; to practise the past simple/continuous

- Explain the task.
- Give Ss time to consider their answers and complete the task.
- Check Ss' answers.
- Alternatively, assign the task as HW and ask various Ss to read out their stories to the class.
- To help Ss, you can write the following words on the board and tell Ss they can use them to help them continue the story: (confused, name, think, strange, gone, corridor, old map, key, car waiting, nervously).

Suggested Answer Key

Laura was confused. She looked at the envelope in her hand and saw her name written in very neat writing on the front. She was thinking how strange this was when she heard the compartment door open. When she looked up, the man was gone. She ran into the corridor, but he was not there.

Laura opened the envelope and inside was an old map and a key. She got off the train, carefully put the envelope in her bag and walked towards the car which was waiting for her. "What shall I do?" she thought nervously. She decided to get into the car.

3c Skills in Action

Vocabulary

1 Aim To present vocabulary for feelings

- Go through the words in the list and elicit their meaning. You can mime the meaning of each word if you like.
- Give Ss time to complete the sentences with the words in the list.
- Check Ss' answers.

Answer Key

1 puzzled
2 thrilled
3 anxious
4 proud
5 frightened
6 angry
7 relieved
8 sad

Extra activity

Mime one of the feelings in Ex. 1. Your partner guesses how you are feeling.

2 Aim To identify sounds

- Ask Ss to read the list of sounds and think about what they actually sound like.
- Play the recording. Ss listen and match the sounds they hear to the descriptions.
- Check Ss' answers around the class.

Answer Key

A 4   B 1   C 3   D 6   E 5   F 2

3 Aim To continue a story; to practise creative writing

- Ask Ss to use the phrases in Ex. 2 to continue the story.
- Elicit answers from Ss around the class.

Suggested Answer Key

... He looked around and saw a dog chasing after a cat. Suddenly, the dog jumped over the wall and ran into the road. John ran after it and tried to grab the lead that was behind it. Then he heard a car's brakes screeching.

John flew through the air and landed on the road. He saw the dog on the other side of the road. The sound of sirens wailing was the last thing he remembered.

John spent two weeks in hospital before he was able to go back home. One day, he was reading a book while he was listening to rain falling. Suddenly, he heard someone knocking on the door. It was the owner of the dog, who wanted to thank him for saving his dog.

4 Aim To listen for specific information (multiple matching)

- Ask Ss to read the lists.
- Play the recording. Ss listen and complete the task.
- Check Ss' answers.

Answer Key

1 d   2 b   3 a   4 c

Everyday English

5 Aim To practise the past simple and the past continuous

- Give Ss time to complete the task.
- Play the recording for Ss to check their answers.

Answer Key

1 were you	7 saw
2 was	8 tried
3 were you doing	9 Did you see
4 was cutting	10 saw
5 happened	11 wrote
6 heard	12 was driving

6 Aim To act out a dialogue

- Explain the task and ask Ss to act out a similar dialogue to the one in Ex. 5 in pairs using the prompts.
- Write this diagram on the board for Ss to follow.

A	B
Ask B about location. *So, ... where were you ...?*	Give details. *I was ... .*
Ask B about activity at time. *What were you doing ...?*	Give details. *I was ... .*
Ask about event. *What happened ...?*	Give details. *I ... and ... .*
Ask for description. *Did you see ...?*	Respond *No, I'm afraid not, but I ... .*
Comment and thank B. *That's really helpful. Thank you.*	Respond. *You're welcome.*

- Monitor the activity around the class and offer assistance as necessary.
- Then ask some pairs to act out their dialogues in front of the class.

Suggested Answer Key

A: So, Miss Green, where were you at the time of the robbery?
B: I was on Old Road.
A: What were you doing?
B: I was coming out of the post office.
A: What happened exactly?
B: Well, I heard the bank alarm go off and I saw two men in black. They ran out of the bank and jumped into a blue van and sped off.
A: Did you see their faces?
B: No, I'm afraid not, but I managed to write down the registration number on the van.
A: That's really helpful. Thank you.
B: You're welcome.

Pronunciation

7 Aim To practise pronunciation of stressed words

- Explain that a strong stress on one word can change the contrastive meaning suggested by a sentence. Read the first sentence aloud, emphasising **six**, and again, emphasising **here**. Elicit difference in meaning (if we emphasise **six**, we mean this time not another one. If we emphasise **here**, this means at this place not somewhere else).

- Play the recording. Ss listen and underline the stressed words.
- Then have Ss tick the correct meaning for each sentence.
- Check Ss' answers around the class, then play the recording again. Ss listen and repeat, chorally and individually.
- Check Ss' pronunciation and intonation.

Answer Key

1 six = not at seven o' clock
2 woman = not a young man
3 both = not just one of them

Reading

8 Aim To read for gist

Read out the writing tip and then ask Ss to read the story and then elicit how the writer sets the scene.

Answer Key

A	8	C	6	E	3	G	5
B	2	D	1	F	7	H	4

Suggested Answer Key

The writer sets the scene by telling the reader where and when the story takes place, who the main character is, what the weather is like and what happened first.

9 Aim To identify adjectives

- Read out the Writing Tip and then ask Ss to read the story again and find the adjectives the writer uses for the nouns in the list.
- Check Ss' answers around the class.

Suggested Answer Key

gentle breeze
huge, yellow balloon
happy smile
dark clouds

10 Aim To practise using adverbs

- Give Ss time to look through the story again and identify the adverbs and then match them to the adjectives in the list.
- Elicit how we form adverbs.
- Check Ss' answers.

Answer key

1 brightly
2 slowly
3 cheerfully
4 suddenly
5 hard
6 loudly
7 anxiously
8 safely

In most cases, we form adverbs by adding -ly to an adjective. If the adjective ends in **-y**, we replace the **-y** with **-i** and add **-ly**. If the adjective ends in **-able**, **-ible**, or **-le**, we replace the **-e** with **-y**. If the adjective ends in **-ic**, we add **-ally**. Some adverbs have the same form as the adjective e.g. early, fast, hard.

Writing

11 a) Aim To listen for order of events

- Explain the task and ask Ss to read the events in the list.
- Play the recording. Ss listen and order them.
- Check Ss' answers.
- Then ask various Ss to use the events to retell the story.

Answer Key

A	6	C	2	E	4	G	3
B	1	D	7	F	5		

Suggested Answer Key

Mark and Dan pushed their canoe onto the river. Later, they stopped to have some coffee when suddenly, they saw a kingfisher. After, they got back into their canoe. They then saw they were approaching a waterfall. Luckily, two fishermen pulled their canoe to safety. In the end, they thanked the fishermen.

b) Aim To write a story

- Give Ss time to write their story using the events in Ex. 11a and the plan to help them.
- Check Ss' answers.
- Alternatively, assign the task as HW and check Ss' answers in the next lesson.

NOTE: To help Ss, you can give them the first sentence of each paragraph in the model answer and ask them to complete the story.

Suggested Answer Key

The Waterfall

A cold wind was blowing, but there was a bright blue sky that morning. Dan and Mark pushed their canoe out onto the water.

Two hours later, they stopped to have some coffee. Suddenly, they saw a kingfisher. They quickly got back into the canoe and started following it. Later, they decided to turn around when they saw a waterfall. Their canoe was quickly approaching it.

At that moment, they heard someone shout from the riverbank. "Here! Catch!" Mark quickly caught the rope that came towards him. He looked up and saw two fishermen. It was their rope, and they pulled the canoe to safety.

A few minutes later, Dan and Mark were sitting on the grassy river bank. They thanked the fishermen. They were tired and frightened but relieved to be alive.

3

Values

Ss try to explain the quotation in their mother tongue. If Ss have difficulty, explain the quotation. Ask Ss to memorise this quotation and check in the next lesson.

The quotation means that if you use your imagination, you can do anything. A perfect example is when the Wright Brothers used their imagination to help them invent the first working flying machine. It literally gave them wings to fly, so if you use your imagination, you can do great things.

Culture 3

Listening & Reading

1 Aim To introduce the topic and predict the content of the text; to listen and read for gist

- Read the rubric aloud and elicit what Ss think happened to Shackleton and his team.
- Play the recording. Ss listen and read and find out.

Suggested Answer Key

Their boat sank.

2 Aim To read for specific information

- Ask Ss to read the sentence stems 1-4 and then read the text again and complete them accordingly.
- Check Ss' answers.

Suggested Answer Key

1 ship
2 cross Antarctica
3 ice destroyed the ship
4 get help to save his men

- Then give Ss time to look up the meanings of the words in bold in the Word List or in their dictionaries.
- Elicit definitions from Ss around the class.

Suggested Answer Key

destroying (v): damaging sth to a level that it can't be used
sank (past simple of sink) (v): went under a surface
relieved (adj): happy that sth happened/didn't happen
save (v): to rescue sb from being hurt
left (past simple of leave) (v): to not take sb/sth; to go
reach (v): to get to a place
rescue (v): to help sb that is in a dangerous situation
survive (v): to live despite danger

- Give Ss time to look up the meanings of the words in the **Check these words** box in the Word List.
- Play the video for Ss and elicit their comments.

Speaking & Writing

3 Aim THINK To develop critical thinking skills

- Give Ss time to consider their answers.
- Elicit answers from Ss around the class.

Suggested Answer Key

I felt happy and relieved that we were going to be alright.

4 Aim ICT To write a short text about an explorer from your country

- Explain the task and give Ss time to collect information about an explorer from their country and write a short text.
- Then ask various Ss to read their text to the class.
- Alternatively, assign the task as HW and ask Ss to read out their texts in the next lesson.

Suggested Answer Key

Henryk Arctowski was a Polish scientist and explorer. He was one of the first people to spend winters in Antarctica and became an internationally renowned meteorologist. In 1895, he applied to take part in the Belgian Antarctic Expedition, the first expedition to spend the winter in the Antarctic. Also on the expedition were Roald Amundsen and Frederick Cook. He coordinated the scientific work and made physical observations.

Review 3

Vocabulary

1 Aim To practise vocabulary from the unit

- Explain the task.
- Give Ss time to complete it.
- Check Ss' answers.

Answer Key

1 hurricane   4 clouds
2 tsunami   5 blizzard
3 lightning

2 Aim To practise vocabulary from the unit

- Explain the task.
- Give Ss time to complete it.
- Check Ss' answers.

Answer Key

1 blowing   3 dropped   5 raining
2 poured   4 snapped

3 **Aim** To practise vocabulary from the unit
- Explain the task.
- Give Ss time to complete it.
- Check Ss' answers.

Answer Key

1 thick   3 stormy   5 anxious
2 heavy   4 thrilled

Grammar

4 **Aim** To practise the past simple and past continuous
- Explain the task.
- Give Ss time to complete it.
- Check Ss' answers.

Answer Key

1 were you doing   4 wasn't riding
2 bought   5 did you call
3 didn't see

5 **Aim** To practise the past simple and the past continuous
- Explain the task.
- Give Ss time to complete it.
- Check Ss' answers.

Answer Key

1 found, sat, took
2 Did you see, were driving
3 was blowing, was pouring
4 was reading, didn't hear
5 visited

Everyday English

6 **Aim** To choose the correct responses in exchanges
- Explain the task.
- Give Ss time to complete it.
- Check Ss' answers.

Answer Key

1 b   2 a   3 a   4 b

Competences

Ask Ss to assess their own performance in the unit by ticking the items according to how competent they feel for each of the listed activities.

Optional activity

Chain story. Ss, one after the other, continue the story.
I was surfing the Net when ...

A Values: Diversity

1 **Aim** **To listen and read for specific information**
- Ask Ss to look at the images.
- Elicit what they think 'diversity' means.
- Ask Ss to read the text and find out.

Answer Key

Diversity means difference i.e. from different backgrounds, countries and races.

- Play the video for Ss and elicit their comments.

2 **Aim** **To read for key information**
- Ask Ss to read the headings.
- Give Ss time to read the text again and then ask them to match the headings to the paragraphs.
- Then give Ss time to explain the meanings of the words in bold from the context or by looking up the meanings in their dictionaries if necessary.

Answer Key

1 D 2 C 3 A 4 B

Suggested Answer Key

basically (adv): *in the most basic way*
unique (adj): *being the only one of its kind*
physical (adj): *relating to the body*
introduce (v): *to bring sth to others' attention for the first time*
enjoy (v): *to take pleasure from*

3 **Aim** **THINK** **To develop critical thinking skills**
- Play the recording. Ss listen and read the text.
- Then ask Ss to work in closed pairs and discuss the question.
- Ask some pairs to share their answers with the class.

Suggested Answer Key

A: Of course it's OK to be different. We can't all be the same – it's impossible.
B: Exactly and we shouldn't judge someone based on their appearance.
A: You're right. We should get to know someone from a different background to learn more about them and the world we live in. etc.
B: Absolutely. Different is interesting.

4 **Aim** **To talk about diversity**
- Ask Ss to talk in small groups about people in a different country.
- Give Ss time to prepare a PowerPoint presentation and show it to the class.

Suggested Answer Key

The people from Jamaica are very different in some ways to the people from my country, Greenland. We both live on an island, but the sea around ours is very cold, while theirs is very warm. They have a tropical climate, too, so lots of tourists go to their country. So they live outside a lot, they spend a lot of time in the water or on the beach. We have an Arctic climate, so we are indoors a lot. We use the sea to catch our food, but we don't swim in it! We don't see the sun as much. In fact, during the winter the days are just hours long. Many Jamaican people have dark skin and hair. We have lighter skin, though we have black hair.

Public Speaking Skills A

1 Aim To present a public speaking task

Read the theory box, then ask Ss to read the task. Elicit the purpose of the presentation.

Answer Key

The purpose is to inform the audience about something they may not know.

2 Aim To analyse a model public speaking task; to revise/present opening/closing techniques

- Play the recording. Ss listen and read the model.
- Elicit the opening/closing remarks used from the list provided.

Answer Key

The presenter addresses the listeners directly to open, and asks a rhetorical question to close.

3 Aim To prepare for a presentation

- Ask Ss to copy the spidergram into their notebooks and give them time to complete it with information about their country and people.
- Then ask Ss to use their notes and the model to help them prepare a presentation on their country and people.

Suggested Answer Key

location, climate & nickname: Southern Europe, Mediterranean climate, the Boot

reasons to visit: fascinating sights, rich cultural history, warm-hearted people

Country

people's appearance & character: brown hair, brown eyes, olive skin, friendly, helpful, generous, fashionable, kind, loud, happy, proud of their history

lifestyle, food & free time:
lifestyle: live in towns/cities, city life, busy and noisy, interesting ancient sites, lively street culture, outdoor cafés, **food:** typically Mediterranean, fresh ingredients, olive oil, pasta, pizza, **free time:** watch sports matches, theatre, go for coffee

4 Aim To give a presentation

- Ask various Ss to give their presentation to the class.
- Alternatively, assign the task as HW and have Ss give their presentations in the next lesson.

Suggested Answer Key

Hello everyone! My name's Anna.

Do you know where I'm from? My country is in southern Europe, its got a Mediterranean climate and ancient temples. Let me give you a clue – its people call it the Boot. That's right – it's Italy! Italy is a beautiful country, but what makes it really special is its people.

Italians usually have brown hair, brown eyes and olive skin. The Italians are friendly people who are well-known for being helpful, generous, fashionable and kind. We are a loud, happy people and we are very proud of our history.

A lot of people in Italy live in towns and cities. Italian cities are busy and noisy, but there are also interesting ancient sites. Every town and city has a lively street culture and lots of outdoor cafés.

Family life is very important in Italy. The food is typically Mediterranean and usually includes fresh ingredients and olive oil. Typical dishes are pasta and pizza. In our free time we love watching sports matches, going to the theatre and going for coffee.

Italy is one of the most wonderful counties to visit. Its fascinating sights, rich cultural history and warm-hearted people make it unique.

49 million visitors a year can't be wrong, can they? Thank you for listening.

4 Planning ahead

Topic
In this unit, Ss will explore the topics of jobs and job qualities.

4a Reading & Vocabulary	30-31
Lesson objectives: To listen for specific information (multiple matching), to read for specific information (multiple matching), to learn phrases with *make* and *do*, to learn prepositional phrases, to talk about people's dream jobs, to write a forum entry **Vocabulary:** Jobs *(animal trainer, app/software developer, builder, doctor, event planner, fashion designer, firefighter, gardener, lifeguard, nurse, public relations specialist, social media editor, stuntman, tour guide, video game tester, web designer)*; Noun *(venue)*; Verbs *(pass, suit, agree)*; Phrase *(entrance test)*	

4b Grammar in Use	32-33
Lesson objectives: To learn/revise *will – going to – present continuous – present simple*, to learn conditionals type 1	

4c Skills in Action	34-35
Lesson objectives: To learn vocabulary for job qualities, to listen for specific information (multiple choice), to read for cohesion and coherence (missing words), to act out a dialogue and practise everyday English for having a job interview, to learn the pronunciation of *'ll*, to write an email applying for a job **Vocabulary:** Job qualities *(brave, patient, imaginative, sociable, hard-working, caring, careful)*	

Culture 4	36
Lesson objectives: To listen and read for gist, to read for specific information (multiple matching), to talk about jobs, to write about jobs in your country **Vocabulary:** Nouns *(receipt, promotion, industry)*; Verbs *(develop, scan)*; Adverb *(outdoors)*; Phrases *(have a head for figures, clash with)*	

Review 4	37
Lesson objectives: To test/consolidate vocabulary and grammar learnt throughout the unit; to practise everyday English	

Go through the objectives box and tell Ss that these are the topics, skills and activities this unit will cover.

4a

Vocabulary

1 a) Aim To introduce vocabulary for jobs

Ask Ss to look at the pictures and elicit which of the jobs in the list they can see.

Answer Key

A stuntman   E event planner
B animal trainer   F video game tester
C lifeguard   G social media editor
D firefighter   H fashion designer

b) Aim To match skills to jobs

• Ask Ss to read the types of skills and explain/ elicit the meanings of any unknown words.
• Elicit which jobs in Ex. 1a require which types of skills.

Suggested Answer Key

physical skills: builder, firefighter, gardener, lifeguard, stuntman, video game tester
computer skills: app/software developer, social media editor, web designer, video game editor
creative skills: fashion designer, web designer
social skills: event planner, nurse, public relations specialist, tour guide
communication skills: animal trainer, doctor, event planner, nurse, public relations specialist, tour guide
organisational skills: event planner, public relations specialist, tour guide

2 a) Aim To match jobs to people's interests

• Explain the task and give Ss time to choose the correct job for each speaker 1-6.
• Check Ss' answers.

Answer Key

1 social media editor   4 event planner
2 gardener   5 nurse
3 tour guide   6 builder

b) Aim To consolidate new vocabulary

• Explain the task and ask two Ss to model the example.
• Then have Ss work in closed pairs and ask and answer questions about the jobs following the example.

- Monitor the activity around the class and then ask various Ss to share their answers with the rest of the class.

Suggested Answer Key

A: Which job would you most like to do?
B: I'd like to work as an event planner because I love organising parties.

Listening & Reading

3 Aim To listen for specific information

- Give Ss time to read the lists of people, jobs and reasons.
- Play the recording. Ss listen and match them.

Answer Key

Ito wants to be a firefighter because he wants to save lives.
Chiara wants to be an event planner because she has great organisational skills.
Neil wants to be a doctor because he wants to treat sick people.

4 Aim To read for specific information (multiple matching)

- Ask Ss to read questions 1-6.
- Give Ss time to read the text and then answer the questions.
- Check Ss' answers.
- Elicit explanations for the words in bold.

Answer Key

1 A, C   2 A   3 B   4 C   5 B   6 A

Suggested Answer Key

save: rescue
fit: healthy and trained
work out: do an exercise programme
degree: university qualification
arrange: organise
set up: start
otherwise: or else
long hours: a lot of hours all at once

- Give Ss time to look up the meanings of the words in the **Check these words** box in the Word List.
- Play the video for Ss and elicit their comments.

5 Aim To consolidate new vocabulary

- Give Ss time to complete the phrases with the words in the list.
- Check Ss' answers. Then give Ss time to write sentences using the completed phrases.
- Elicit answers from Ss around the class.

Answer Key

1 set up   5 organisational
2 make   6 training
3 long   7 full-time
4 have   8 entrance

Suggested Answer Key

1 I'd like to set up my own software company.
2 I made a decision to become a dancer when I was young.
3 Doctors have to work long hours.
4 My brother has no idea what he wants to do after school.
5 Event planners need good organisational skills.
6 Firefighters have to go on a training course.
7 It took Sam a long time to get a full-time job.
8 Some jobs ask you to take an entrance test.

6 Aim To consolidate new vocabulary

- Explain the task and give Ss time to complete it.
- Check Ss' answers.

Answer Key

1 passed   3 follow
2 studying   4 job

7 Aim To learn phrases with *make* and *do*

- Explain/Elicit the meanings of any unknown words and explain the task.
- Give Ss time to complete the task.
- Check Ss' answers around the class.

Answer Key

1 make   5 do   9 do
2 make   6 make   10 do
3 do   7 make
4 make   8 do

Suggested Answer Key

1 When we make mistakes, we can learn something.
2 Can I use your mobile to make a phone call?
3 Danny always does his homework before dinner.
4 Martha was busy making the beds when the phone rang.
5 My dad usually does the washing-up after dinner.
6 My brother doesn't only work to make money – he loves his job!
7 Our neighbours next door sometimes make a lot of noise!
8 My family does the weekly shopping on Friday evenings.
9 I really don't like doing the ironing!
10 My friend Tom did his best to pass his driving test but he failed.

8 Aim To learn prepositional phrases

- Ask Ss to fill in the correct prepositions.
- Check Ss' answers and then give Ss time to make sentences using the prepositional phrases.
- Elicit answers from Ss around the class.

Answer Key

1 from	3 at	5 with
2 for	4 of	

Suggested Answer Key

1 Rafael is from Portugal.
2 You have to study to be ready for a test.
3 Sam is good at Maths.
4 I've just thought of a great idea!
5 I agree with you that it's a fantastic job.

Speaking

9 Aim To consolidate information in a text

- Ask Ss to read the text again and copy the headings into their notebooks.
- Give Ss time to make notes under the headings. Then ask various Ss to use their notes to talk about the people in the text in front of the class.

Suggested Answer Key

Ito's ambition is to become a firefighter because he wants to save lives. He has to be fit and strong. He works out twice a week to be ready for the entrance test and then he's going to begin a training course and he's going to work really hard.
Chiara's ambition is to be an event planner because she's got great organisational skills, which the job needs. She's going to set up her own company.
Neil's ambition is to become a doctor because he wants to treat sick people. He is studying now. When he finishes his studies, he is going to start a full-time job in a hospital.

Writing

10 Aim THINK To write a forum entry

- Explain the task and give Ss time to write a forum entry about a job they would like to do and why.
- Remind Ss to follow the style of the other forum entries.
- Ask various Ss to read out their forum entry to the class.

Suggested Answer Key

Hi Ellie. I agree with the others. Find something you're good at or something you are interested in and you will be happy. I want to protect people and help my community so I want to be a police officer. I'm going to study hard at school and then take the entrance test. Good luck with your decision!

Optional activity

Play in pairs or teams. Think of a job. Say a few sentences about your daily work routine without saying what your job is. The other person or team guesses what the job is.

4b Grammar in Use

1 Aim To present/revise *will* – *be going to* – present continuous – present simple

- Present the future simple *(will)*. Say then write on the board: I'm thirsty. *I will drink some water.* and *I think my parents will buy me a laptop for my birthday.* Underline *I will drink* and *my parents will buy* and explain that these verbs are in the future simple. Explain that we use **will** + **the base form of the main verb** to form the affirmative. Explain that we use this tense to talk about on-the-spot decisions and predictions based on what we think or imagine.
- Say then write on the board: *Will you go out tonight? No, it's raining. I will not/won't go out tonight.* Underline *Will you go* and *I will not/won't go* and explain that these are the interrogative and negative forms of the future simple. Give examples for all persons and explain that we form the negative with **will** + **not** + **the base form of the main verb** and the interrogative with **will** + **personal pronoun** + **the base form of the verb**.
- Present *be going to*. Say then write on the board: *Now that I have enough money, I am going to buy a smartphone.* Explain that we use **be going to** + **infinitive** to talk about plans and intentions for the future. Say then write on the board: *Look out! You're going to fall!* Explain that we also use **be going to** for predictions based on what we can see or know.
- Explain that we use the present continuous with a future meaning to talk about fixed future arrangements.
- Explain that we use the present simple with a future meaning to talk about timetables/schedules/programmes.
- Ask Ss to read the theory.
- Elicit examples from the advert.

Answer Key

What are you doing next week?
There are going to be, starts, finishes

2 Aim To practise *will/be going to*

- Explain the task and give Ss time to read the dialogue and complete it.
- Check Ss' answers.

Answer Key

1 are going to
2 I'm going to
3 I'm picking up
4 I'll
5 I'll
6 I'll
7 I'll

3 **Aim** To practise *will/be going to*

- Explain the task and give Ss time to complete it.
- Check Ss' answers.

Answer Key

1 won't
2 will
3 am going to
4 is going to
5 will

4 **Aim** To listen for specific information; to practise *be going to*

- Ask Ss to read the notes and ask two Ss to model the exchange.
- Play the recording. Ss tick (√) the ones they hear.
- Have Ss ask and answer in closed pairs following the example and using the notes.
- Monitor the activity around the class and then ask some Ss to tell the class.

Answer Key

2, 4, 5, 7, 8

Suggested Answer Key

A: Is Robin going to work as a waiter this summer?
B: Yes, he is. He is going to work as a waiter.

A: Is Robin going to volunteer at a summer camp this summer?
B: No, he isn't. He isn't going to volunteer at a summer camp.

A: Is Robin going to buy a car this summer?
B: Yes, he is. He is going to buy a car.

A: Is Robin going to take driving lessons this summer?
B: Yes, he is. He is going to take driving lessons.

A: Is Robin going to move house this summer?
B: No, he isn't. He isn't going to move house.

A: Is Robin going to study Maths this summer?
B: Yes, he is. He is going to study Maths.

A: Is Robin going to join a gym this summer?
B: Yes, he is. He is going to join a gym.

Speaking

5 **Aim** To practise *be going to*

- Ask Ss to use the ideas to talk about what they are/aren't going to do after work/college today.
- Ask various Ss to tell the class.

Suggested Answer Key

I'm going to drive home. I'm not going to go shopping. I'm going to have a snack. I'm not going to visit friends. I'm going to listen to music. I'm not going to do my homework. I'm going to watch a film. I'm not going to clean my house. I'm going to get some exercise. I'm not going to have a dance class. I'm not going to have a board game night. I'm going to watch an episode of my favourite TV show.

6 **Aim** To practise the present continuous and the present simple (future use)

- Explain the task and give Ss time to read the texts and then complete the task.
- Check Ss' answers.

Answer Key

1 is giving, begins, finishes
2 are travelling, leaves, arrives
3 am going, is picking
4 starts, are meeting

7 **Aim** To practise future forms

- Explain the task and then give Ss time to complete it.
- Check Ss' answers and then ask Ss to act out similar dialogues using the prompts.
- Monitor the activity around the class and then ask some pairs to act out their dialogues in front of the class.

Answer Key

1 are going to visit, are you leaving
2 is going to rain
3 are you going to study, will choose

Suggested Answer Key

A: What are your plans for the winter break?
B: We are going to visit Switzerland.
A: Wow! When are you leaving?
B: On 20th December.

A: It's very cold today.
B: Yes. I think it's going to snow.

A: Which languages are you going to study next year?
B: I'm not sure yet, but I think I will choose Spanish and French.

8 **Aim** To present conditionals type 1

- Present conditionals type 1. Say then write on the board: *If you call me, I will answer.* Ask Ss to identify the **if-clause** (*If you call me*) and which tense we use (*the present simple*). Ask Ss to

identify the **main clause** (*I will answer*) and the tense used (*the future simple*). Explain that this is a type 1 conditional and we use them to talk about a real or probable situation in the present or future.
- Ask Ss to read the table, study the examples and complete the rule. Check Ss' answers and then elicit an example from the advert on p. 32.

Answer Key

If + present simple → **future simple** + infinitive without **to**

Example: If you come on Monday, you will get the chance to meet the Chairman of the Board of the hospital.

9 **Aim** To practise type 1 conditionals
- Explain the task and give Ss time to complete it, adding commas where necessary.
- Check Ss' answers around the class.

Answer Key
1 If you study hard, you will pass the test.
2 When she starts works as a taxi driver, she won't be at home very often.
3 He will become a doctor if he gets a degree in Medicine.
4 You will be fitter if you work out at the gym three times a week.
5 Unless you work full-time, you won't earn much money.
6 If they open their own café, they will work long hours.

10 **Aim** THINK To practise type 1 conditionals; to develop critical thinking skills
- Explain the task and read out the example.
- Give Ss time to complete the task in pairs and then ask various pairs to share their answers with the class.

Suggested Answer Key

A: What will you do if your car breaks down?
B: If my car breaks down, I will call a breakdown service. What will you do if it's a sunny day tomorrow?
A: If it's a sunny day tomorrow, I'll go to the beach. What will you do if you get hungry?
B: If I get hungry, I'll order a pizza. What will you do if you go to London?
A: If I go to London, I'll go on the London Eye and visit Buckingham Palace.

4c Skills in Action

Vocabulary

1 **Aim** To present vocabulary for job qualities
- Give Ss time to complete the sentences with the words in the list.
- Ask Ss to look up the meanings of any words they don't know in their dictionaries.
- Check Ss' answers.

Answer Key

1 careful   5 imaginative
2 hard-working   6 patient
3 caring   7 brave
4 sociable

Listening

2 **Aim** To listen for specific information (multiple choice)
- Ask Ss to read the questions and answer choices.
- Play the recording. Ss listen and choose their answers.
- Check Ss' answers around the class.

Answer Key

1 C   2 B   3 B   4 A   5 A

Everyday English

3 a) **Aim** To read for cohesion and coherence (missing words)

Ask Ss to read the job adverts. Then ask them to read the dialogue and fill in the missing words.

b) **Aim** To listen for confirmation
- Play the recording. Ss listen and check their answers in Ex. 3a.
- Elicit which advert it matches.

Answer Key

1 What   3 tell   5 Do
2 Can   4 How   6 Can

It matches advert B.

4 **Aim** To role play a job interview
- Explain the task and ask Ss to act out a similar dialogue to the one in Ex. 3 in pairs using advert A.
- Write this diagram on the board for Ss to follow.

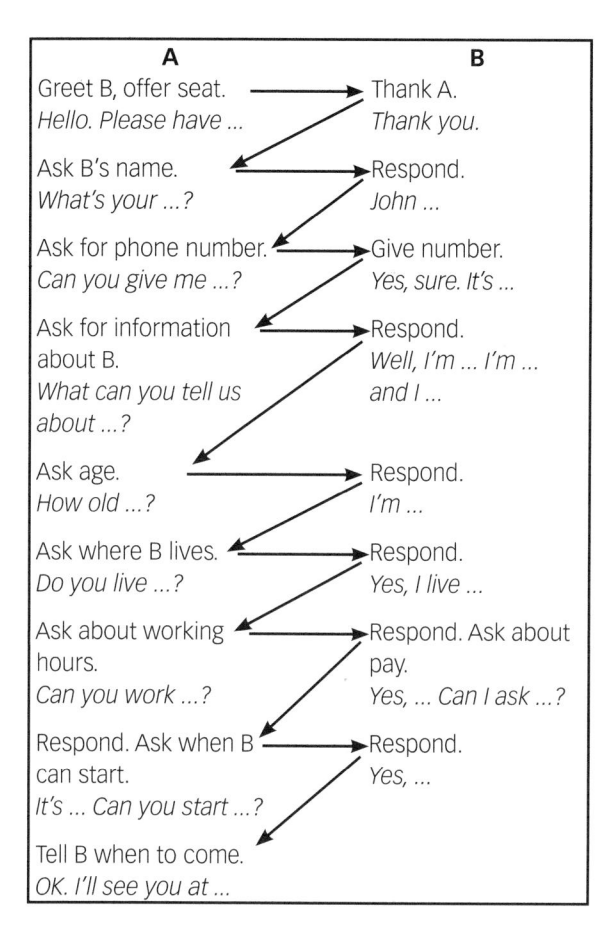

A	B
Greet B, offer seat. Hello. Please have …	Thank A. Thank you.
Ask B's name. What's your …?	Respond. John …
Ask for phone number. Can you give me …?	Give number. Yes, sure. It's …
Ask for information about B. What can you tell us about …?	Respond. Well, I'm … I'm … and I …
Ask age. How old …?	Respond. I'm …
Ask where B lives. Do you live …?	Respond. Yes, I live …
Ask about working hours. Can you work …?	Respond. Ask about pay. Yes, … Can I ask …?
Respond. Ask when B can start. It's … Can you start …?	Respond. Yes, …
Tell B when to come. OK. I'll see you at …	

- Monitor the activity around the class and offer assistance as necessary.
- Then ask some pairs to act out their dialogues in front of the class.

Suggested Answer Key

A: Hello. Please have a seat.
B: Thank you.
A: What's your full name?
B: John Smith.
A: Can you give me a contact number?
B: Yes, sure. It's 0789541236.
A: OK. What can you tell us about yourself, Mr Smith?
B: Well, I'm a student, studying English. I'm very friendly and hard-working and I need a job.
A: How old are you?
B: I'm 20.
A: Do you live near the shop?
B: Yes, I live at 44 Princess Avenue.
A: Can you work in the mornings?
B: Yes, no problem. Can I ask how much the salary is?
A: It's £7.50 per hour. Can you start this Monday?
B: Yes, I'd be happy to.
A: OK. I'll see you at 9 am, then.

Pronunciation ('ll)

5 Aim To learn the pronunciation of 'll

- Play the recording with pauses for Ss to repeat, chorally and/or individually.
- Check Ss' pronunciation and intonation.

Reading & Writing

6 Aim To substitute informal phrases for formal ones

- Read out the Writing Tip and remind Ss that the style of letters/emails of application is formal.
- Ask Ss to read the email and then the list of formal phrases a-h.
- Give Ss time to complete the task and then check their answers.

Answer Key

1 d	3 h	5 e	7 g
2 f	4 b	6 a	8 c

Writing

7 Aim To complete a CV

- Explain to Ss that when we write a letter/email applying for a job, it is common to also enclose our CV (so that the prospective employer can see our personal details in note form).
- Ask Ss to read the text and then give them time to use the information to complete the CV.
- Explain/Elicit the meanings of any unknown words.
- Check Ss' answers around the class.

Answer Key

Date of birth: 03/07
Place of residence: 12 Cambridge Drive, Bodley
Contact number: 0161 430 7873
Email address: SarahJ_01@gmail.com
Education: student at Bodley Heath High School
Work experience: Bodley Library, assistant in the online reference section, last summer
Skills & Qualities: good with computers, excellent communication skills, very sociable

8 Aim To write an email applying for a job

- Give Ss time to read the advert and use their answers in Ex.7 to write an email applying for a job and following the plan.
- Ask various Ss to read their email to the class.
- Alternatively, assign the task as HW and then check Ss' answers in the next lesson.

Suggested Answer Key

From: SarahJ_01@gmail.com
To: techshack@live.co.uk
Subject: Summer job

Dear Sir/Madam,
I am writing to enquire about the summer job at Tech Shack. I am 17 years old and I am a student in my last year at Bodley Heath High School. My subjects are Maths, Computer Science and ICT.
I worked in the Bodley Library last summer as an assistant in the online reference section. I am very good with computers and have excellent communication skills. Moreover, I am very friendly and sociable and enjoy helping people find the information they need.
I am available to work from June to September. Thank you for taking the time to read my application. I look forward to hearing from you.
Yours faithfully,
Sarah Jones

Values

Ss try to explain the quotation in their mother tongue. If Ss have difficulty, explain the quotation. Ask Ss to memorise this quotation and check in the next lesson.
The quotation means that for something to grow, in particular I think it means a business, then you must work hard.

Culture 4

Listening & Reading

1 **Aim** **To introduce the topic and predict the content of the text; to listen and read for gist**

- Read the rubric aloud and elicit what Ss think it's like to work as a cashier and a car wash attendant.
- Play the recording. Ss listen and read and find out.

Suggested Answer Key

It's quite easy to work as a cashier, but you need to be good with money and friendly and polite to customers. You don't earn much money, but you might get a higher position. On the other hand, it can be a boring job.
Car wash attendants can find a job easily and work when they don't have lessons. They don't need any special skills and it can be sociable working with other attendants. But the wages are low and sometimes you work outside.

2 a) **Aim** **To read for specific information (multiple matching)**

- Ask Ss to read the questions 1-6 and then read the text again and match them to the jobs accordingly.
- Check Ss' answers.

Answer Key

1 A 2 B 3 B 4 A 5 A 6 B

b) **Aim** **To consolidate vocabulary from a text**

- Give Ss time to look up the meanings of the words in the **Check these words** box in the Word List.

Suggested Answer Key

customer: sb who buys a product or service
wages: money paid in exchange for work or services done (usually weekly)
qualification: formal education or training
fit: strong and healthy

- Play the video for Ss and elicit their comments.

Speaking & Writing

3 **Aim** **THINK** **To relate the topic to your culture; to express an opinion**

- Give Ss time to consider their answers.
- Elicit answers from Ss around the class.

Suggested Answer Key

Two part-time jobs for students in my country are waiting and working as shop assistants. I think waiting jobs are the most difficult. You often work long shifts, it's tiring work and the pay is quite low. Also, you sometimes have to serve difficult, rude customers.

4 **Aim** **ICT** **To develop research skills; to write about typical student jobs in your country**

- Explain the task and give Ss time to research online and collect information about typical student jobs in their country and write a short text.
- Then ask various Ss to present the jobs to the class.
- Alternatively, assign the task as HW and ask Ss to read out their texts in the next lesson.

Suggested Answer Key

Part-time jobs for students in my country include waiting, pet sitting, assisting at sports and music events, tutoring and creating social media content.
Waiting staff can work in many different places like restaurants, hotels and cafés. It's tiring because they are on their feet all the time but they can earn good tips as well as their pay.
People in my country love animals so pet sitting is a popular job. Pet sitters have a nice job taking dogs for walks outdoors and grooming and feeding pets. It is a big responsibility, though. Pet sitters are usually paid by the hour and can earn quite good money.
Assisting at sports and music events is usually casual rather than part-time – that is, you only work for a short

period. But there are so many of these events going on in our capital city that a student can find work almost all the time. The only thing is, they can't choose what times they work as these events have a set programme. I think the rate of pay is quite high.

Tutoring and creating social media content are jobs for students with the right qualifications. Tutoring can be teaching almost any subject to younger pupils, from a foreign language to Maths and Sciences. It's pleasant teaching something you know. Some younger students might not always be easy to teach, however. Students who have computer skills can get a job with companies who want help to create their social media profile. This job has the advantage that a lot of it can be done from home, in between a student's lessons. It means working on your own, which might not suit all people. Both these jobs are highly paid.

Review 4
Vocabulary

1 **Aim** **To practise vocabulary from the unit**
- Explain the task.
- Give Ss time to complete it.
- Check Ss' answers.

Answer Key

| 1 c | 3 f | 5 a | 7 d |
| 2 e | 4 g | 6 h | 8 b |

2 **Aim** **To practise vocabulary from the unit**
- Explain the task.
- Give Ss time to complete it.
- Check Ss' answers.

Answer Key

1 works   3 do   5 passed
2 make   4 followed

3 **Aim** **To practise vocabulary from the unit**
- Explain the task.
- Give Ss time to complete it.
- Check Ss' answers.

Answer Key

1 brave   3 sociable   5 careful
2 imaginative   4 patient

Grammar

4 **Aim** **To practise *will – be going to***
- Explain the task.
- Give Ss time to complete it.
- Check Ss' answers.

Answer Key

1 're going to   4 'll
2 will   5 'm going to
3 'm going to

5 **Aim** **To practise future forms**
- Explain the task.
- Give Ss time to complete it.
- Check Ss' answers.

Answer Key

1 are seeing   4 will get
2 will go   5 are going to break
3 starts

6 **Aim** **To practise type 1 conditionals**
- Explain the task.
- Give Ss time to complete it.
- Check Ss' answers.

Answer Key

1 passes, will become   4 work, will earn
2 go, 'll catch   5 won't go, is
3 won't be, wakes

7 **Aim** **To practise conjunctions used with type 1 conditionals**
- Explain the task.
- Give Ss time to complete it.
- Check Ss' answers.

Answer Key

1 if   2 when   3 If   4 when

Everyday English

8 **Aim** **To choose the correct responses in exchanges**
- Explain the task.
- Give Ss time to complete it.
- Check Ss' answers.

Answer Key

1 b   2 a   3 a

Competences

Ask Ss to assess their own performance in the unit by ticking the items according to how competent they feel for each of the listed activities.

Optional activity

Discuss your weekend plans, then decide to do sth together.

5 Food, glorious food!

Topic
In this unit, Ss will explore the topics of food & drinks and fast food dishes & drinks.

5a   Reading & Vocabulary   36-37
Lesson objectives: To learn vocabulary for food & drinks, to act out dialogues about food & cooking methods, to listen and read for gist, to read for specific information (multiple choice), to learn prepositional phrases, to design a day's menu
Vocabulary: Food & drinks *(fried rice with chicken and prawns, pizza and Buffalo wings, poached salmon, lamb & mashed potatoes, spaghetti Bolognese & garlic bread, steak with jacket potato, fish and chips with peas, lasagne, yoghurt, mussels, wholemeal bread, mayonnaise, bread rolls, doughnut, watermelon, melon, fruit salad, apple juice, carrot juice, cheesecake)*; Nouns *(submarine, crew, vegetarian)*; Adjectives *(well stocked, frozen, tinned)*; Phrases *(on board, keep spirits up)*

5b   Grammar in Use   38-39
Lesson objectives: To learn/revise countable/uncountable nouns – quantifiers, to learn/revise *some – any – no – every* & compounds, to learn/revise conditionals type 0

5c   Skills in Action   40-41
Lesson objectives: To learn vocabulary for fast food dishes & drinks, to listen for cohesion (multiple choice), to act out a dialogue and practise everyday English for ordering a takeaway, to learn the pronunciation of *like – 'd like*, to read for cohesion & coherence (missing words), to write an online review
Vocabulary: Fast food dishes & drinks *(fried chicken, burger, kebab, cheeseburger, fish & chips, chips, garlic bread, green salad, onion rings, ice cream (vanilla, chocolate, strawberry), cheesecake, apple pie, pancakes & syrup, chocolate brownie, tea, milk, coffee, cola, lemonade, water [still/sparkling])*

Culture 5   42
Lesson objectives: To listen and read for specific information, to read for key information (answer questions), to talk and write about a festival sweet in your country
Vocabulary: Nouns *(oven, oatmeal)*; Verbs *(wrap, fail)*; Phrasal verbs *(blow up)*; Adjectives *(festive, dried, spicy)*; Phrase *(ground nuts)*

Review 5   43
Lesson objectives: To test/consolidate vocabulary and grammar learnt throughout the unit; to practise everyday English

Go through the objectives box and tell Ss that these are the topics, skills and activities this unit will cover.

5a

Vocabulary

1 Aim To introduce subject-related vocabulary; to classify food

- Play the recording with pauses for Ss to repeat chorally and/or individually.
- Check Ss' pronunciation and intonation.
- Explain that the title of the unit is the title of a song, and that glorious is a synonym of wonderful. Explain/Elicit the meaning of *healthy, low-fat foods, fatty foods* and *junk food*, and write these on the board as headings.
- Elicit from Ss which heading(s) each item in the pictures should go under, and write their answers on the board. A variety of answers is possible, as some foods are healthy when eaten in moderation, the fat content of various foods depends on the method of cooking, certain foods which do not contain fat are nonetheless fattening, etc. Ss copy the lists into their notebooks.

Suggested Answer Key

healthy foods: chicken, prawns, poached salmon, lamb, mashed potatoes, garlic, steak, jacket potato, peas, yoghurt, mussels, wholemeal bread, bread rolls, watermelon, melon, fruit salad, apple juice, carrot juice
low-fat foods: watermelon, melon, fruit salad, apple juice, carrot juice, mussels, prawns, wholemeal bread, jacket potato
fatty foods: fried rice, pizza, Buffalo wings, fried fish, chips, mayonnaise, cheesecake, lasagne, spaghetti Bolognese
junk food: pizza, Buffalo wings, chips, doughnut

2 Aim To practise vocabulary related to cooking methods

Divide the class into teams. Give each team a minute to think of as many foods as they can that can be cooked with the cooking methods in the list. Then write the cooking methods on the board and elicit answers from each team, one at a time. Each correct answer gets a point. The team with the most points after all the answers have been shared is the winner.

Suggested Answer Key

bake: fish, potatoes, cake, biscuits, pizza
boil: vegetables (e.g. carrots, broccoli), potatoes, rice, egg, pasta, chicken
poach: salmon, egg, fish
steam: vegetables (e.g. broccoli, spinach), rice
fry: fish, steak, chips, egg, chicken

3 Aim To practise vocabulary relating to food & drinks; to act out dialogues talking about food and cooking methods

- Explain the task and ask two Ss to act out the example dialogue.
- Then ask Ss to act out dialogues using the food in the list and following the example.
- Monitor the activity around the class and then ask some pairs to act out their dialogues in front of the class.

Suggested Answer Key

A: How do you like your mushrooms?
B: Fried. What about you?
A: I prefer them baked.

A: How do you like your chicken?
B: Roasted. What about you?
A: I prefer it fried.

A: How do you like your fish?
B: Fried. What about you?
A: I prefer it grilled.

A: How do you like your rice?
B: Boiled. What about you?
A: I prefer it fried.

A: How do you like your broccoli?
B: Boiled. What about you?
A: I prefer it poached.

A: How do you like your prawns?
B: Fried. What about you?
A: I prefer them baked.

A: How do you like your salmon?
B: Baked. What about you?
A: I prefer it grilled.

Reading & Listening

4 Aim To introduce the topic and read for gist

- Elicit Ss' guesses as to the food on a submarine.
- Ss read the text quickly to find out.

Suggested Answer Key

The food on a submarine is excellent.

5 Aim To read for specific information (multiple choice)

- Ask Ss to read the questions and answer choices.
- Give Ss time to read the text and then choose their answers.
- Check Ss' answers.

Answer Key

1 B   2 C   3 A   4 C

- Give Ss time to look up the meanings of the words in bold in the Word List or in their dictionaries.
- Elicit definitions from Ss around the class.

Suggested Answer Key

ingredient (n) = sth you use to make a food dish
mission (n) = an important task
produce (n) = fruit and vegetables
voyage (n) = a journey by ship, plane or space ship
popular (adj) = well-known and liked
make sense (phr) = to be easy to understand
wave (n) = a raised line of water that moves along the surface

- Give Ss time to look up the meanings of the words in the **Check these words** box in the Word List.
- Play the video for Ss and elicit their comments.

6 Aim THINK To listen and read for gist; to develop critical thinking skills

Give Ss time to consider their answers to the questions and then ask various Ss around the class to tell the rest of the class, giving reasons.

Suggested Answer Key

I think the food on a submarine is healthy because there are a lot of fruit and vegetables on the menu. They have pizza and Buffalo wings, which are not very healthy, but these are only on the menu once a week. I would add a wider variety of fruit to the menu.

7 Aim To consolidate new vocabulary

- Play the recording. Ss listen to and read the text.
- Give Ss time to complete the sentences with the words in the list.
- Check Ss' answers.

Answer Key

1 cramped   5 well   9 midnight
2 healthy   6 frozen   10 salad
3 typical   7 tinned
4 store   8 fresh

Suggested Answer Key

1 The crew on the submarine live in cramped conditions.
2 The submarine's chef uses healthy ingredients in his cooking.
3 The chef makes sure there is enough food to last the crew on a typical mission.
4 The store cupboard on the submarine is where the chef keeps his ingredients.

5 The chef makes sure the cupboards are well stocked, so the crew won't go hungry.
6 The chef uses frozen rather than fresh meat.
7 The crew eat lots of tinned food during a mission.
8 The chef orders fresh produce such as fruit and vegetables before every trip.
9 Crew members who work night shifts might want to eat a midnight snack.
10 The salad bar offers a variety of salads for those who don't eat meat.

8 Aim To practise prepositional phrases

- Give Ss time to complete the phrases with the correct preposition.
- Check Ss' answers.
- Then give Ss time to write sentences using the phrases.
- Elicit answers from Ss around the class.

Answer Key

1 on   2 to   3 on   4 with

Suggested Answer Key

1 There is excellent food on board a submarine.
2 Ben Hayes talked to chef Tom Walsh.
3 Submarines may go on a mission for months.
4 The salad bar is popular with vegetarians.

Speaking & Writing

9 Aim THINK To design a menu; to develop critical thinking skills

- Ask Ss to work in small groups and give them time to consider their answers and design a menu for airline flight, including the points listed.
- Then ask various groups to present their menu to the class.

Suggested Answer Key

breakfast: omelette, fruit, bread roll with jam and butter
lunch: pasta with tomato sauce, salad, walnut cake
dinner: chicken, broccoli and rice, salad, chocolate sponge
drinks: fruit juice, water, cola, tea, coffee

5b Grammar in Use

1 Aim To present/revise countable/uncountable nouns

- Explain that some nouns can be counted (e.g. e-book reader, smartphone, etc) and these are countable and some nouns can't be counted (e.g. data, information etc). These are uncountable nouns.
- Then ask Ss to list all the countable/uncountable nous in the dialogue.

Answer Key

Countable: prawn salads, lettuce leaves, cucumber slices, bowls, tomatoes, prawns, shells
Uncountable: fish, dressing, tomato ketchup, lemon juice, lime juice, mayonnaise

2 Aim To present/revise quantifiers

- Explain that we use **a/an** with countable nouns and **some** with uncountable nouns.
- Explain that we use **some** in affirmative sentences and we use **any** in negative sentences and interrogative sentences.
- Explain that we use **(how) much/(a) little** with uncountable nouns and **(how) many/(a) few** with countable nouns.
- Explain that we use **a lot of** with countable / uncountable nouns.
- Elicit the answers to the questions from Ss around the class.

Answer Key

Affirmative sentences: an, some, a lot of/lots of, a few, few, a little, little, no
Negative sentences: many, much, any
Questions: an, any, much, many

3 Aim To practise countable/uncountable nouns

- Explain the task and give Ss time to complete it.
- Check Ss' answers.

Answer Key

3 honey U
4 potato C potatoes
5 salmon U
6 yoghurt U
7 lettuce U
8 peach C peaches
9 tea U
10 strawberry C strawberries
11 grape C grapes
12 lamb U
13 pea C peas
14 burger C burgers

4 a) Aim To practise a/an/some

- Explain the task and give Ss time to complete it.
- Check Ss' answers around the class.

Answer Key

a: burger, banana, jacket potato, biscuit, peach
an: apple, apricot
some: pasta, chips, sweets, orange juice, tea, coffee, milk, chocolates, eggs, grapes, cheese

b) Aim To practise a/an/some

- Ask two Ss to model the example dialogue and then have Ss act out similar short dialogues in closed pairs using the items in Ex. 4a.

- Monitor the activity around the class and then ask some Ss to act out their dialogues in front of the class.

Suggested Answer Key

A: Would you like some chips?
B: Yes, please. And can I have a burger too?
A: Of course. Do you want an apricot?
B: No, thanks. I'd rather have a banana.

5 Aim To practise nouns of quantity

- Explain the task and give Ss time to complete it.
- Then check Ss' answers.

Answer Key

3	bread	8	salmon
4	lettuce	9	fish
5	butter	10	potatoes
6	meat	11	mayonnaise
7	pizza	12	coffee

6 a) Aim To practise quantifiers

- Explain the task and give Ss time to read the dialogue and complete the gaps with the correct words.
- Check Ss' answers.

Answer Key

13	some	17	some	21	any	25	some
14	any	18	much	22	a little		
15	many	19	much	23	any		
16	a few	20	a little	24	any		

b) Aim To practise quantifiers

- Have Ss act out similar short dialogues in closed pairs using the items in the lists.
- Monitor the activity around the class and then ask some Ss to act out their dialogues in front of the class.

Suggested Answer Key

A: Have we got what we need for the omelette?
B: Let me see. Well, there are some eggs, but there aren't any onions at all.
A: How many onions do you need?
B: Just a few. I need some cheese, too.
A: How much cheese is there in the fridge?
B: Not much, but I only need a little.
A: Is there any milk left?
B: Only a little, but we don't need much, so don't buy any. We haven't got any butter at all, though.
A: I'll buy some, then.

A: Have we got what we need for the pizza?
B: Let me see. Well, there are some mushrooms, but there aren't any tomatoes at all.

A: How many tomatoes do you need?
B: Just a few. I need some chicken, too.
A: How much chicken is there in the fridge?
B: Not much, but I only need a little.
A: Is there any olive oil left?
B: Only a little, but we don't need much, so don't buy any. We haven't got any cheese at all, though.
A: I'll buy some, then.

Optional activity

Play in pairs or teams. Say a sentence using a quantifier or a noun of quantity wrongly. The other person or team corrects the sentence.

A: I want **some** burger.
B: I want **a** burger.

7 Aim To present *some – any – no – every* & compounds

- Explain that for people we use *someone/somebody* (affirmative statements), *no one/nobody* (negative statements) and *anyone/anybody* (questions and negative statements). For things/places we use *something/somewhere* (affirmative statements), *nothing/nowhere* (negative) and *anything/anywhere* (questions and negative). We use *everyone/everybody/everything/everywhere* in affirmative and interrogative sentences.
- Ask Ss to read the theory and then give them time to compete the table. Check Ss' answers and then elicit examples from the dialogue on p. 40.

Answer Key

1	someone	3	no one	5	everyone
2	anything	4	everything		

Examples: anything, some, any, everyone

8 Aim To practise *some – any – no – every* & compounds

- Give Ss time to complete the task.
- Check Ss' answers around the class.

Answer Key

1 any (question)
2 something (affirmative)
3 any (negative)
4 somewhere (affirmative)
5 anyone (negative)
6 some (affirmative)
7 nothing (affirmative with negative meaning)
8 anywhere (negative)
9 nothing (affirmative with negative meaning)
10 Everyone (affirmative; all)

47

9 Aim To practise *some – any – no – every* & compounds

- Explain the task and read out the example.
- Give Ss time to complete it.
- Check Ss' answers.

Answer Key

1 anyone, everyone/everybody
2 anything, some
3 nothing, something
4 somewhere, No one/Nobody

10 Aim To present/revise/practise Type 0 conditionals

- Say, then write on board: *If you freeze water, it turns to ice.* Explain that this is a type 0 conditional sentence and that it contains an if-clause and a main clause. Tell Ss that we put a comma after the *if*-clause.
- Explain that we use type 0 conditional to talk about a general truth or things that always happen and we use the present simple in both clauses.
- Explain the task and read out the example.
- Give Ss time to complete the task.
- Check Ss' answers.

Answer Key

2 If/When you heat butter, it melts.
3 If/When you mix red and white, you get pink.
4 If/When it rains regularly, it helps flowers to grow.
5 If/When I eat a lot of chocolate, I get spots.

5c Skills in Action

Vocabulary

1 Aim To present vocabulary for fast food dishes & drinks

- Give Ss time to complete the menu with the words in the list.
- Ask Ss to look up the meanings of any words they don't know in their dictionaries.
- Check Ss' answers.

Answer Key

1 Chicken   5 Vanilla
2 Fish   6 Apple
3 Bread   7 Shake
4 Green   8 Lemonade

2 Aim To talk about fast food dishes

Elicit a variety of answers from Ss around the class.

Suggested Answer Key

My favourite fast food is pizza. I eat fast food once a week and takeaways once a month.

Listening

3 Aim To listen for cohesion (multiple choice)

- Ask Ss to read the answer choices.
- Play the recording. Ss listen and complete the task.
- Check Ss' answers.

Answer Key

1 A   2 B   3 B   4 B   5 A

Everyday English

4 a) Aim To complete a dialogue

- Ask Ss to read the sentences.
- Give Ss time to complete the task.

Answer Key

1 I'd like a kebab, please.
2 Would you like chips with it?
3 Anything to drink?
4 Would you like anything else?
5 Is that to eat in or take away?
6 How much is it?
7 Here you are.

b) Aim To listen for confirmation

Play the recording for Ss to check their answers to Ex. 4a.

5. Aim To act out a dialogue ordering food

- Explain the task and ask Ss to act out a similar dialogue to the one in Ex. 4 in pairs using the menu in Ex. 1 and the Language box to help them.
- Write this diagram on the board for Ss to follow.

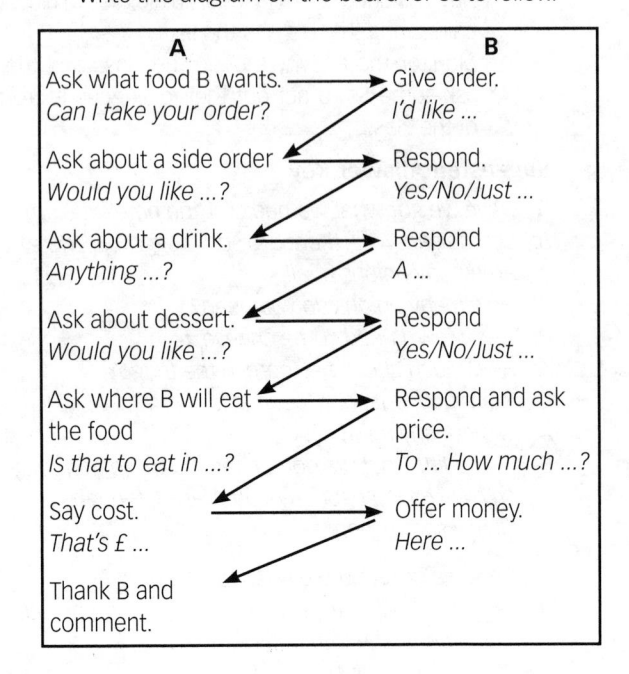

A	B
Ask what food B wants. *Can I take your order?*	Give order. *I'd like …*
Ask about a side order *Would you like …?*	Respond. *Yes/No/Just …*
Ask about a drink. *Anything …?*	Respond *A …*
Ask about dessert. *Would you like …?*	Respond *Yes/No/Just …*
Ask where B will eat the food *Is that to eat in …?*	Respond and ask price. *To … How much …?*
Say cost. *That's £ …*	Offer money. *Here …*
Thank B and comment.	

- Monitor the activity around the class and offer assistance as necessary.
- Then ask some pairs to act out their dialogues in front of the class.

Suggested Answer Key

A: Can I take your order?
B: Yes, I'd like a cheeseburger, please.
A: Would you like chips with it?
B: Just a small portion.
A: Anything to drink?
B: A lemonade.
A: Fine. Would you like dessert?
B: No, thanks.
A: Is that to eat in or take away?
B: To take away, please. How much is it?
A: That's £3.30, please.
B: Here you are.
A: Thank you. Enjoy your meal.

Pronunciation

6 **Aim** To learn the pronunciation of *like* – *'d like*

- Explain that Ss will hear six sentences, some with **like** and some with **'d like** [=would like].
- Play the recording. Ss listen and repeat, chorally and/or individually.
- Check Ss' pronunciation and intonation.

Reading & Writing

7 **Aim** To read for cohesion and coherence (missing words)

- Ask Ss to read the restaurant review and complete the gaps with the words in the list.
- Check Ss' answers.

Answer Key

1 heart   5 homemade
2 disappointed 6 top
3 starter   7 high
4 treat   8 friendly

8 **Aim** To practise language for recommending

- Read out the phrases in the list and give Ss time to use them to complete the sentences.
- Check Ss' answers around the class.

Answer Key

1 you'll love   3 worth visiting
2 highly recommend 4 a thumbs down

9 **Aim** To read for specific information

- Ask Ss to read the restaurant review again and give Ss time to find the good/bad points and recommendation.
- Elicit answers from Ss around the class.

Answer key

Good points – beautiful restaurant, excellent prawn starter, (the fish and chips with peas) was an absolute treat, everything was perfect, gave the food top marks, great food served by friendly, professional staff
Bad points – the prices were a bit high
Recommendation – I would definitely recommend the place! There's nowhere better for Sunday lunch!

10 a) **Aim** To practise using adjectives

- Explain the task, then give Ss time to complete it.
- Elicit answers from Ss around the class.

Answer Key

restaurant – beautiful, little
river – small
Sunday lunch – great, quiet
apple pie – homemade
prices – high
food – great
staff – friendly, professional
setting – beautiful

b) **Aim** To practise using adjectives

- Explain the task. Then, give Ss time to complete it.
- Elicit answers from Ss around the class.

Answer Key

1 friendly   4 delicious   7 crowded
2 beautiful   5 popular   8 daily
3 sociable   6 tasty

Writing

11 **Aim** To write an online review

- Read out the Writing Tip and tell Ss this advice will help them to complete the task successfully.
- Give Ss time to write their review using the plan to help them.
- Check Ss' answers.
- Alternatively, assign the task as HW and check Ss' answers in the next lesson.

Suggested Answer Key

Monty's is a new fast-food restaurant on the high street in the centre of Chester. I visited it last week to try it out. There is a varied menu at Monty's which includes a fantastic salad bar, a wide choice of vegetarian dishes and five types of delicious hamburgers. I tried the Mexican Sizzler — a spicy hamburger with chilli sauce in a soft, white bread roll. It was very tasty. Monty's staff were helpful, friendly and polite and the good music, clean tables and comfortable seating all helped to give Monty's an excellent atmosphere.

However, I thought that Monty's was a bit too expensive. Also, the service was slow and one of the cashiers gave me the wrong change.

On the whole, Monty's is a good fast food restaurant. However, unless they lower the prices and the staff work faster with fewer mistakes, I don't think I'll go there again.

Values

Ss try to explain the saying in their mother tongue. If Ss have difficulty, explain the saying. Ask Ss to memorise this saying and check in the next lesson.
The saying means that you should be happy with what you have and always remember that it could be worse.

Culture 5

Listening & Reading

1 **Aim** To introduce the topic and listen and read for specific information

- Read the rubric aloud and elicit when Ss think the British eat the sweets in the pictures.
- Play the recording. Ss listen and read and find out.

Suggested Answer Key

The British eat Clootie dumpling on Burns Night. They eat Simnel cake on Mother's Day and they eat parkin on Bonfire Night.

2 **Aim** To read for specific information/detailed understanding (answer questions)

- Ask Ss to read the questions 1-6 and then read the text again and answer them.
- Check Ss' answers.

Answer Key

1 On 25th January.
2 It's a tradition from the time when people didn't have ovens to cook in.
3 On Mother's Day.
4 The man and his wife who invented Simnel cake.
5 Someone tried to blow up the Houses of Parliament in London but failed.
6 They watch fireworks displays and eat parkin.

- Give Ss time to look up the meanings of the words in bold in the Word List or in their dictionaries.
- Elicit definitions from Ss around the class.

Suggested Answer Key

Clootie dumpling (n): a traditional Scottish dessert
national (adj): from or of a country
mixture (n): two or more substances combined to make another substance
a pan of (phr): a metal bowl with handles used for cooking
Simnel cake (n): a British cake with yellow topping people eat on Mother's Day
invented (v): thought of and created for the first time
shortened (v): made smaller
celebrates (v): takes part in enjoyable activities to show that an event is important
parkin (n): a British cake made with oatmeal that people eat on Bonfire night
treat (n): sth special and enjoyable

- Give Ss time to look up the meanings of the words in the **Check these words** box in the Word List.
- Play the video for Ss and elicit their comments.

Speaking & Writing

3 **Aim** **THINK** To expand the topic

- Give Ss time to consider their answers.
- Elicit answers from Ss around the class.
- Alternatively, assign the task as HW and encourage Ss to video themselves and show the video in the next lesson.

Suggested Answer Key

In Italy at Christmas, we eat panettone. It is a sweet, dome-shaped bread loaf with raisins and candied fruit. The dough takes several days to make and it is nice to eat with a cup of coffee.

4 **Aim** To write a short text about a festive sweet from your country

- Explain the task and give Ss time to write a short text about a festive sweet from their country.
- Then ask various Ss to read their text to the class.
- Alternatively, assign the task as HW and ask Ss to read out their texts in the next lesson.

Suggested Answer Key

In Italy at Christmas, we eat panettone. It is a sweet, dome-shaped bread loaf with raisins and candied fruit. The dough takes several days to make and it is nice to eat with a cup of coffee.

Review 5

Vocabulary

1 **Aim** To practise vocabulary from the unit
- Explain the task.
- Give Ss time to complete it.
- Check Ss' answers.

Answer Key

1 olive 3 low-fat 5 garlic
2 tinned 4 poached

2 **Aim** To practise vocabulary from the unit
- Explain the task.
- Give Ss time to complete it.
- Check Ss' answers.

Answer Key

1 sparkling 4 wholemeal
2 fried 5 dessert
3 syrup

3 **Aim** To practise vocabulary from the unit
- Explain the task.
- Give Ss time to complete it.
- Check Ss' answers.

Answer Key

1 Bake 3 run 5 cosy
2 popular 4 on board

Grammar

4 **Aim** To practise quantifiers
- Explain the task.
- Give Ss time to complete it.
- Check Ss' answers.

Answer Key

1 many 4 no 7 a few
2 a little 5 any 8 some
3 a lot of 6 too many

5 **Aim** To practise some, any, no, every & compounds
- Explain the task.
- Give Ss time to complete it.
- Check Ss' answers.

Answer Key

1 anywhere, somewhere 3 No one, something
2 anyone, everyone 4 Someone, nothing

6 **Aim** To practise type 0 conditionals
- Explain the task.
- Give Ss time to complete it.
- Check Ss' answers.

Answer Key

1 If you boil sugar and fruit, you get jam.
2 If I eat too much, I get a stomach ache.
3 If people eat a lot of sweets, they put on weight.
4 If we don't water plants, they die.

Everyday English

7 **Aim** To choose the correct responses in exchanges
- Explain the task.
- Give Ss time to complete it.
- Check Ss' answers.

Answer Key

1 D 2 E 3 A 4 B 5 C

Competences

Ask Ss to assess their own performance in the unit by ticking the items according to how competent they feel for each of the listed activities.

Optional activity

Play in pairs or team. Say a word from the unit that collocates with another word. The other person or team says the word.
e.g. A: fried
B: fish – mashed
A: potatoes, etc.

Possible phrases to be used: *fried rice, poached salmon, garlic bread, jacket potato, wholemeal bread, apple juice, fruit salad, frozen meat, salad bar, ice cream, onion rings,* etc.

6 Health

Topic
In this unit, Ss will explore the topics of health, illnesses & remedies, parts of the body & injuries.

6a Reading & Vocabulary	46-47

Lesson objectives: To learn vocabulary for illnesses & remedies, to act out dialogues about illnesses & remedies, to listen and read for gist, to read for specific information (multiple choice), to distinguish between words easily confused, to learn prepositions, to talk about natural remedies, to write a forum post giving advice
Vocabulary: Illnesses & Remedies *(a toothache, a cold, a sore throat, a temperature, a cough, an earache, a headache, a stomach ache, see the dentist, stop eating chocolates, take some cough medicine, go to bed)*; Nouns *(nettle, fluid, fever, vinegar, infection)*; verb *(soak)*; Adjectives *(smelly, medical)*; Phrase *(in doubt)*

6b Grammar in Use	48-49

Lesson objectives: To learn/revise the present perfect, to compare the present perfect and the past simple, to learn the present perfect continuous

6c Skills in Action	50-51

Lesson objectives: To learn vocabulary for parts of the body & injuries, to listen for specific information (multiple matching), to act out a dialogue and practise everyday English at the doctor's, to learn the pronunciation of /ɪd/, to read for cohesion & coherence (missing sentences), to write an email narrating an experience
Vocabulary: Parts of the body & injuries *(cut finger, sprain ankle, break wrist, bump head, burn hand, bruise leg)*

Culture 6	52

Lesson objectives: To listen and read for gist, to read for cohesion & coherence (missing sentences), to talk about the Flying Doctors Service, to write about a similar service in your country
Vocabulary: Nouns *(outback, community, check-up, shot, donation)*; Adjectives *(Aboriginal, remote)*

Review 6	53

Lesson objectives: To test/consolidate vocabulary and grammar learnt throughout the unit; to practise everyday English

Go through the objectives box and tell Ss that these are the topics, skills and activities this unit will cover.

6a

Vocabulary

1 Aim To present and practise vocabulary for illnesses & remedies

- Play the recording with pauses for Ss to repeat chorally and/or individually.
- Check Ss' pronunciation and intonation.
- Read out the example sentences and then elicit sentences from Ss around the class for the remaining pictures.

Suggested Answer Key

2 Mike has got a stomach ache.
3 Jasmine has got a sore throat.
4 Sonia has got a temperature.
5 Trevor has got a cough.
6 Jimmy has got an earache.
7 Felix has got a toothache.
8 Anne has got a cold.

Speaking

2 Aim To act out dialogues about illnesses & remedies

- Ask two Ss to model the example dialogue and then have Ss complete the task in closed pairs using the prompts.
- Monitor the activity around the class and then ask various pairs to act out their dialogues in front of the rest of the class.

Suggested Answer Key

A: What's the matter?
B: I've got a toothache.
A: Why don't you see the dentist?

A: What's the matter?
B: I've got a stomach ache.
A: Why don't you drink some ginger tea?

A: What's the matter?
B: I've got a cough.
A: Why don't you take some cough medicine?

A: What's the matter?
B: I've got a temperature.
A: Why don't you take an aspirin?

Listening & Reading

3 Aim To listen and read for gist

- Elicit Ss' guesses as to how nettle tea, rice water and vinegar are related to a cold.
- Play the recording. Ss listen and read to find out.

Suggested Answer Key

They are different natural remedies. According to the text, nettle tea can cure a cold. Rice water and vinegar can bring down a temperature.

4 Aim To read for specific information (multiple choice)

- Ask Ss to read the questions and answer choices.
- Give Ss time to read the text and then choose their answers.
- Check Ss' answers.

Answer Key

1 A   2 B   3 A   4 A

- Give Ss time to look up the meanings of the words in the **Check these words** box in the Word List.
- Play the video for Ss and elicit their comments.

5 Aim THINK To develop critical thinking skills; to express an opinion

Give Ss time to consider their answers to the question and then ask various Ss around the class to tell the rest of the class giving reasons.

Suggested Answer Key

I think people try home remedies because going to the doctor is inconvenient and can be expensive. Also, I think that people don't like to see the doctor for minor things like a cough or a cold because they may feel they are wasting the doctor's time.

6 Aim To present and practise verbs of the senses

- Read out the theory box and elicit further examples from Ss around the class (e.g. It looks like spring is here. It feels like winter today. It tastes like chicken.)
- Then give Ss time to complete the task and check their answers.

Answer Key

1 –   2 like   3 –   4 –   5 like   5 like

Background Information

Switzerland is in Western-Central Europe. It consists of 26 cantons. Bern is the seat of the federal authorities.

---

7 Aim To distinguish between words easily confused

- Give Ss time to read the sentences and complete the task.
- Have Ss check their answers by looking up the words in their dictionaries.

Answer Key

1 pain   4 prescription
2 sore   5 treatment
3 hurt   6 disease

8 Aim To practise prepositional phrases

- Give Ss time to complete the phrases with the correct preposition.
- Check Ss' answers.

Answer Key

1 of   2 for   3 for   4 in   5 on

Speaking & Writing

9 Aim ICT To develop research skills; to talk about natural remedies

- Ask Ss to work in small groups and give them time to research home cough remedies online and collect information about different home remedies from around the world.
- Then ask various groups to share their information with the class.

Suggested Answer Key

A Japanese home remedy for a cough is to grate lots of ginger, add lemon and honey and hot water and drink it. In South Africa, a home remedy involves grinding fresh garlic and adding it to soups.
A Native American home remedy tells people to add two tablespoons of chickweed herb and mullein leaves to boiling water. Stir and then leave it for 30 minutes and then drink it warm, one cup every three hours.
In Scotland, drinking nettle tea and going for a walk to get sea air is a home remedy for a cough.

10 Aim To write a forum post giving advice

- Explain the task and give Ss time to complete it using the beginning provided.
- Elicit answers from Ss around the class.

Suggested Answer Key

Sorry you're so ill, Julie. I think you should take a painkiller and then see a doctor. You might have an ear infection from your cold. You can also try putting some warm olive oil on a piece of cotton wool and putting it in your ear to relieve the pain until you get to the doctor. It really helps!

Background Information

Scotland is part of the UK. Its capital city is Edinburgh.

India is a country in South Asia. Its capital city is New Delhi.

6b Grammar in Use

1. **Aim** To present/revise the present perfect

   - Say, then write on the board: *I have finished my homework. Tom hasn't finished his homework.* Underline: *have finished* and *hasn't finished*.
   - Explain that this verb is in the present perfect and that we form it in the affirmative with **have/has** + past participle and in the negative with **haven't/hasn't** + past participle.
   - Explain that we use the present perfect to talk about an action that started in the past and continues to the present, an action which happened at an unstated time in the past, a recent action with a visible result in the present and personal experiences.
   - Explain that we form questions in the present perfect with **have/has** + personal pronoun + past participle.
   - Explain/Elicit that we form short answers with **Yes/No** + personal pronoun + **have/has/haven't/hasn't**.
   - Ask Ss to read the theory and then elicit examples from the dialogue, and which usage each is. Ask Ss to provide more examples for each use.

   Answer Key

   has gone, hasn't spread, I've decided, you've made, has had, has he gone, haven't seen, he's gone, has given

2. **Aim** To practise the present perfect

   - Explain the task and give Ss time to complete it.
   - Check Ss' answers.

   Answer Key

   1 has it been, haven't visited
   2 has your husband had, hasn't had
   3 have just had, Have you seen, haven't come
   4 has hit, Have you put
   5 haven't been, have been

3. **Aim** To practise the present perfect (*have gone/have been*)

   - Explain the task and give Ss time to complete it.
   - Check Ss' answers.

   Answer Key

   1 have, been
   2 has gone
   3 have gone
   4 has been

4. **Aim** To practise adverbs used with the present perfect

   - Explain the task and give Ss time to complete it.
   - Check Ss' answers around the class. Elicit reasons.

   Answer Key

   1 just (recently completed action)
   2 ever (question)
   3 yet (negative sentence)
   4 for (a period of time)
   5 since (a specific time)
   6 yet (question)
   7 never (statement with negative meaning)
   8 already (completed action)

5. **Aim** To compare the present perfect and the past simple

   Ask Ss to read the theory and then elicit how the tenses are different.

   Suggested Answer Key

   We use the present perfect for an action which happened at an unstated time in the past or an uncompleted action and we use the past simple for a completed action which happened at a stated time in the past.

6. **Aim** To practise the present perfect and the past simple

   - Explain the task and give Ss time to complete it.
   - Then check Ss' answers.

   Answer Key

   1 Did, did   4 Has, haven't
   2 Has, hasn't   5 Has, has
   3 Did, didn't

Optional activity

Ss in teams make sentences using these words: *yet, ago, already, since, for, just, ever, yesterday, two weeks ago, last summer*. Point out that Ss need to use the present perfect or the past simple.

7. **Aim** To present the present perfect continuous

   - Present the present perfect continuous. Say then write on the board: *Tom has been talking to the doctor for half an hour.* Underline: *has been talking* and explain that the verb is in the present perfect continuous.

- Explain that we use this tense to place emphasis on the duration of an action which started in the past and continues up to the present and to describe a completed past action with a result visible in the present.
- Elicit how we form the present perfect continuous, how it differs from the present perfect and examples from the dialogue.
- Check Ss' answers.

Answer Key

We form the present perfect continuous in the affirmative with the personal pronoun + **have/has** + **been** + main verb with **-ing**.
We form the negative with personal pronoun + **haven't/hasn't** + **been** + main verb with **-ing**.
We form the questions with **have/has** + personal pronoun + **been** + main verb with **-ing**.
It differs from the present perfect because the emphasis is on the duration of the action.
Examples: have you been taking

8 **Aim** To practise the present perfect continuous and the time adverbs *for/since*

- Explain the task and give Ss time to complete it.
- Check Ss' answers.

Answer Key

1 have been waiting, for
2 Has your aunt been working, since
3 hasn't been feeling, since
4 has been talking, for
5 has been raining, since

9 **Aim** To practise the present perfect continuous interrogative

- Explain the task and read out the example.
- Give Ss time to complete the task in pairs and then ask various Ss to share their answers with the class.

Answer Key

2 A: How long have you been living in Japan?
  B: I've been living in Japan since last August.
3 A: How long have you been working here?
  B: I've been working here since 2012.
4 A: How long have you been waiting here?
  B: I've been waiting here for a few minutes.

10 **Aim** To practise the present perfect, the present perfect continuous and the past simple

- Give Ss time to complete the task.
- Check Ss' answers around the class.

Answer Key

1 has probably told
2 started
3 has been
4 have been working
5 have been trying
6 haven't had
7 have been
8 have worked
9 have you ever regretted
10 did you know
11 have started

6c Skills in Action

Vocabulary

1 **Aim** To present vocabulary for parts of the body & injuries

- Explain the task and ask two Ss to model the example dialogue.
- Give Ss time to complete the task in pairs.
- Monitor the activity around the class.

Answer Key

2 E   3 D   4 A   5 C   6 F

2 A: What's wrong with Max?
  B: He's sprained his ankle.
  A: How did he do that?
  B: He was running.
3 A: What's wrong with Sandy?
  B: She's broken her wrist.
  A: How did she do that?
  B: She was playing tennis.
4 A: What's wrong with John?
  B: He's bumped his head.
  A: How did he do that?
  B: He was cleaning up the garage.
5 A: What's wrong with Carla?
  B: She's burnt her hand.
  A: How did she do that?
  B: She was making coffee.
6 A: What's wrong with Sam?
  B: He's bruised his foot.
  A: How did he do that?
  B: He was playing football.

Listening

2 **Aim** To listen for key information (multiple matching)

- Ask Ss to read the lists.
- Play the recording. Ss listen and complete the task.
- Check Ss' answers.

Answer Key

1 F   2 E   3 C   4 D   5 B

6

Everyday English

3 Aim To predict the content of a dialogue and listen and read for gist

- Ask Ss to read the first exchange and try to answer the questions.
- Play the recording. Ss listen and read and find out if their guesses were correct.

Answer Key/Suggested Answer Key

The patient has a cough and a temperature. I think the doctor will suggest antibiotics.

4 Aim To act out a dialogue describing a health problem

- Explain the task and ask Ss to act out a similar dialogue, to the one in Ex. 3 in pairs using the prompts and the language in the box to help them.
- Write this diagram on the board for Ss to follow.

A	B
Greet B and ask about problem. *Good afternoon Mr/Mrs ... What seems ...?*	Say problem. *I've got ... and ...*
Ask about symptoms. *I see. How long ...?*	Respond. *Today's the ... day.*
Offer to examine B. Make diagnosis and say treatment plan. *Let me ... It looks/doesn't look like ... I'm going to give you ...*	Ask about ability to work/action to take. *Can I go to work?/What shall I do?*
Give advice. *I (don't) think it's a good idea to ...*	Take advice and thank A. *I will, doctor. Thank you.*

- Monitor the activity around the class and offer assistance as necessary.
- Then ask some pairs to act out their dialogues in front of the class.

Suggested Answer Key

A: Good afternoon, Miss Jones. What seems to be the problem?
B: I've got an earache and a temperature that just won't go away.
A: I see. How long have you had a temperature?
B: Today's the third day.
A: Let me look at your ear. Yes, it looks like you've got an infection. I'm going to give you a prescription for some antibiotics and some aspirin for the pain.
B: Can I go to work?

A: I don't think it's a good idea to go out for a day or two. You need to stay indoors.
B: I will, doctor. Thank you.

A: Good afternoon, Mr Smith. What seems to be the problem?
B: I've got a headache and a sore throat.
A: I see. How long have you had a sore throat?
B: Today's the second day.
A: Let me look at your throat. Well, it doesn't look like you've got an infection.
B: What shall I do?
A: I think you should get plenty of rest and drink lots of hot tea.
B: I will, doctor. Thank you.

Pronunciation

5 Aim To identify verbs ending in /ɪd/

- Explain that Ss will hear a number of words and they have to identify the /ɪd/ ending by ticking them.
- Play the recording. Ss listen and repeat, chorally and/or individually.
- Check Ss' pronunciation and intonation and elicit which words end in /ɪd/.

Answer Key

wanted, treated, decided, succeeded

We say /ɪd/ after verbs ending in -d or -t.

Reading & Writing

6 Aim To read for cohesion and coherence (missing sentences)

- Ask Ss to read the email and complete the gaps with the sentences in the list.
- Check Ss' answers.

Answer Key

1 D   2 A   3 E   4 C

7 Aim To read for detailed understanding

- Read out the people/things in the list and give Ss time to match them to the underlined words in the text.
- Check Ss' answers around the class.

Answer Key

1 I   3 he   5 one
2 you   4 it   6 that

8 Aim To practise error correction

- Read out the Writing Tip and tell Ss this advice will help them to complete the task successfully.
- Give Ss time to complete the task and then check Ss' answers.

Answer Key

Sorry I haven't **written** for a while but I have **broken** my wrist.
I was playing tennis last Wednesday when I **slipped** and fell. They **took** me to hospital and the doctor put it in cast. It's really **painful**. I don't think I'll be able to take part in the tennis tournament ~~in~~ this year.

Writing

9 a) Aim To analyse a rubric

- Ask Ss to read the rubric and answer the questions.
- Check Ss' answers.

Answer key

I am writing to my English relative.
I am going to write an email.
I should write 100-120 words.

b) Aim To prepare for a writing task; to brainstorm for ideas

Explain the task and give Ss time to make notes under the headings in their notebooks.

Suggested Answer Key

When: last year
Where: at school
What was wrong: had a pain in my chest and couldn't breathe very well (pneumonia)
How doctor treated you: he gave me an X-ray, antibiotics and two weeks of rest
How you felt after: much better

10 Aim To write an email narrating a health issue

- Give Ss time to write their email using the plan to help them.
- Check Ss' answers.
- Alternatively, assign the task as HW and check Ss' answers in the next lesson.

Suggested Answer Key

Hi Sam,
Thanks for your email. How are you? I hope you are feeling better now. I was once ill with something similar last year.
I was working when I suddenly felt a terrible pain in my chest and I couldn't breathe very well. I went to the hospital. I was very worried. The doctor gave me an X-ray and he found out that I had pneumonia. He gave me antibiotics. It took me two weeks before I could go back to work. Anyway, I've got to go now.
Take care,
Louis

Values

Ask Ss to try to explain the saying in their mother tongue. If Ss have difficulty, explain the saying. Ask Ss to memorise this saying and check in the next lesson.
The saying means that good health is priceless and worth more than anything else in the world.

Culture 6

Listening & Reading

1 Aim To introduce the topic and listen and read for gist

- Ask Ss to look at the pictures, title and subheadings in the text. Elicit Ss' guesses as to what the Royal Flying Doctors Service does.
- Play the recording. Ss listen and read and find out.

Suggested Answer Key

The Royal Flying Doctors Service provides emergency care in remote areas in Australia.

2 Aim To read for cohesion and coherence (missing sentences)

- Ask Ss to read the sentences A-E and then read the text again and fill the gaps.
- Check Ss' answers.

Answer Key

1 D   2 E   3 A   4 C

- Give Ss time to look up the meanings of the words in the **Check these words** box in the Word List.
- Play the video for Ss and elicit their comments.

Speaking & Writing

3 Aim THINK To consolidate information in a text and express an opinion

- Give Ss time to consider their answers.
- Elicit answers from Ss around the class.

Suggested Answer Key

The good thing about being a doctor in the Royal Flying Doctors Service in Australia is that you get to travel all over the country. You also have the satisfaction that you are providing a valuable service and possibly saving people's lives every time you go to a call. The disadvantages might be that you have to work long hours or unsociable hours and that sometimes you might not get to a patient in time.

6

4 **Aim** ICT To develop research skills; to write a short text about a medical service in your country or another country

- Explain the task and give Ss time to make notes and then write a short text about a medical service similar to the Royal Flying Doctors Service in their country or another country.
- Ask various Ss to read their text to the class.
- Alternatively, assign the task as HW and ask Ss to read out their texts in the next lesson.

Suggested Answer Key

name: Greek Flying Doctors
history: started in 1992
services: transports patients by air ambulance from the Greek islands to the mainland or to other countries for medical assistance
funding: private company (costs covered by health insurance)

The Greek Flying Doctors started in 1992. It is a service which transports patients by air ambulance from the Greek islands to the mainland or to other countries for medical assistance. It is a private company, but the patient doesn't pay any costs; they are covered by health insurance.

Review 6

Vocabulary

1 **Aim** To practise vocabulary from the unit

- Explain the task.
- Give Ss time to complete it.
- Check Ss' answers.

Answer Key

1 throat   4 infection
2 toothache   5 ache
3 temperature

2 **Aim** To practise vocabulary from the unit

- Explain the task.
- Give Ss time to complete it.
- Check Ss' answers.

Answer Key

1 did   3 getting   5 get
2 took   4 go   6 see

3 **Aim** To practise vocabulary from the unit

- Explain the task.
- Give Ss time to complete it.
- Check Ss' answers.

Answer Key

1 burnt   3 ankle   5 bumped
2 broke   4 cut   6 bruised

Grammar

4 **Aim** To practise the past simple, the present perfect and present perfect continuous

- Explain the task.
- Give Ss time to complete it.
- Check Ss' answers.

Answer Key

1 gone   4 been   7 been
2 went   5 already   coughing
3 just   6 never   8 for

5 **Aim** To practise the present perfect and the present perfect continuous

- Explain the task.
- Give Ss time to complete it.
- Check Ss' answers.

Answer Key

1 have visited
2 Have you ever spent
3 haven't been waiting
4 has read
5 hasn't finished
6 Have you been sleeping

Everyday English

6 **Aim** To match exchanges

- Explain the task.
- Give Ss time to complete it.
- Check Ss' answers.

Answer Key

1 D   2 C   3 A   4 B

Competences

Ask Ss to assess their own performance in the unit by ticking the items according to how competent they feel for each of the listed activities.

Optional activity

Say verbs. Ss in teams say the past participle. e.g.
　　T:　go
Team AS1:　gone
　　T:　Correct! 1 point for Team A, break
Team AS2:　broken, etc.

58

Values: Volunteering   B

1 Aim To identify the context and purpose of a text

- Ask Ss to look at the title and elicit where you might see a text like this.
- Then elicit what they think the purpose of a text like this is.
- Give Ss time to read the text and check.

Suggested Answer Key

I think you can find a text like this on the Internet, in an online magazine or blog.

I think the purpose of the text is to describe because it is giving information. I also think the purpose of the text is to persuade because it describes the benefits of volunteering and uses persuasive language.

2 Aim To listen and read for cohesion and coherence

- Ask Ss to read the sentences A-E and then give them time to read the text and fill the gaps with the missing sentences.
- Play the recording. Ss listen and read the text and check their answers.

Answer Key

1 B   2 E   3 A   4 C

Suggested Answer Key

forget: *not remember*
benefits: *helps*
stressed: *feeling under pressure*
simple: *not difficult or complicated*
local: *near where you live*

- Play the video for Ss and elicit their comments.

3 Aim ICT To research local volunteering opportunities

- Ask Ss to work in pairs or small groups and research local volunteering opportunities.
- Then ask various Ss to share their information with the class.

Ss' own answers

4 Aim THINK To develop critical thinking skills

- Explain the situation and give Ss time to consider their answers, drawing on the text as well as their own ideas.
- Ask various Ss to share their answers with the class.

Suggested Answer Key

Volunteering at an old people's home and chatting to the elderly was a very positive experience for me. It has changed my life because I felt useful and helpful and I could see that I was really making a difference in someone's life. It made me feel happy and contented.

5 Aim To create a promotional video

- Ask Ss to work in pairs and prepare a promotional video on volunesia. Tell Ss to use their answers from Ex. 4 as well as the ideas in the text and write a short script which they can film using their smartphone or other electronic devices.
- Ask various Ss to share their videos with the class.

Ss' own answers

B Public Speaking Skills

1 **Aim** To present a public speaking task

Ask Ss to read the task. Elicit the purpose of the presentation.

Answer Key

The purpose is to make a presentation about a famous person from your country who spends time helping others.

2 **Aim** To analyse a model public speaking task; to introduce the use of cue cards

- Read out the **Study Skills** box and tell Ss that this is a helpful tip to assist them when giving a presentation.
- Play the recording. Ss listen and read the model and number the cue cards in the correct order.
- Check Ss' answers.

Answer Key

A 3   B 1   C 5   D 2   E 4

3 **Aim** ICT To give a presentation

- Ask Ss to think of a famous person from their country who helps others and research online for information about them and then make notes under the headings provided.
- Tell Ss to then use their notes to prepare cue cards and number them.
- Ask various Ss to give their presentation to the class.
- Alternatively, assign the task as HW and have Ss give their presentations in the next lesson.

Suggested Answer Key

- *born 5/2/1985*
- *Funchal, Madeira, Portugal*
- *Age 12 – Sporting CP youth team*
- *Age 16 – first team*
- *Manchester United - 18*
- *Real Madrid 6 years later*
- *Awards and titles*
- *Record-breaking goal scorer*
- *Charity donations*
- *Spokesperson for global campaigns*
- *Global Artist Ambassador for Save the Children*

Suggested Answer Key

Good morning/afternoon everyone. I'm Mateus Frankez. The man I'm going to talk about today is one of the best footballers of all time – but he's so much more than that. Cristiano Ronaldo was born on 5th February, 1985 in Funchal, Madeira, Portugal. He grew up in poverty in a poor neighbourhood sharing a room with his brother and sisters. As a child, he played for various amateur teams and then at 12, Sporting CP signed him for their youth team. By 16 he was playing for their first team.

He quickly attracted international attention and at the age of 18 he started playing for Manchester United. After a successful career there, he moved to Real Madrid six years later. During his career he has won 5 Ballon d'Or awards, 4 European Golden Shoes, 5 league titles, 4 UEFA Champions League titles, and a UEFA European Championship. Cristiano Ronaldo is one of the greatest footballers of all time and a record-breaking goal scorer.

But there is so much more to Cristiano Ronaldo than just football. He has never forgotten his poor background and works to help children all over the world today. He has donated money to charity and has helped individuals and communities in many ways. He is the international spokesperson for two global campaigns fighting childhood hunger and obesity and another that conserves biodiversity, and he is the Global Artist Ambassador for Save the Children.

As Cristiano Ronaldo said, "Many people look at me and think they know me but they don't at all. This is the real me. I am a humble person, a feeling person. A person who cares about others, who wants to help others." Even when he became the biggest football star in the world, he never stopped helping others. Thank you for listening.

Stick to the rules! 7

Topic
In this unit, Ss will explore the topics of rules & regulations and chores.

7a Reading & Vocabulary	56-57
Lesson objectives: To learn vocabulary for rules & regulations, to listen and read for gist, to read for specific information (multiple choice), to learn prepositions, to revise the imperative, to talk about rules & regulations, to write a leaflet of rules **Vocabulary:** Rules & regulations *(Keep your dog on a lead. Don't light fires. Recycle your rubbish. Do your washing-up in the area provided. No loud music after 11 pm. Use the campsite kitchen for cooking. Keep your campsite clean. No litter. Park your car near your tent.)*; Nouns *(safety, fire pit, litter, lead)*; Verbs *(supply, annoy, respect, disturb)*	

7b Grammar in Use	58-59
Lesson objectives: To learn/revise modals *(have/need to – don't have/need to – must/mustn't – may/might/could – can/can't – be allowed to – should/shouldn't)*; to learn/revise past modals *(had/didn't have to – could/couldn't – was/were[n't] able to)*	

7c Skills in Action	60-61
Lesson objectives: To learn vocabulary for chores, to listen for specific information (multiple matching), to act out a dialogue and practise everyday English asking about/explaining the rules, to learn the pronunciation of can /kæn/, can't /kɑːnt/, to read for gist (matching headings to paragraphs), to write an advert about a flat for rent **Vocabulary:** Chores *(take out the rubbish, clean the bathroom, sweep the floors, clean the windows, dust the furniture, vacuum the carpets, do the laundry, do the washing-up, do the ironing, clean the oven)*	

Culture 7	62
Lesson objectives: To listen and read for gist, to read for specific information (T/F/DS), to present a race in your country **Vocabulary:** Nouns *(yacht, competitor, wave, crew member, limit, challenge, spectator)*; Verb *(face)*; Phrases *(set sail, sail against)*	

Review 7	63
Lesson objectives: To test/consolidate vocabulary and grammar learnt throughout the unit; to practise everyday English	

Go through the objectives box and tell Ss that these are the topics, skills and activities this unit will cover.

7a

Vocabulary

1 **Aim** To present vocabulary for campsite rules & regulations

- Play the recording with pauses for Ss to repeat chorally and/or individually.
- Check Ss' pronunciation and intonation.

Listening & Reading

2 **Aim** To listen and read for gist/author's purpose

- Elicit Ss' guesses as to the purpose of the text.
- Play the recording. Ss listen and read to find out.

Suggested Answer Key

The purpose of the text is to inform people of the rules and regulations of the campsite.

3 **Aim** To read for specific information (multiple choice)

- Ask Ss to read the questions and answer choices.
- Give Ss time to read the text and then choose their answers.
- Check Ss' answers.

Answer Key

1 B   2 C   3 B   4 A

- Elicit the meanings of the words in bold from Ss around the class. They may use their dictionaries if necessary.

Suggested Answer Key

light (v): to start a fire
extremely (adv): very
tidy (adj): to have everything in order
pick up (phr v): to collect
charge (n): an amount asked for sth
freely (adv): without being controlled
daily (adj): happening every day
caravan (n): a vehicle used for living and/or travelling

- Then give Ss time to look up the meanings of the words in the **Check these words** box in the Word List.
- Play the video for Ss and elicit their comments.

61

4 Aim To consolidate vocabulary from the text

- Explain the task and give Ss time to complete it.
- Check Ss' answers and then give them time to make sentences using the phrases.
- Elicit answers from Ss around the class.

Answer Key

1 relaxing	4 rubbish	7 loud
2 simple	5 fellow	
3 fire	6 daily	

Suggested Answer Key

Have a relaxing stay at our campsite.
There are a few simple rules to follow.
A fire pit is a safe place to light a campfire.
The campsite provides free rubbish bags.
People should respect their fellow campers.
There is a special area where dogs can take their daily exercise.
Please don't play loud music at the campsite after 11 pm.

5 Aim To consolidate vocabulary from a text

- Ask Ss to read the verbs in the list and then give them time to complete the sentences.
- Check Ss' answers around the class.

Answer Key

1 play	3 light	5 pick up
2 recycle	4 take	6 keep

6 Aim To practise prepositions

- Give Ss time to complete the phrases with the correct preposition.
- Check Ss' answers and then give them time to make sentences using the phrases.
- Elicit answers from Ss around the class.

Answer Key

1 of	3 on	5 from	7 to
2 at	4 of	6 in	

Suggested Answer Key

In the interests of peace and quiet, no loud music.
We stayed at the campsite for a week.
Keep your dog on a lead!
You can have a soft drink free of charge.
The film lasts from 6 pm to 8 pm.
Your car's in the way of my bike!
I sit next to Jim in class.

7 Aim To identify and revise the imperative

Elicit the imperative forms in the text and then elicit how we form the imperative from Ss around the class.

Answer Key

Imperative forms: please use the areas provided, please keep your dog on a lead, don't park your car in the way
We form the imperative with the base form of the main verb and the negative with 'do not' and the base form of the main verb.

Speaking

8 Aim To consolidate information about rules and regulations

Ask various Ss around the class to talk about the rules and regulations at the Green Forest Campsite without looking at the leaflet.

Suggested Answer Key

At Green Forest Campsite, campers should keep their dogs on a lead. They shouldn't light fires except in a fire pit. They should recycle their rubbish and do their washing-up in the area provided. They can't play loud music after 11 pm. They should only use the campsite kitchen for cooking. They should keep their campsite clean and pick up all their litter. Finally, they should park their car near their tent and not in the way of other campers.

Writing

9 Aim THINK To write a leaflet about rules for camping in the mountains; to develop critical thinking skills

- Explain the task and give Ss time to complete it in small groups using the prompts provided.
- Ask various Ss to present their leaflet to the class.
- Alternatively, assign the task as HW and ask Ss to present their leaflets in the next lesson.

Suggested Answer Key

Rules for camping on the mountain
Fire safety
Cook meals with a portable stove. Do not build a fire. Fires destroy forest resources and can easily get out of control.
Damaging trees/plants
Make sure to stick to the trails and don't tread on plants. Do not cut trees and do not take any rocks or plants away from their natural environment.

Litter
Always pick up all of your litter.
Disturbing wildlife
The mountain is home to a wide range of animals. If you are lucky enough to see some, do not disturb them. Thank you for your cooperation. We wish you happy camping!

7b Grammar in Use

1 Aim To present/revise modals *(have/need to – don't have/need to – must/mustn't)*

- Ask Ss to read the theory and find examples in the dialogue.
- Then ask various Ss around the class to identify their uses.

Answer Key

Examples: *you have to sign, do I have to pay, you don't need to give, you must let me know*

*We use **have to** to talk about necessity.*
*We use **don't need to** to talk about lack of necessity.*
*We use **must** to talk about very strong advice.*

2 Aim To practise modals *(have/need to – don't have/need to – must/mustn't)*

- Explain the task and give Ss time to complete it.
- Check Ss' answers.

Answer Key

1	have to	5	don't have to
2	mustn't	6	mustn't
3	has to	7	must
4	must	8	doesn't have to

3 a) Aim To listen for specific information and consolidate modals *(have/need to – don't have/need to – must/mustn't)*

- Explain the task and ask Ss to read the questions.
- Play the recording. Ss listen and complete the task.
- Check Ss' answers.

Answer Key

	Chris	Ann
2	–	✓
3	✓	–
4	✓	–
5	–	✓

b) Aim To practise *have to/don't have to*

- Explain the task and read out the examples.
- Then give Ss time to complete the task and check Ss' answers around the class.

Suggested Answer Key

Chris doesn't have to go to a lesson on Saturday mornings.
Ann has to go to a lesson on Saturday mornings.
Chris has to help out at the Student's Union.
Ann doesn't have to help out at the Student's Union.
Chris has to do housework on Sundays.
Ann doesn't have to do housework on Sundays.
Chris doesn't have to pay for college lunches.
Ann has to pay for college lunches.

4 Aim To practise *have to/don't have to*

- Explain the task, read out the example and give Ss time to complete the dialogue in pairs using the ideas provided as well as their own.
- Monitor the activity around the class and then have some Ss share their answers with the class.

Suggested Answer Key

A: Tomorrow, I have to clean up my room.
B: So do I, but I don't have to mop the floors.
A: Neither do I. I have to do the laundry this week.
B: I don't have to do the laundry, but I have to tidy the garage.

Optional activity

Write your weakly chores. Tell your partner.

5 Aim To revise/present/practise *may/might/could*

- Ask Ss to read the theory box on p. 58 and then read the advice and the results and match them.
- Give Ss time to make sentences following the example and then elicit answers from Ss around the class.

Answer Key

1 B   2 C   3 A

Suggested Answer Key

Always be careful when cooking with hot oil. It may/might/could set on fire.
Never throw water on an oil fire. The fire may/might/could spread.

7

6 **Aim** To revise/present/practise *can/can't – be allowed to – should/shouldn't*

- Ask Ss to read the theory box and explain any points Ss are unsure of.
- Then elicit examples from the dialogue.

Answer Key

Example: *Am I allowed to have visitors …? … they can stay here. … you can't have pets here.*

7 **Aim** To practise *can/can't – be allowed to*

- Explain the task and ask two Ss to model the example dialogue.
- Then give Ss time to compete the task in pairs.
- Monitor the activity around the class and then ask some pairs to act out their short dialogues in front of the rest of the class.

Suggested Answer Key

2 A: Can my son come to the hospital?
  B: No, I'm afraid he can't. He isn't allowed to come to the hospital. You have to leave him at home.
3 A: Can we eat in here?
  B: No, I'm afraid you can't. You aren't allowed to eat in here. You have to eat your food outside.
4 A: Can I wear shorts in this restaurant?
  B: No, I'm afraid you can't. You aren't allowed to wear shorts in this restaurant. You have to wear a suit and a tie.
5 A: Can I take this olive oil on the plane with me?
  B: No, I'm afraid you can't. You aren't allowed to take olive oil on the plane. You have to leave it with airport security.

8 **Aim** To practise *should/shouldn't*

- Explain the task and give Ss time to complete it.
- Check Ss' answers.

Answer Key

| 1 should | 3 shouldn't |
| 2 shouldn't | 4 should |

9 **Aim** To revise/present/practise past modals (*had to/didn't have to – could/couldn't – was/were[n't] able to*)

- Ask Ss to read the theory and explain any points that Ss are unsure of.
- Explain the task and give Ss time to complete it.
- Check Ss' answers.

Answer Key

1 could	4 couldn't
2 didn't have to	5 had to
3 had to	6 wasn't able to

10 **Aim** To practise modals

- Give Ss time to complete the task.
- Check Ss' answers around the class.

Answer Key

1 need	5 may
2 can't	6 mustn't
3 don't have to	7 should
4 must	8 shouldn't

7c Skills in Action

Vocabulary

1 **Aim** To present vocabulary for chores

- Play the recording with pauses for Ss to repeat chorally and/or individually.
- Check Ss' pronunciation and intonation.

2 **Aim** To practise new vocabulary

- Ask Ss to talk in pairs about which chores they have to do this weekend.
- Ask various Ss to tell the class.

Suggested Answer Key

A: I have to take out the rubbish, do the laundry and vacuum the carpets. How about you?
B: I have to clean the bathroom and clean the windows.

Listening

3 **Aim** To listen for key information (multiple matching)

- Ask Ss to read the lists.
- Play the recording. Ss listen and complete the task.
- Check Ss' answers.

Answer Key

1 c   2 g   3 f   4 a   5 d

Everyday English

4 **Aim** To listen and read for coherence

- Ask Ss to read the dialogue and choose the correct items.
- Play the recording. Ss listen and read and check their answers.

64

Answer Key

1	have to	3	mustn't	5	have to
2	should	4	can	6	can

5 **Aim** **To act out a dialogue**

- Explain the task and ask Ss to act out a similar dialogue to the one in Ex. 4 in pairs using the prompts and the language in the box to help them.
- Write this diagram on the board for Ss to follow.

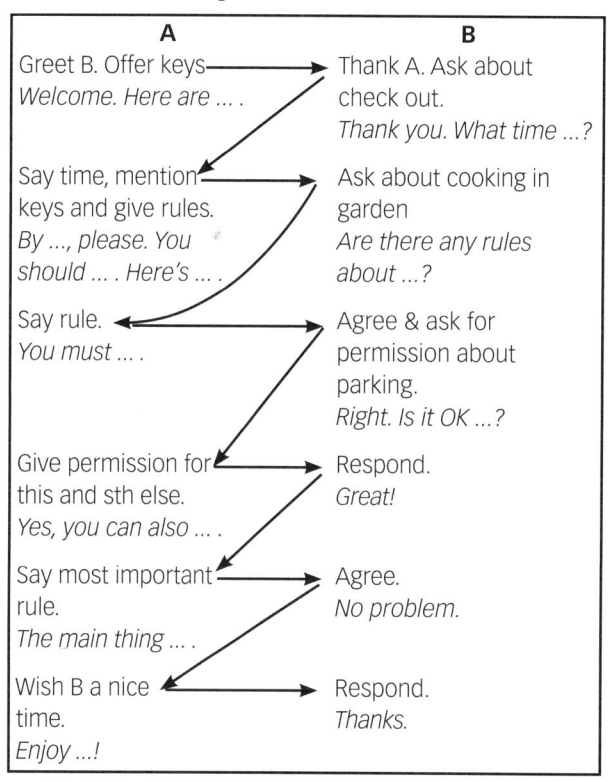

A	B
Greet B. Offer keys. *Welcome. Here are ... .*	Thank A. Ask about check out. *Thank you. What time ...?*
Say time, mention keys and give rules. *By ..., please. You should ... . Here's ... .*	Ask about cooking in garden *Are there any rules about ...?*
Say rule. *You must ... .*	Agree & ask for permission about parking. *Right. Is it OK ...?*
Give permission for this and sth else. *Yes, you can also ... .*	Respond. *Great!*
Say most important rule. *The main thing ... .*	Agree. *No problem.*
Wish B a nice time. *Enjoy ...!*	Respond. *Thanks.*

- Monitor the activity around the class and offer assistance as necessary.
- Then ask some pairs to act out their dialogues in front of the class.

Suggested Answer Key

A: Welcome. Here are your keys.
B: Thank you. What time do we have to check out on Monday?
A: By 2 pm please. You should leave the keys in the letterbox. Here's a full list of rules.
B: OK. Are there any rules about cooking in the garden?
A: You have to use the barbecue provided.
B: Right. Is it OK to park my bike at the main entrance?
A: Yes, you can. You can also put it in the garage.
B: Great!

A: The main thing is you mustn't leave rubbish outside the bins.
B: No problem at all!
A: Enjoy your stay!
B: Thanks.

Pronunciation

6 **Aim** **To learn the pronunciation of** *can* /kæn/, *can't* /kɑːnt/

- Play the recording. Ss listen and repeat, chorally and/or individually.
- Check Ss' pronunciation and intonation.

Reading & Writing

7 **Aim** **To read for gist (matching headings to paragraphs)**

- Ask Ss to read the advert and fill in the missing headings from the list.
- Check Ss' answers and elicit where you can see an advert like this.

Answer Key

1	The Space	3	House Rules
2	Facilities	4	Cancellations

You can see an advert like this on the Internet on a holiday booking site.

8 **Aim** **To analyse the layout of an advert.**

- Ask Ss to read the Writing Tip and tell them that this tip will help them to complete the writing task successfully.
- Ask them to look at the advert in Ex. 7 and elicit answers from Ss around the class.

Suggested Answer Key

The advert is properly laid out. It has headings before each section and bullet points to list ideas.

9 **Aim** **To identify facilities/rules**

- Ask Ss to read through the list and categorise each one under the headings.
- Check Ss' answers around the class.

Answer Key

Facilities: *laptop-friendly workspace, fully air-conditioned, weekly cleaning service, large balcony*
House Rules: *report any damage to property, lock all doors and windows when leaving, park in the garage not on the street, sort rubbish into recycling bins*

Writing

10 a) Aim To analyse a rubric
- Ask Ss to read the rubric and underline the key words.
- Check Ss' answers.

Answer key

Key words: flat, block of flats, city centre, advert, holiday homes website, full details, 100-120 words

b) Aim To brainstorm for ideas

Explain the task and give Ss time to brainstorm for ideas and make notes under the headings in Ex. 7.

Suggested Answer Key

THE SPACE: large spacious flat in a block of flats in city centre, close to public transport, perfect for a sightseeing holiday
FACILITIES: fully air-conditioned, large balcony with great views, fully-fitted kitchen, washing machine, dishwasher, Wi-Fi, wide-screen TV
HOUSE RULES: report any damage to property, lock all doors and windows when out, keep the flat clean and tidy, no pets, no loud music after 11 pm
CANCELLATIONS: cancel up to 30 days before your trip for a full refund

c) Aim To write an advert about a flat for rent
- Give Ss time to write their email using their ideas in Ex. 10b to help them.
- Check Ss' answers.
- Alternatively, assign the task as HW and check Ss' answers in the next lesson.

Suggested Answer Key

City Centre Flat in Rome
4 guests 2 bedrooms 2 double beds 1 bathroom
THE SPACE
This lovely large spacious flat is in a modern block of flats in the city centre. It is close to public transport and is perfect for a sightseeing holiday.
FACILITIES
- fully air-conditioned
- large balcony with great views
- fully-fitted kitchen with washing machine and dishwasher
- Wi-Fi
- wide-screen TV

HOUSE RULES
- Guests must report any damage to property.
- Guests must lock all doors and windows when out.
- Please keep the flat clean and tidy.
- No pets are allowed.
- Guests must not play loud music after 11 pm.

CANCELLATIONS
Cancel up to 30 days before your trip for a full refund.

Values

Ask Ss to try to explain the saying in their mother tongue. If Ss have difficulty, explain the saying. Ask Ss to memorise this saying and check in the next lesson.

The saying means that when you visit a place, use a facility or rent a house/flat you should leave it as clean and as tidy as you would like to find it yourself and not leave a mess for the next person.

Culture 7

Listening & Reading

1 Aim To introduce the topic and listen and read for gist
- Ask Ss to look at the pictures. Elicit Ss' guesses as to what type of race it is, where it takes place and how long it lasts.
- Play the recording. Ss listen and read to find out.

Suggested Answer Key

It is a yacht race from Sydney to Hobart that takes place over six days.

2 Aim To read for specific information (T/F/DS)
- Ask Ss to read the statements. Then give them time to read the text and mark them according to what they read.
- Check Ss' answers.

Answer Key

1 F   2 F   3 DS   4 T   5 T

- Elicit the meanings of the words in bold from Ss around the class. They may use their dictionaries if necessary.

Suggested Answer Key

take part (phr): to participate in sth
last (v): to continue over a period of time
join (v): to get involved in an activity

limit (of age) (n): the age at which one can do or not do sth
gather (v): to come together
spot (n): a place

- Give Ss time to look up the meanings of the words in the **Check these words** box in the Word List.
- Play the video for Ss and elicit their comments.

3 Aim THINK To consolidate information in a text and express an opinion

- Give Ss time to consider their answers.
- Elicit answers from Ss around the class.

Suggested Answer Key

I would like to take part in the Sydney to Hobart Yacht Race because I think it sounds challenging and exciting and I like sailing. / I would not like to take part in the Sydney to Hobart Yacht Race because it sounds dangerous and I don't like sailing.

4 Aim ICT To develop research skills; to write a short text about a race in your country

- Explain the task and ask Ss to work in small groups. They research online and then write a short text about a race in their country.
- Ask various groups to read their text to the class.
- Alternatively, assign the task as HW and ask Ss to read out their texts in the next lesson.

Suggested Answer Key

Where/When is it? *Lake Szale, Kalisz, Poland, 1-3 June*
What is it? *International Windsurfing Regatta, started in 2012, 3 days of racing, over 100 competitors,*
What are the rules?: *from 12 years old with different age groups and classes, have a windsurfing board, register, pay a fee and have insurance, take part in up to 11 races in challenging conditions*
Why go? *Challenge for competitors and great fun for spectators, prize money for competitors and great atmosphere and evening barbecues for everyone*

Poland is home to a very exciting windsurfing competition for young people. People travel from all over Europe to take part. It takes place on Lake Szale near Kalisz, in Poland every year from 1-3 June.
The competition is the International Windsurfing Regatta. It started in 2012 and it is one of the most exciting windsurfing competitions for young people today. There are 3 days of racing with over 100 competitors.

To join the competition, you must be at least 12 years old and you must have a windsurfing board. You also have to register, pay a fee and have insurance. Then you can take part in up to 11 races with different age groups and classes in challenging conditions.
The regatta is a challenge for competitors and great fun for spectators. There is prize money for the competitors and a great atmosphere and evening barbecues for everyone.

Review 7

Vocabulary

1 Aim To practise vocabulary from the unit
- Explain the task.
- Give Ss time to complete it.
- Check Ss' answers.

Answer Key

1 area	4 ironing	7 lead
2 litter	5 pit	8 rubbish
3 charge	6 fire	

2 Aim To practise vocabulary from the unit
- Explain the task.
- Give Ss time to complete it.
- Check Ss' answers.

Answer Key

1 D   2 F   3 B   4 A   5 C   6 E

Grammar

3 Aim To practise modals
- Explain the task.
- Give Ss time to complete it.
- Check Ss' answers.

Answer Key

1 have to	3 don't have to
2 need to	4 mustn't

4 Aim To practise modals
- Explain the task.
- Give Ss time to complete it.
- Check Ss' answers.

Answer Key

1 can't	4 mustn't
2 should	5 have to
3 may	

5 Aim To practise modals

- Explain the task.
- Give Ss time to complete it.
- Check Ss' answers.

Answer Key

1 could, couldn't, had to
2 didn't have to
3 wasn't able to, was able to

Everyday English

6 Aim To match exchanges

- Explain the task.
- Give Ss time to complete it.
- Check Ss' answers.

Answer Key

1 E 2 D 3 B 4 A 5 C

Competences

Ask Ss to assess their own performance in the unit by ticking the items according to how competent they feel for each of the listed activities.

Optional activity

Work in groups Think of various places *(e.g. museum, hotel, etc.)*. Write 5 sentences explaining the rules & regulations there. Use modal verbs.

e.g. *(museum). You mustn't touch the exhibits. You can't take photos inside the museum. You can have a snack at the café, etc.*

Landmarks 8

Topic
In this unit, Ss will explore the topics of geographical features, landmarks and materials.
8a Reading & Vocabulary   64-65
Lesson objectives: To learn vocabulary for geographical features, to listen and read for gist, to read for specific information (sentence completion), to learn prepositions, to talk about Wieliczka Salt Mine, to write a blog entry
Vocabulary: Geographical features *(falls, lakes, mine, canyon, caves, mountains, rainforests, valley)*; Nouns *(mine, surface, well, lump)*; Verbs *(dig, carve)*
8b Grammar in Use   66-67
Lesson objectives: To learn the passive
8c Skills in Action   68-69
Lesson objectives: To learn vocabulary for man-made landmarks & materials, to listen for specific information (gap fill), to act out a dialogue and practise everyday English asking for information, to learn intonation in passive questions, to read for cohesion & coherence (missing tense forms), to write an article about Angkor Wat
Vocabulary: Man-made landmarks *(The Shard, The Guggenheim Museum, The Parthenon, Golden Gate Bridge, Stonehenge The Royal Albert Hall, The Trojan Horse statue, The ancient city of Chan Chan)*; Materials *(glass, concrete, marble, steel, stone, brick, wood, clay)*
Culture 8   70
Lesson objectives: To listen and read for specific information, to read for key information (multiple matching), to talk about landmarks, to prepare a poster about interesting landmarks in your country
Vocabulary: Nouns *(trade, figure, chalk, emblem, tribe, explorer, beast, ceramic tile, time capsule)*
Review 8   71
Lesson objectives: To test/consolidate vocabulary and grammar learnt throughout the unit; to practise everyday English

Go through the objectives box and tell Ss that these are the topics, skills and activities this unit will cover.

8a

Vocabulary

1 a) Aim To present vocabulary for geographical features

- Ask Ss to look at the pictures and then read the words in the list and complete the gaps.
- Check Ss' answers.

Answer Key

1 Canyon	4 Rainforests	7 Falls
2 Lakes	5 Caves	8 Mine
3 Valley	6 Mountains	

b) Aim To ask and answer about geographical features

- Explain the task and ask two Ss to model the example. Then have Ss ask and answer in pairs following the example.
- Monitor the activity around the class.

Suggested Answer Key

A: Where is the Plitvice Lakes National Park?
B: It's in Croatia. Where is the Viñales Valley?
A: It's in Cuba. Where are the Rainforests of Atsinanana?
B: They're in Madagascar. Where are the Elephanta Caves?
A: They're in India. Where are the Greater Blue Mountains?
B: They're in Australia. Where are the Victoria Falls?
A: They're in Zambia. Where is the Wieliczka Salt Mine?
B: It's in Poland.

2 Aim To match pictures to descriptions

- Ask Ss to look at the pictures and read the descriptions. Then give Ss time to match them.
- Check Ss' answers.

Answer Key

1 B   2 D   3 C   4 A   5 E

Listening & Reading

3 Aim THINK To listen and read for gist

- Elicit Ss' guesses as to what makes Wieliczka Salt Mine unique.
- Play the recording. Ss listen and read to find out.

Suggested Answer Key

The Wieliczka Salt Mine is unique because it has some wonderful sights and it dates from the 13th century.

69

8

4 **Aim** To read for specific information (sentence completion)

- Ask Ss to read the sentence stems.
- Give Ss time to read the text and then complete them.
- Check Ss' answers.

Suggested Answer Key

1 near Kraków (in Poland)
2 museum
3 natural salt crystals (in strange shapes)
4 the miners
5 were digging a well

- Elicit the meanings of the words in bold from Ss. They may use their dictionaries if necessary.

Suggested Answer Key

attractions (n): things worth seeing
chambers (n): large rooms
decorated (adj): made beautiful
shapes (n): forms
ceiling (n): the top of a room
legend (n): myth
servants (n): people that look after sb rich
hidden (adj): out of sight
chance (n): opportunity

- Give Ss time to look up the meanings of the words in the **Check these words** box in the Word List.
- Play the video for Ss and elicit their comments.

5 **Aim** To consolidate vocabulary from the text

- Explain the task and give Ss time to complete it.
- Check Ss' answers and then give them time to make sentences using the phrases.
- Elicit answers from Ss around the class.

Answer Key

1 famous
2 huge
3 underground
4 salt
5 strange
6 rock
7 high
8 ancient

Suggested Answer Key

The salt mine is one of the famous attractions in Kraków. There are huge chambers in the mine as well as underground lakes and natural salt crystals in strange shapes. There are interesting statues that the miners carved out of rock salt and beautiful lights hanging from the high ceiling in the main chamber. There is even an ancient legend linked to the Wieliczka Salt Mine.

6 **Aim** To consolidate vocabulary from a text through antonyms

- Read out the Writing Tip and tell Ss this is useful advice when learning new vocabulary.
- Ask Ss to read the adjectives in the list and then give them time to match them to their antonyms 1-6.
- Check Ss' answers around the class.

Answer Key

1 unknown
2 tiny
3 low
4 boring
5 ugly
6 modern

7 **Aim** To practise prepositions

- Give Ss time to choose the correct preposition in each of the phrases.
- Check Ss' answers and give them time to make sentences using the phrases.
- Elicit answers from Ss around the class.

Answer Key

1 in
2 by
3 with
4 out
5 from
6 to
7 on
8 by

Suggested Answer Key

1 The mine was first opened in the 13th century.
2 Miners dug it out by hand.
3 Tunnels and caves are decorated with salt crystals.
4 Miners carved statues out of rock salt.
5 Beautiful lights hang from the ceiling.
6 According to legend, Princess Kinga threw her ring into a salt mine.
7 Princess Kinga was on her way to Poland.
8 Tourists are amazed by the mine's unforgettable sights.

Speaking & Writing

8 a) **Aim** To consolidate information in a text

- Ask Ss to write the headings in their notebooks and then give them time to write the phrases under the correct headings.
- Check Ss' answers around the class.

Answer Key

Place/Location: Wieliczka Salt Mine, near Kraków in Poland
History: horses used after 1620, opened in 13th century, salt dug out by hand
Things to see: natural salt crystals, interesting statues, huge chambers, underground lakes, tunnels & caves, beautiful lights

Legend: *servants dug well, threw ring into mine, Hungarian princess Kinga, ring was found*
Recommendation: *should visit it*

b) Aim To talk about a place of interest, to consolidate information in a text

Ask various Ss around the class to take the role of a tour guide and use their notes from Ex. 8a to tell visitors about the Wieliczka Salt Mine.

Suggested Answer Key

Today we're visiting the Wieliczka Salt Mine near Krakow in Poland. The mine opened in the 13th century. Back then the miners dug out the salt by hand. Then in 1620, they started using horses.

There is plenty to see here. There are natural salt crystals, interesting statues carved out of rock salt, huge chambers, underground lakes, tunnels and caves as well as beautiful lights and lots more.

According to legend, a Hungarian princess called Kinga threw her ring into a mine. Then she came to Wieliczka and told her servants to dig a well. When they dug the well, they found salt instead of water and they found her ring.

9 Aim To write a blog entry

- Explain the task and give Ss time to complete it.
- Ask various Ss to read their blog entry to the class.
- Alternatively, assign the task as HW and ask Ss to present their blog entries in the next lesson.

Suggested Answer Key

Hi everyone! I've just visited the Wieliczka Salt Mine near Kraków in Poland. It was amazing and so interesting. It opened in the 13th century. Back then the miners dug out the salt by hand. Then in 1620, they started using horses. I saw so much there. I saw natural salt crystals, interesting statues, huge chambers, underground lakes, tunnels and caves as well as beautiful lights and lots more. Wieliczka Salt Mine is an unforgettable place. You should visit it!

8b Grammar in Use

1 Aim To present the passive

- Explain that we use the passive to talk about an action when we don't know who performed it or when it is obvious who performed it from the context or when the action is more important than the person who performed it.
- Explain/Elicit that we form the passive tense with the verb *to be* + the past participle of the main verb.

- Ask Ss to read the theory and the announcement and then use the passive forms in the announcement to complete the table.
- Check Ss' answers around the class.

Answer Key

	Active	Passive
Present simple	invite	are invited
Past simple	completed	was completed
will	will open	will be opened
modals	must not use	must not be used

2 Aim To present the agent in the passive

- Elicit which word denotes the agent (by).
- Elicit which sentences do not include the agent.
- Then elicit the reason.

Answer Key

2 – We do not know who performed the action.
3 – The people who performed the action (miners) are obvious from the context.

3 Aim To present/practise the passive

- Explain that to change an active sentence to a passive sentence the object of the active verb becomes the subject of the passive verb and the active form changes to a passive form while the subject becomes the agent.
- Give Ss time to complete the task and then check their answers.

Answer Key

1 should not be touched 5 can be seen
2 built 6 confuse
3 will be visited 7 was completed
4 was designed 8 is admired

4 Aim To practise the passive

- Explain the task and ask two Ss to model the example.
- Then give Ss time to complete the task in pairs.
- Monitor the activity around the class and then ask some Ss to ask and answer in front of the rest of the class.

Suggested Answer Key

A: *What is this ring made of?*
B: *It is made of gold.*
A: *Where was it made?*
B: *It was made in France.*

A: *What is this watch made of?*
B: *It is made of silver.*
A: *Where was it made?*
B: *It was made in Switzerland.*

A: What is this jacket made of?
B: It is made of wool.
A: Where was it made?
B: It was made in Spain.

A: What is this shirt made of?
B: It is made of silk.
A: Where was it made?
B: It was made in China.

A: What are these skirts made of?
B: They are made of cotton.
A: Where were they made?
B: They were made in England.

A: What is this toy made of?
B: It is made of plastic.
A: Where was it made?
B: It was made in Japan.

A: What are these desks made of?
B: They are made of wood.
A: Where were they made?
B: They were made in Germany.

5 Aim To practise the passive

- Explain the task, read out the example and give Ss time to complete it.
- Check Ss' answers.

Suggested Answer Key

2 largest diamond is owned by
3 is visited by millions of tourists
4 must be repaired
5 will be opened by the mayor
6 wasn't invented by

6 a) Aim To practise the passive

- Explain the task and give Ss time to complete it.
- Elicit answers from Ss around the class.

Answer Key

1 b   2 a   3 b   4 a   5 a   6 b

b) Aim To practise the passive

- Ask two Ss to read out the example dialogue and then give Ss time to act out similar dialogues using their answers in Ex. 6a.
- Monitor the task around the class.

Answer Key

A: It was invented by Alexander Graham Bell. When was it invented?
B: It was invented in 1876. Who was The Café Concert painted by?
A: It was painted by Édouard Manet. When was it painted?
B: It was painted in 1878. Who was the Gherkin designed by?
A: It was designed by Foster and Partners. Who was Wuthering Heights written by?
B: It was written by Emily Brontë. When was it written?
A: It was written in 1845. Who was The Blue Danube composed by?
B: It was composed by Johann Strauss. When was it composed?
A: It was composed in 1867.

7 Aim To practise the passive

- Explain the task and ask two Ss to model the example exchange.
- Then give Ss time to compete the task in pairs.
- Monitor the activity around the class and then ask some pairs to act out their exchanges in front of the rest of the class.

Answer Key

1 was started   4 are kept
2 was used   5 is visited
3 was opened

Suggested Answer Key

b A: What was it used as until 1682?
  B: It was used as a royal palace until 1682.
c A: When was the Louvre opened to the public?
  B: The Louvre was opened to the public in 1793.
d A: What is kept in the Louvre?
  B: Many of the world's most famous paintings as well as sculptures, jewellery and other forms of art are kept in the Louvre.
e A: How many people is it visited by every year?
  B: It is visited by millions of people every year.

8 Aim To practise the passive

- Tell Ss to work in pairs. Student A looks at the information in text A and covers text B. Student B covers text A and asks questions which Student A answers. Then ask Student A to present the Burj Khalifa.
- Then Ss swap roles and repeat the task for text B.
- Monitor the activity around the class and then ask various Ss to present the Burj Khalifa or The Sydney Opera House to the rest of the class.

Suggested Answer Key

B: Where is the Burj Khalifa located?
A: It is located in Dubai, in the United Arab Emirates.
B: Who was it designed by?

A: It was designed by Adrian Smith.
B: When was it completed?
A: It was completed in 2010.
B: What is it made of?
A: It is made of steel, glass and concrete.
B: Why was it built?
A: It was built as a place both to live and work in.

The Burj Khalifa is located in Dubai. It was designed by Adrian Smith. It was completed in 2010. It is made of steel, glass and concrete. It was built as a place both to live and work in.

A: Where is the Sydney Opera House located?
B: It is located in Sydney, Australia.
A: Who was it designed by?
B: It was designed by Jørn Utzon.
A: When was it completed?
B: It was completed in 1973.
A: What is it made of?
B: It is made of concrete.
A: Why was it built?
B: It was built as a performing arts centre.

The Sydney Opera House is located in Sydney, Australia. It was designed by Jørn Utzon. It was completed in 1973. It is made of concrete. It was built as a performing arts centre.

9 **Aim** ICT **To write a fact file; to present a landmark**

- Give Ss time to research online and collect information about a landmark and write a fact file about it like the ones in Ex.8. Tell Ss to add a photo.
- Then ask various Ss to present the landmark to the class.

Suggested Answer Key

Name: Taj Mahal, Agra, India
Designer: Ustad Ahmad Lahauri
Completed: 1653
Material: white marble
Built as: a mausoleum for the wife of Shah Jahan

The Taj Mahal is located in Agra, India. It was designed by Ustad Ahmad Lahauri. It was completed in 1653. It is made of white marble. It was built as a mausoleum for the wife of Shah Jahan.

Optional activity

Memory game: Put some objects on a desk. Ask Ss to look at them carefully. Change the position of the objects without Ss seeing the changes. Ask Ss to find the differences using the passive. e.g. *The book was moved next to the pencil case.*

8c Skills in Action

Vocabulary

1 **Aim** **To present vocabulary for man-made landmarks & materials**

- Explain the task and read out the example.
- Ask Ss to look at the pictures and read the descriptions and make similar sentences.
- Elicit answers from Ss around the class.

Answer Key

2 The Guggenheim Museum is made of concrete.
3 The Parthenon is made of marble.
4 The Golden Gate Bridge is made of steel.
5 Stonehenge is made of stone.
6 The Royal Albert Hall is made of brick.
7 The Trojan Horse statue is made of wood.
8 The ancient city of Chan Chan is made of clay.

Listening

2 **Aim** **To listen for specific information (gap-fill)**

- Ask Ss to read the information in the box.
- Play the recording. Ss listen and complete the task.
- Check Ss' answers.

Answer Key

| 1 6 | 3 tours | 5 library |
| 2 bus | 4 17.50 | |

Everyday English

3 **Aim** **To listen and read for coherence**

- Ask Ss to read the dialogue and fill in the missing words.
- Play the recording. Ss listen and read and check their answers.

Answer Key

| 1 tell | 3 Who | 5 afraid |
| 2 located | 4 take | 6 you |

4 **Aim** **To act out a dialogue asking for information**

- Explain the task and ask Ss to act out a similar dialogue to the one in Ex. 3 in pairs using the prompts and the language in the box to help them.
- Write this diagram on the board for Ss to follow.

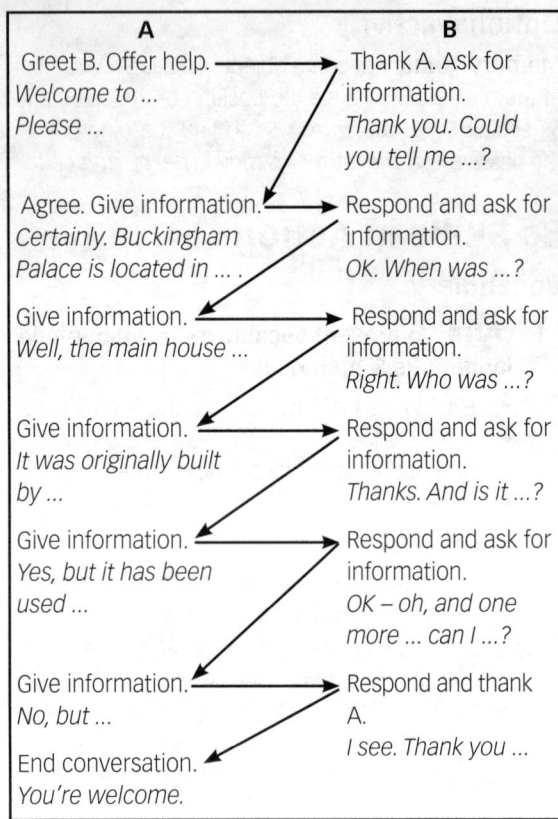

A	B
Greet B. Offer help. *Welcome to ... Please ...*	Thank A. Ask for information. *Thank you. Could you tell me ...?*
Agree. Give information. *Certainly. Buckingham Palace is located in ... .*	Respond and ask for information. *OK. When was ...?*
Give information. *Well, the main house ...*	Respond and ask for information. *Right. Who was ...?*
Give information. *It was originally built by ...*	Respond and ask for information. *Thanks. And is it ...?*
Give information. *Yes, but it has been used ...*	Respond and ask for information. *OK – oh, and one more ... can I ...?*
Give information. *No, but ...*	Respond and thank A. *I see. Thank you ...*
End conversation. *You're welcome.*	

- Monitor the activity around the class and offer assistance as necessary.
- Then ask some pairs to act out their dialogues in front of the class.

Suggested Answer Key

A: *Welcome to Buckingham Palace. Please feel free to ask me anything.*
B: *Thank you. Could you tell me what part of London we are in?*
A: *Certainly. Buckingham Palace is located in the City of Westminster.*
B: *OK. When was it built?*
A: *Well, the main house was built in 1703 and it was expanded over the years. It was completed in 1913.*
B: *Right. Who was it built by?*
A: *It was originally built by the Duke of Buckingham.*
B: *Thanks. And is it true that it was used as a townhouse at first?*
A: *Yes, but it has been used as a royal residence since 1837.*
B: *OK – oh, and one more thing – can I take photographs?*
A: *No, cameras are not allowed anywhere except in the palace garden, I'm afraid.*
B: *I see. Thank you for your help.*
A: *You're welcome.*

Intonation

5 **Aim** To practise intonation in passive questions

- Play the recording. Ss listen and underline the stressed words.
- Play the recording again with pauses for Ss to repeat, chorally and/or individually.
- Check Ss' pronunciation and intonation.

Answer Key

1 made
2 written
3 discovered
4 found
5 built
6 chosen

Reading & Writing

6 **Aim** To read for cohesion & coherence; to practise the passive

- Ask Ss to read the article and fill in the gaps with the correct passive forms of the verbs in brackets.
- Check Ss' answers.

Answer Key

1 is located
2 are made
3 (are) connected
4 was built
5 were killed
6 is visited
7 are amazed
8 was used
9 will be thrilled

7 **Aim** To decide on best titles to an article

- Ask Ss to read the Writing Tip and tell Ss that this tip will help them to complete the task successfully.
- Then ask Ss to read through the list of titles and select the most appropriate ones.
- Check Ss' answers around the class.

Answer Key

A, C – both short and make you want to read more. A uses an interesting adjective and C uses the imperative.

8 **Aim** To analyse a rubric

- Ask Ss to read the rubric and answer the questions.
- Check Ss' answers.

Answer key

It asks me to write about a famous landmark in my country for readers of an international online travel magazine.

9 **Aim** To listen for specific information; to prepare for a writing task

- Play the recording. Ss listen and complete the gaps.
- Check Ss' answers.

Answer Key

1	north	4	12th/twelfth
2	two/2	5	two/2
3	stone	6	towers

10 **Aim** **To write an article about a place of interest**

- Give Ss time to write their article using the notes in Ex. 9 and the plan to help them.
- Check Ss' answers.
- Alternatively, assign the task as HW and check Ss' answers in the next lesson.

Suggested Answer Key

Are you planning to visit Cambodia? Then, don't miss out on the ancient city of Angkor Wat. It is located in Siem Reap in the north of the country. There are two square kilometres of temples, courtyards, terraces, palaces and beautiful sculptures all made of stone.

Angkor Wat was built in the 12th century and it was used as a place of worship until the 15th century. It was first opened to the public in the 20th century.

It is now visited by over 2 million people a year. Visitors can admire the temple ruins. The main temple has five towers.

You will be thrilled by the beauty of Angkor Wat. As Cambodia's most famous landmark, it is a must-see.

Values

Ask Ss to try to explain the saying in their mother tongue. If Ss have difficulty, explain it to them. Ask Ss to memorise this saying and check in the next lesson.

The saying means that we should get our inspiration for buildings from nature.

Culture 8

Listening & Reading

1 **Aim** **To introduce the topic and listen and read for gist**

- Ask Ss to look at the pictures. Elicit Ss' guesses as to what two things all the landmarks have in common and what they symbolise.
- Play the recording. Ss listen and read and find out.

Suggested Answer Key

The landmarks are all man-made and they all depict animals. The Kelpies are horses' heads that symbolise the importance of the horse in Scottish trade and transport. The Uffington White Horse may symbolise an ancient tribe or a Celtic horse goddess. The Animal Wall symbolises the mysterious and exotic animals the explorers of the 19th century would have seen. The Big Fish symbolises a legendary wise fish in Irish mythology and Belfast's past.

2 **Aim** **To read for key information (multiple matching)**

- Ask Ss to read the questions and then match them to the texts.
- Check Ss' answers.

Answer Key

1	A	2	C	3	B	4	D

- Give Ss time to look up the meanings of the words in the **Check these words** box in the Word List.
- Play the video for Ss and elicit their comments.

Speaking & Writing

3 **Aim** **THINK** **To consolidate information in a text and express an opinion**

- Give Ss time to consider their answers.
- Elicit answers from Ss around the class.

Suggested Answer Key

I think it is interesting that Kelpies were water spirits with the strength of ten horses.

I think it is interesting that no one knows for certain why the Uffington White Horse was made.

I think it is interesting that the statues in the Animal Wall still have their glass eyes.

I think it is interesting that the Big Fish is called the Salmon of Knowledge after the one in Irish mythology.

> **Background Information**
>
> **'The Salmon of Knowledge'** comes from an Irish legend about a salmon that ate one acorn from each of the nine trees of knowledge and ended up with all the knowledge in the world.

4 **Aim** **ICT** **To develop research skills; to prepare a poster about man-made landmarks in your country**

- Explain the task and give Ss time to make notes and then prepare a poster about interesting landmarks in their country or in other countries.
- Ask various Ss to present their poster to the class.
- Alternatively, assign the task as HW and ask Ss to present their posters in the next lesson.

Suggested Answer Key

Man-Made Landmarks in Spain

Sagrada Família is a church in Barcelona designed by Antoni Gaudí. The design includes ten spires, each one symbolising an important figure from the Bible.

The City of Arts and Sciences is an architectural complex in the city of Valencia. It looks like an eye and it symbolises having ones' eyes opened by science.

The Bull Statue is in Plaza De Toros in El Puerto De Santa Maria, Cadiz, Spain. It is made of bronze and it symbolises the long tradition of bullfighting in Spain.

El Cid is Burgos's most famous citizen and the statue there is a monument to him. It symbolises his victories in many battles.

Review 8

Vocabulary

1 **Aim** To practise vocabulary from the unit
- Explain the task.
- Give Ss time to complete it.
- Check Ss' answers.

Answer Key

1 decorated	3 carved	5 hang
2 amazed	4 made	6 dug

2 **Aim** To practise vocabulary from the unit
- Explain the task.
- Give Ss time to complete it.
- Check Ss' answers.

Answer Key

1 wood	3 canyon	5 stone
2 glass	4 cave	6 rainforest

Grammar

3 **Aim** To practise the passive
- Explain the task.
- Give Ss time to complete it.
- Check Ss' answers.

Answer Key

1 by	4 by	7 served
2 be taken	5 weren't	8 will be
3 was	6 asked	

4 **Aim** To practise the passive
- Explain the task.
- Give Ss time to complete it.
- Check Ss' answers.

Answer Key

1 is situated	6 is made
2 was built	7 be arranged
3 was designed	8 be driven
4 is visited	9 be taken
5 are supported	10 be missed

Everyday English

5 **Aim** To match exchanges
- Explain the task.
- Give Ss time to complete it.
- Check Ss' answers.

Answer Key

1 D	2 B	3 C	4 A

Competences

Ask Ss to assess their own performance in the unit by ticking the items according to how competent they feel for each of the listed activities.

Optional activity

Work in groups of four. In pairs, research information about things you use (e.g. watch, pencil, smartphone, etc) and who invented them. Write the names of the objects and the inventors on different pieces of paper. The other two members guess who invented each object.

hand backpack	Martin Cooper
ballpoint pen	the Chinese
handheld cellular mobile phone	László Biró
the umbrella	Gerry Cunningham

1 The hand backpack was invented by Gerry Cunningham.
2 The handheld cellular mobile phone was invented by Martin Cooper.
3 The ballpoint pen was invented by László Biró.
4 The umbrella was invented by the Chinese.

Live and let live 9

Topic
In this unit, Ss will explore the topics of endangered animals and green activities.
9a Reading & Vocabulary 72-73
Lesson objectives: To learn vocabulary for endangered animals, to listen and read for gist, to read for specific information (comprehension questions), to learn prepositional phrases, to learn about similes with animals, to talk about endangered animals, to write a tweet **Vocabulary:** Endangered animals (*mountain gorilla, polar bear, Asian elephant, African penguin, Amazon River dolphin, Indian rhino, Philippine eagle, Bengal tiger*); Animal body parts (*horn, hooves, stripes, whiskers, fur, paws, feathers, hooked beak, claws, fins, webbed feet, tusks, trunk, fur, tail*); Nouns (*oil spill, response, ivory, seal, source, treetops, logger*); Verb (*hunt*)
9b Grammar in Use 74-75
Lesson objectives: To learn/revise the past perfect, to learn/revise conditionals type 2, to learn/revise reflexive pronouns
9c Skills in Action 76-77
Lesson objectives: To learn vocabulary for green activities, to listen for specific information (multiple choice), to act out a dialogue and practise everyday English for making & agreeing/disagreeing with suggestions, to learn intonation in exclamations, to read for key information, to write an article providing solutions to a problem **Vocabulary:** Green activities (*drinks can, drop, bin, recycle, car, public transport, bike, fruit and vegetables, supermarket, market, garden, rubbish, bagful, recycled, eco-friendly, air pollution, plant trees, greenery, fresh air*)
Culture 9 78
Lesson objectives: To listen and read for gist, to read for specific information (comprehension questions), to present an eco-festival in your country **Vocabulary:** Nouns (*outfit, service*); Verb (*celebrate*); Phrases (*free of charge, in the heart of*)
Review 9 79
Lesson objectives: To test/consolidate vocabulary and grammar learnt throughout the unit; to practise everyday English

Go through the objectives box and tell Ss that these are the topics, skills and activities this unit will cover.

9a

Vocabulary

1 Aim To present endangered animals

- Read out the list of endangered animals and ask Ss to look at the poster and complete the labels.
- Play the recording with pauses for Ss to check their answers.

Answer Key

1 Indian rhino
2 African penguin
3 mountain gorilla
4 Bengal tiger
5 Philippine eagle
6 Asian elephant
7 polar bear
8 Amazon River dolphin

2 Aim To present and practise vocabulary for animals' body parts

- Ask Ss to use their dictionaries to look up the meanings of the words in bold and then give them time to answer the questions using the animals in Ex. 1.
- Check Ss' answers around the class.

Answer Key

A 1 C 7 E 8 G 6
B 4 D 5 F 2 H 3

Optional activity

Choose an animal from Ex. 1 and describe it to your partner. Make three mistakes. Your partner corrects the mistakes.

Reading

3 a) Aim To read for gist

- Give Ss time to skim the tweets and match them to the animals in Ex. 1.
- Check Ss' answers.

Answer Key

Tweet 1: no animal (introduction)
Tweet 2: African penguin
Tweet 3: Asian elephant
Tweet 4: polar bear
Tweet 5: Philippine eagle

b) Aim To match endangered species to problems

- Ask Ss to predict which of the problems affect which of the endangered animals in Ex. 1.
- Play the recording. Ss listen and read to check.

77

9

Answer Key

African penguin – water pollution
Asian elephant – hunting
polar bear – melting ice
Philippine eagle – disappearing forests

4 Aim To read for specific information (comprehension questions)

- Ask Ss to read the questions.
- Give Ss time to read the text again and then answer the questions.
- Check Ss' answers.

Answer Key

1 to raise awareness about the most endangered animals because it's Earth Day
2 an oil spill
3 50,000
4 seals
5 in 1995

- Elicit the meanings of the words in bold from Ss. They may use their dictionaries if necessary.

Answer Key

take action (phr): to do sth (about a problem)
volunteers (n): people who offer their time to do sth without payment
hunters (n): people who kill or capture wild animals, e.g. for sport
fatten (v): to become fatter, to gain weight
dropped (v): gone down

- Give Ss time to look up the meanings of the words in the **Check these words** box in the Word List.
- Play the video for Ss and elicit their comments.

5 Aim To practise prepositional phrases

- Explain the task and give Ss time to complete it.
- Check Ss' answers.

Answer Key

1 in   3 in, in   5 on
2 on   4 in, in

6 Aim To consolidate vocabulary from a text

- Ask Ss to read the words in the list and then give them time to complete the text.
- Check Ss' answers.

Answer Key

1 national   4 endangered
2 numbers   5 source
3 action

7 Aim To present and practise similes with animals

Read out the animals in the list and give Ss time to use them to complete the similes.
Have Ss check their answers in their dictionaries.

Answer Key

1 bat   4 bird   7 mouse
2 lion   5 peacock   8 dog
3 bee   6 kitten

Speaking

8 Aim THINK To talk about endangered animals

Read out the question and give Ss time to discuss it. Then elicit answers from Ss around the class.

Suggested Answer Key

A: I think the Indian rhino is endangered because of hunting.
B: Yes, I think you're right. They are hunted for their horns. Maybe there's nowhere for them to live, too. etc.

> **Background Information**
>
> **California** is a state on the west coast of the USA. Its capital is Sacramento.
>
> **Oregon** is a state on the West Coast of the USA. Its capital city is Salem.
>
> **The Philippines** is a country in Southeast Asia. Its capital city is Manila.

Writing

9 Aim ICT To develop research skills; to write a tweet

- Explain the task and give Ss time to complete it using the tweets in the text as models.
- Ask various Ss to read their tweet to the class.

Suggested Answer Key

The 3,555 Indian rhinos left in the wild are in danger because the grasslands where they live are getting smaller and smaller every day due to global warming and human activity. #mostwanted

9b Grammar in Use

1 Aim To present/revise the past perfect

- Present the past perfect. Say then write on the board: *I had seen the accident.* Underline *had seen*

and explain that this verb is in the past perfect. Point to a S and say: *You had seen the accident.* Then write it on the board. Point to a male S and say: *He had seen the accident.* Then write it on the board. Present the other persons in the same way.
- Explain that we form the past perfect simple in the affirmative with *had* and the past participle of the main verb, we form the negative by putting *not* after *had* and we form questions by putting *had* before the subject.
- Explain that we use this tense to talk about an action which had finished in the past before another past action.
- Explain/Elicit that past participles of regular verbs are usually formed by adding **-ed** *(work – worked)*, verbs ending in -e add **-d** *(love – loved)*, verbs ending in consonant + -y lose -y and add **-ied**, *(study – studied)*, verbs ending in a vowel + -y add -ed *(play – played)*, verbs ending in a vowel + l, p, k, b, etc. double the consonant and add **-ed** *(travel – travelled)*.
- Ask Ss to read the theory and elicit examples from the forum discussion. Ss give more examples using this tense.

Answer Key

Examples: *had already lived, had all disappeared*

Background Information

Mauritius is an island nation in the Indian Ocean about 2,000 km off the southeastern coast of Africa.

Brazil is in South America. Its capital city is Brasilia.

2 Aim To practise the past perfect
- Explain the task and give Ss time to complete it.
- Check Ss' answers.

Answer Key

1	had cleaned	3	hadn't noticed
2	had injured	4	Had he booked

3 Aim To practise the past perfect and the past simple
- Explain the task and give Ss time to complete it.
- Check Ss' answers.

Answer Key

1	had left	7	had taken
2	had fallen	8	raised
3	had stopped	9	hadn't managed
4	hadn't seen	10	had ever seen
5	had heard	11	turned
6	felt	12	had gone

4 Aim To practise the past perfect
- Explain the task and ask Ss to read the phrases and match them to form sentences.
- Check Ss' answers and elicit which action happened first.

Answer Key

1 b the people sat down
2 e I read the text
3 a the clean-up started
4 d the lecture ended
5 c Kim finished her work

5 Aim To present/revise type 2 conditionals
- Say then write on the board: *If I had enough money, I would buy a new computer.* Ask Ss to identify the *if*-clause *(If I had enough money)* and which tense we use *(the past simple)*. Ask Ss to identify the main clause *(I would buy a new computer)* and the verb form used *(would + bare infinitive)*. Explain that this is a type 2 conditional and we use it to talk about an unreal or unlikely situation in the present or future. Also point out that we can use *were* instead of *was* in all persons.
- Read out the theory box and elicit examples from the forum discussion.

Answer Key

We use type 2 conditionals to talk about unreal, imaginary or highly unlikely situations in the present or future.
Examples: *What would you do if you were the leader of your country for a day? If I were the leader of my country, I would stop loggers from cutting down the forests. If I were the president, I would create national parks where animals could live safely.*

6 Aim To practise type 2 conditionals
- Explain the task and give Ss time to complete it adding commas where necessary.
- Check Ss' answers.

Answer Key

1 If you took your bicycle, you would get there faster.
2 If he had showers rather than baths, he would save on water.
3 Our beaches would be much cleaner if people didn't drop litter.
4 You'd save on electricity if you turned off lights you don't need.
5 If hunters stopped killing Bengal tigers, they wouldn't be an endangered species.
6 The air would be cleaner if we all planted more trees.
7 There would be more forests if people didn't cut down trees.

8 If people used public transport instead of driving their cars, there would be less air pollution in big cities.

7 Aim To practise type 2 conditionals
- Explain the task and read out the example.
- Give Ss time to make sentences following the example and then elicit answers from Ss around the class.

Answer Key

2 If there were more bins in towns and cities, there would not be so much litter on our streets.
3 If we didn't pollute our lakes and rivers, we would have clean drinking water.
4 If we recycled all of our waste, there would be no rubbish.
5 If we stopped cutting down rainforests, animals would not lose their homes.

8 Aim To practise type 2 conditionals
- Explain the task and ask two Ss to model the example dialogue.
- Then give Ss time to complete the task in pairs.
- Monitor the activity around the class and then ask some pairs to act out their short dialogues in front of the rest of the class.

Suggested Answer Key

2 A: What would you do if you found a sick cat?
   B: If I found a sick cat, I'd take it to the vet.
3 A: What would you do if you were able to travel back in time?
   B: If I were able to travel back in time, I would visit my grandparents when they were young.
4 A: What would you do if you had one wish for the environment?
   B: If I had one wish for the environment, I would wish for an end to pollution.
5 A: What would you do if your friend threw litter on the ground?
   B: If my friend threw litter on the ground, I would tell him/her to pick it up and put it in a bin.

9 Aim To practise type 2 conditionals
- Explain the task and read out the example.
- Have Ss complete the task in pairs.
- Monitor the activity around the class and then ask some pairs to tell the class.

Suggested Answer Key

2 A: If I won £1,000,000, I would buy a big house.
   B: If I bought a big house, I would have a big garden.
   A: If I had a big garden, I would keep animals.
3 A: If I saw a stray animal, I would give it some food.
   B: If I gave it some food, it would not starve.

4 A: If I saw a bear, I would be scared.
   B: If I was scared, I would stand still.
   A: If I stood still, the bear would not attack.

10 Aim To revise/present reflexive pronouns
- Ask Ss to read the theory and explain any points that Ss are unsure of.
- Elicit the reflexive pronouns in the forum discussion.

Answer Key

Examples: itself, themselves

11 Aim To practise reflexive pronouns
- Give Ss time to complete the task.
- Check Ss' answers around the class.

Answer Key

1 themselves   3 yourself   5 myself
2 itself   4 ourselves

12 Aim THINK To consolidate the topic through type 2 conditionals

Give Ss time to consider their answers and write some sentences. Then ask various Ss around the class to share their answers with the rest of the class.

Suggested Answer Key

If I were the leader of my country, I would ban all hunting. I would also ban all cars and make people have electric cars to reduce pollution. I would also ban plastic bags and plastic packaging and make people recycle everything.

9c Skills in Action

Vocabulary

1 Aim To present vocabulary for green activities
- Give Ss time to read the quiz and complete it.
- Tell Ss to look up the meanings of any unknown words in their dictionaries.
- Ask various Ss to tell the class how 'green' they are.

Ss' own answers

Listening

2 Aim To listen for specific information (multiple choice)
- Ask Ss to read the questions and look at the picture answers.
- Play the recording and have Ss complete the task.
- Check Ss' answers.

Answer Key

1 B 2 A 3 C

Everyday English

3 **Aim** To listen and read for specific information

- Tell Ss the situation and elicit their guesses as to three suggestions they might make.
- Play the recording. Ss listen and read and see if their suggestions were mentioned.

Suggested Answer Key

Plant trees, put plants in halls and classrooms, recycle the rubbish

The speakers mention hiring bikes and putting bins everywhere.

4 **Aim** To substitute functional language for suitable alternatives; to expand vocabulary

- Give Ss time to replace the underlined phrases in the dialogue with suitable alternatives from the useful language box.
- Elicit answers from Ss around the class.

Suggested Answer Key

Yes, let's = All right.
I see your point, but = I'm afraid I don't agree because
How about = Shall we
What a good idea! = I couldn't agree more.
Why don't we = Why not
I couldn't agree more. = What a good idea!

5 **Aim** To role play a dialogue making & agreeing/disagreeing with suggestions

- Explain the task and ask Ss to act out a similar dialogue to the one in Ex. 3 in pairs using the prompts and the language in the box to help them.
- Write this diagram on the board for Ss to follow.

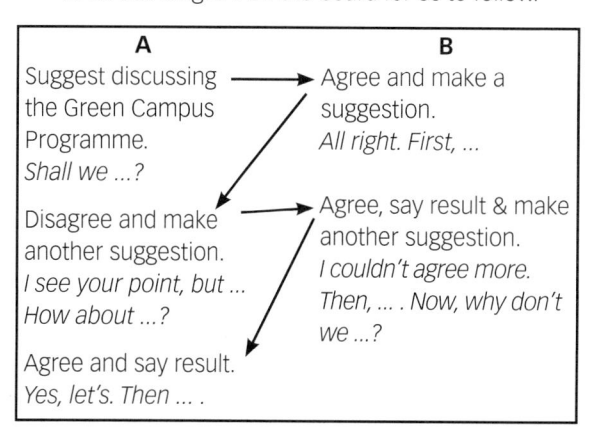

A	B
Suggest discussing the Green Campus Programme. *Shall we ...?*	Agree and make a suggestion. *All right. First, ...*
Disagree and make another suggestion. *I see your point, but ... How about ...?*	Agree, say result & make another suggestion. *I couldn't agree more. Then, ... Now, why don't we ...?*
Agree and say result. *Yes, let's. Then ... .*	

- Monitor the activity around the class and offer assistance as necessary.

- Then ask some pairs to act out their dialogues in front of the class.

Suggested Answer Key

A: Shall we discuss the Green College Programme?
B: All right. First, more public transport would mean fewer cars.
A: I see your point, but that is up to the council not us. How about planting more trees?
B: I couldn't agree more. Then the air quality would improve. Now, why don't we recycle more?
A: Yes, let's. Then we would produce less rubbish.

Intonation

6 **Aim** To learn & practise intonation in exclamations

- Ask Ss to read the items 1-6.
- Play the recording. Ss listen and circle how the speaker sounds.
- Then play the recording again with pauses for Ss to repeat, chorally and/or individually.
- Check Ss' pronunciation and intonation.

Answer Key

1 shocked 3 annoyed 5 angry
2 excited 4 worried 6 bored

Reading & Writing

7 a) **Aim** To read for gist

- Ask Ss to read the article quickly and then choose the most appropriate title from the options provided.
- Check Ss' answers.

Answer Key

b

b) **Aim** To read for specific information

- Ask Ss to read the article again and copy and complete the table in their notebooks.
- Check Ss' answers on the board.

Answer Key

Problem	less than a million hedgehogs left in UK
Causes & effects	killed by cars on new roads, loss of habitat because of new houses
Solutions & results	make gardens 'hedgehog-friendly', put sticks in corner, put out water – hedgehogs have home and way to get around

81

9

8 **Aim** **To identify writing techniques**
- Read the writing tip and check understanding.
- Read the rubric and elicit answers from the class.

Answer key

The writer supports his/her solutions with the sentence: Then, our gardens would be good places for hedgehogs to live and a safe way to get around.

Writing

9 **Aim** **To analyse a rubric**
- Ask Ss to read the rubric and answer the questions.
- Check Ss' answers.

Answer key

I am going to write an article. It is for my teacher/college magazine. It should be 100-120 words.

10 a) **Aim** **To prepare for a writing task; to make connections**
- Explain the task and give Ss time to match the causes (1-5) with the effects (a-e).
- Check Ss' answers.

Answer Key

1 c   2 b   3 a   4 e   5 d

b) **Aim** **To prepare for a writing task; to make connections**
- Explain the task and give Ss time to match the solutions (1-5) with the results (a-e).
- Check Ss' answers.

Answer Key

1 d   2 b   3 a   4 e   5 c

11 **Aim** **To write an article providing solutions to a problem**
- Give Ss time to write their article using the ideas in Ex. 10 and the plan to help them.
- Check Ss' answers.
- Alternatively, assign the task as HW and check Ss' answers in the next lesson.

Suggested Answer Key

Greener Cities

We all want our cities to be nice places to live, so what can we do to make them better?
One problem is air pollution. This is because many people drive cars. Another problem is a lack of fresh air. This is because there are not enough trees and parks.
One solution is to improve public transport. If we do this, there would be fewer cars and less air pollution. Also, if we built cycle paths, more people would use their bicycles. Another solution is to plant more trees and create more parks. Then, people would have fresh air and children would have somewhere to play.
If we took these simple steps, our cities would be better.

Values

Ask Ss to try to explain the saying in their mother tongue. If Ss have difficulty, explain the saying. Ask Ss to memorise this saying and check in the next lesson.

The saying means that the Earth can provide enough for every person to live if they live modestly, but when people get greedy and want more than they need, then that is when the Earth's resources will run out.

Culture 9

Listening & Reading

1 **Aim** **To introduce the topic and listen and read for gist**
- Ask Ss to look at the title and the headings. Elicit Ss' guesses as to what people can do at the festival.
- Play the recording. Ss listen and read and find out.

Suggested Answer Key

At the Footprints Eco Festival, you can listen to music, get your face painted and buy organic food and handicrafts. You can also learn about turning rubbish into art and about bee-keeping or finding food in the wild. You can watch a fashion show and take part in a clothes swap. You can also let them service your bike for free and watch films at the film festival.

2 **Aim** **To read for specific information (comprehension questions)**
- Ask Ss to read the questions and then read the text again and answer them.
- Check Ss' answers.

Answer Key

1 Every August
2 They can learn how to turn rubbish into art.
3 Six
4 A free bike service
5 Whites Creek Valley Park, Sydney, Australia.

- Give Ss time to look up the meanings of the words in the **Check these words** box in the Word List.
- Play the video for Ss and elicit their comments.

82

3 **Aim** **To consolidate new vocabulary**

Give Ss time to look up the meanings of the words in bold in their dictionaries and elicit explanations from Ss around the class.

Suggested Answer Key

gather (v): *to get together*
workshops (n): *meetings where a group of people discuss and take part in an activity/project on a particular subject*
swap (v): *to exchange*
pedal (v): *to move by working the pedals of a bicycle*

Speaking & Writing

4 **Aim** **THINK** **To consolidate information in a text and express an opinion**

- Give Ss time to consider their answers.
- Elicit answers from Ss around the class.

Suggested Answer Key

I think people need to go to festivals like this because it is a way to help the environment and learn more about helping the environment. There is also a lot of entertainment, with fun activities for all the family.

5 **Aim** **ICT** **To develop research skills; to write a short text about an eco festival in your country**

- Explain the task and give Ss time to make notes and then write a short text about an eco festival in their country.
- Ask various Ss to read their text to the class.
- Alternatively, assign the task as HW and ask Ss to read out their texts in the next lesson.

Suggested Answer Key

name of festival: *EcoWest Festival*
where & when it takes place: *17 March – 15 April – Auckland, New Zealand*
what you can do there: *take part in photography workshop, gardening workshops, craft and DIY workshops with recycled materials, go on guided walks, learn bike maintenance, go on bike rides, take part in clean-up events, try street food*
why people enjoy going: *good way to help the environment, learn about the environment and take part in fun events for the whole family*

The EcoWest Festival takes place from the 17th March to the 15th April in Auckland, New Zealand. You can take part in a photography workshop, gardening workshops and craft and DIY workshops with recycled materials. You can go on guided walks. You can also learn about bike maintenance and go on bike rides. You can take part in clean-up events and try delicious street food. People enjoy going to this festival because it is a good way to help the environment and to learn about the environment and take part in fun events for the whole family.

Review 9

Vocabulary

1 **Aim** **To practise vocabulary from the unit**

- Explain the task.
- Give Ss time to complete it.
- Check Ss' answers.

Answer Key

6	thick	8	hooked
7	sharp	9	webbed

2 **Aim** **To practise vocabulary from the unit**

- Explain the task.
- Give Ss time to complete it.
- Check Ss' answers.

Answer Key

1 b   2 d   3 a   4 e   5 c

3 **Aim** **To practise vocabulary from the unit**

- Explain the task.
- Give Ss time to complete it.
- Check Ss' answers.

Answer Key

1	drop	3	save	5	throw
2	take	4	recycle	6	plant

Grammar

4 **Aim** **To practise reflexive pronouns**

- Explain the task.
- Give Ss time to complete it.
- Check Ss' answers.

Answer Key

1	myself	3	herself	5	themselves
2	yourself	4	ourselves		

5 **Aim** **To practise the past perfect**

- Explain the task.
- Give Ss time to complete it.
- Check Ss' answers.

Answer Key

1 hadn't seen   5 hadn't gone
2 had just finished   6 Had Penny ever
3 Had you known   cycled
4 had been

83

9

6 **Aim** To practise type 2 conditionals
- Explain the task.
- Give Ss time to complete it.
- Check Ss' answers.

Answer Key

1 would plant, had
2 found, would
3 wasn't, wouldn't
4 could live, didn't
5 Would, asked
6 couldn't, would

Everyday English

7 **Aim** To match exchanges
- Explain the task.
- Give Ss time to complete it.
- Check Ss' answers.

Answer Key

1 C 3 D
2 A 4 B

Competences

Ask Ss to assess their own performance in the unit by ticking the items according to how competent they feel for each of the listed activities.

Optional activity

Ss work in pairs. One S starts a sentence using the past perfect, the other ends the sentence using the past simple.
  A: *I had finished my essay ...*
  B: *before I went to football practice.*

Values: Good Citizenship

1 **Aim** To predict the content of a text

Ask Ss to look at the title of the text and the introductory paragraph and elicit Ss' guesses as to what the 'circles of citizenship' are.

Suggested Answer Key

The circles of citizenship are the levels of responsibility a person has starting with themselves and expanding to cover the entire world.

2 **Aim** To read for key information

- Ask Ss to read the text and then give them time to match the paragraphs to the circles of citizenship.
- Check Ss' answers and then elicit explanations for the words in bold from Ss around the class.

Answer Key

1 C 2 E 3 B 4 F 5 A 6 D

Suggested Answer Key

obey the law (phr): *to follow the rules of the country as set by the government*
under arrest (phr): *be placed in police custody*
impossible (adj): *cannot be done*
impact (n): *effect*
in public (phr): *in view of other people*
stick (v): *to continue doing sth*
coaching (n): *training and teaching athletes*
gift (v): *to give/donate*

- Play the video for Ss and elicit their comments.

3 **Aim** THINK To expand on the topic

- Play the recording. Ss listen and read.
- Ask Ss to work in pairs and think of one more activity for each circle of citizenship.
- Elicit answers from Ss around the class.

Suggested Answer Key

1 We have a responsibility to ourselves to get enough sleep to stay well rested.
2 We have a responsibility to the people and animals we live with. We should take care of our pets and respect our family members.
3 We should respect our neighbours and not play loud music at night or let our dog bark at night.
4 We should respect the place where we live and not drop litter on the streets.
5 We should pay our taxes and vote for good people to govern us.
6 We should respect other cultures when we travel abroad.

Public Speaking Skills

1 a) Aim To present a public speaking task

Ask Ss to read the task.

b) Aim To analyse a model public speaking task; to identify opening/closing techniques

- Play the recording. Ss listen and read the model and identify the opening/closing techniques.
- Elicit answers from various Ss.

Answer Key

The writer starts his presentation with a rhetorical question and ends by addressing the listeners directly.

2 Aim To introduce the use of transition phrases

- Read out the **Study Skills** box and tell Ss that this is a helpful tip to assist them when giving a presentation.
- Give Ss time to identify the transition phrases in the model and replace them with the ones in the list.
- Check Ss' answers.

Suggested Answer Key

Let's start with – To begin with, there's
But there's more. = But that's not all.
Then there's = Don't forget

3 Aim ICT To give a presentation

- Ask Ss to work in small groups and then research online for information about how to save electricity and then make notes.
- Give Ss time to prepare a presentation.
- Ask various Ss to give their presentation to the class.
- Alternatively, assign the task as HW and have Ss give their presentations in the next lesson.

Suggested Answer Key

Good morning everyone. I'm Carla Ducat. Can you believe that 1.3 billion people in the world live without access to electricity? We have it at our fingertips, but instead of feeling lucky, we waste it all the time. It's time to stop wasting electricity.

To begin with, there is no reason why all homes can't use solar energy. Solar panels are a cost-effective way to save energy and many councils and governments have schemes to help people pay for the installation. Another way to save electricity is to swap all the lightbulbs in your house for energy-efficient ones. These save electricity and money on your energy bills.

But that's not all. Why use an electric light when there is daylight? Use natural light whenever possible and use a small lamp instead of a large overhead light to save electricity. You can also use blinds instead of curtains to let more light into your home.

Then there's cooking. Thawing out food before cooking can save energy. You can also use the cooker less in the summer by making salads and using a barbecue. You can also unplug appliances when you are not using them and buy energy-efficient appliances that use less power than standard ones.

As you can see, you can save electricity by doing these simple things. It's not difficult at all, is it? So, what are you waiting for? Start saving electricity today!

Are there any questions? ... Thank you for listening.

Holiday time 10

Go through the objectives box and tell Ss that these are the topics, skills and activities this unit will cover.

Topic
In this unit, Ss will explore the topics of types of holidays, weather, and hotel services & facilities.

10a Reading & Vocabulary	82-83
Lesson objectives: To learn vocabulary for types of holidays, to scan a text, to listen and read for specific information (T/F/DS), to learn prepositions and prepositional phrases, to talk about the weather, to write a weather forecast **Vocabulary:** Types of holidays *(package holidays, city breaks, cruises, adventure holidays)*; Weather *(fine weather, bright sunshine, high temperatures, wet weather, strong winds, thick clouds, heavy rain)*; Nouns *(budget, deal, fortnight, thunderstorm)*; Verbs *(stroll, dine)*; Phrase *(tick every box)*	

10b Grammar in Use	84-85
Lesson objectives: To learn the *(to)* infinitive/*-ing* form, to learn relatives and defining relative clauses, to revise/learn the uses of the definite article	

10c Skills in Action	86-87
Lesson objectives: To learn vocabulary for hotel services & facilities, to listen for specific information (multiple choice), to act out a dialogue and practise everyday English for checking in at a hotel, to learn pronunciation in rhyming words, to read for specific information (comprehension questions), to write a hotel review **Vocabulary:** Hotel services & facilities *(free Wi-Fi, wake-up call, restaurant, laundry service, hotel porter, gym, swimming pool, hotel parking, room service, airport shuttle, beauty salon, café)*	

Culture 10	88
Lesson objectives: To listen and read for gist, to read for specific information, to create a brochure about different places and types of holidays in one's country **Vocabulary:** Nouns *(capital, eagle, otter, puffin)*; Verb *(wander)*	

Review 10	89
Lesson objectives: To test/consolidate vocabulary and grammar learnt throughout the unit; to practise everyday English	

10a

Vocabulary

1 Aim To present types of holidays; to express preference

- Ask Ss to work in pairs and look at the types of holidays in the adverts. Go through the list of adjectives and explain/elicit the meanings of any unknown words.
- Then have Ss express preferences and respond using the adjectives and following the example.
- Monitor the activity around the class and then ask some pairs to share their preferences with the class.

Answer Key

A: *I prefer to go on city breaks because they are cheap and interesting.*
B: *Well, I prefer package holidays to city breaks because they are relaxing.*

Reading

2 Aim To scan a text for key vocabulary

- Give Ss time to look though the text quickly to find the items required.
- Check Ss' answers around the class.

Answer Key

Holiday activities: *swimming, sunbathing, sightseeing, relaxing on a beach, dining in restaurants, travelling, hiking*
Weather: *showers, freezing cold, bright sunshine, clouds, thunderstorms*

3 Aim To listen and read for specific information (T/F/DS)

- Ask Ss to read the statements.
- Give Ss time to read the text again and then mark the statements according to what they read.
- Check Ss' answers.

Answer Key

1 DS   2 T   3 F   4 T   5 F

- Elicit the meanings of the words in bold from Ss around the class. They may use their dictionaries if necessary.

Suggested Answer Key

get you down (phr): *make you sad*
sights (n): *tourist attractions*

87

on board (phr): on a ship
expedition (n): a journey involving exploring
look after (phr v): take care of

- Give Ss time to look up the meanings of the words in the **Check these words** box in the Word List.
- Play the video for Ss and elicit their comments.

4 **Aim** THINK **To talk about types of holidays and express preferences; to develop critical thinking skills**

Give Ss time to consider their answers and then elicit answers from Ss around the class.

Suggested Answer Key

camping holiday, safari, beach holiday, eco-holiday, volunteering holiday, cultural holiday, sailing holiday, etc.
I prefer camping holidays to the holidays in the adverts because camping is very cheap and you can get very close to nature.

5 **Aim** **To consolidate vocabulary from a text**

- Ask Ss to read the words in the list and then give them time to complete the phrases.
- Check Ss' answers.
- Then give Ss time to use the phrases to make sentences.
- Elicit answers from Ss around the class.

Answer Key

1 warm   4 tropical   7 delicious
2 five-star   5 sandy   8 local
3 capital   6 crystal

Suggested Answer Key

*You can swim in the **warm sea** at Pho Quoc Island.*
*The package holiday includes a stay at a **five-star hotel**.*
*London is the **capital city** of the UK.*
*Pho Quoc is a **tropical island**.*
*There are **sandy beaches**, **crystal waters** and **delicious cuisine** in the Caribbean.*
*A **local guide** will look after you on the adventure holiday.*

6 **Aim** **To practise prepositions and prepositional phrases**

- Explain the task and give Ss time to complete it.
- Check Ss' answers.

Answer Key

1 in   2 on   3 on   4 on   5 from   6 in

7 **Aim** **To consolidate new vocabulary through antonyms**

- Ask Ss to find the highlighted adjectives in the text and read their antonyms in the list and match them.
- Have Ss check their answers in their dictionaries.

Answer Key

1 delicious   4 cold   7 memorable
2 warm   5 bright   8 best
3 long   6 huge

Vocabulary

8 **Aim** **To present and practise vocabulary relating to weather**

- Explain/Elicit the meanings of the adjectives in the list from Ss around the class.
- Then give Ss time to read the weather forecast and complete the task.
- Check Ss' answers.

Answer Key

1 fine   4 wet   7 heavy
2 bright   5 Strong
3 high   6 thick

Speaking

9 **Aim** **To talk about the weather**

Read out the questions and ask Ss to discuss them in pairs and then elicit answers from Ss around the class.

Suggested Answer Key

The weather in my country is cool and sunny in spring. In the summer it is hot with high temperatures. In autumn it is rainy and cloudy and in the winter it is freezing cold.

Writing

10 **Aim** **To write a weather forecast**

- Explain the task and give Ss time to complete it using the forecast in the text in Ex. 8 as a model.
- Ask various Ss to read their weather forecasts to the class.

Suggested Answer Key

Tomorrow it will feel like spring has finally come in many parts of the UK. There will be the highest temperatures of the spring so far and bright sunshine. However, later in the day, there will be some wet and windy weather in the north of England and parts of Scotland. In the evening there will be strong winds and thick clouds in these parts as well, and the rain may lead to thunderstorms in some places.

Background Information

Slovakia is a country of Central Europe. It borders Poland, Ukraine, the Czech Republic, Hungary and Austria. Its capital city is Bratislava. Its official language is Slovak.

10b Grammar in Use

1 **Aim** To present the *(to)* infinitive/*-ing* form

- Present the infinitive forms. Explain that the infinitive is the base form of all verbs. Explain that we can use it with or without *to*. Say then write on the board: *I want to play football. I can play football.* Explain that we use to-infinitive to express purpose and after certain verbs such as *would love, would like, would prefer, agree, ask, decide, expect, forget, hope, manage, need, offer, promise, refuse, seem, want,* etc. Explain that we also use to-infinitive after *too/enough*.
- Explain that we use the infinitive without *to* with modal verbs e.g. *can, could, should, may, might, must, will, would,* etc. (**BUT** not with *have/need to*.)
- Present the *-ing* form. Explain that the *-ing* form is the verb form that ends in *-ing*. Say then write on the board: *Swimming is fun.* Explain that we can use the *-ing* form as a noun and as the subject of a sentence. Say then write on the board: *I like running.* Explain that we use the *-ing* form to talk about an activity, often with the verb *go*. We also use it with the verbs *like, love, dislike, fancy, hate, enjoy, prefer* as well as with the verbs *avoid, admit, deny, finish, forget, keep, mind, miss, remember, risk, stop,* etc., as well as with phrases such as *be busy, it's no use, it's (not) worth, look forward to, there's no point (in), can't stand,* etc.
- Ask Ss to read the theory box and elicit examples in the advert.

Answer Key

Examples: *would you like to spend, to build it, has to be, avoid building, can stay, there's no point bringing, go skiing and dog sledding, enjoy watching*

2 **Aim** To practise the *(to)* infinitive/*-ing* form

- Explain the task and give Ss time to complete it.
- Check Ss' answers.

Answer Key

1 to make	3 camping	5 to stay
2 packing	4 let	6 to buy

3 a) **Aim** To practise the *(to)* infinitive/*-ing* form

- Explain the task. Ask Ss to read the dialogue and complete the task.
- Check Ss' answers.

Answer Key

1 telling	5 doing	9 hiking
2 to spend	6 take	10 visiting
3 to go	7 book	
4 to visit	8 to have	

b) **Aim** To practise the *(to)* infinitive/*-ing* form

- Explain the task and give Ss time to continue the dialogue using the *(to)* infinitive/*-ing* form and the verbs in the list.
- Elicit exchanges from Ss around the class.

Suggested Answer Key

A: Actually, I**'d prefer** to **go** somewhere in the countryside than go to a big city.
B: Right. If you **dislike** visiting cities, we **need** to choose somewhere we will both enjoy.
A: **Can** you suggest anywhere?
B: How about going on an adventure holiday?
A: That sounds like fun. I **love** doing outdoor activities.
A: I do **too**. We **should** look into it and come back with some options to **decide** on.
A: Good idea.

Optional activity

Say various verbs/phrases from the theory box in Ex. 1. Ss in teams make a sentence using it. Ss should use a *(to-)* infinitive or *-ing* form as well.
e.g.   T: agree
     Team AS1:   *We agreed to work together on this project.*

4 **Aim** To present relatives and defining relative clauses

- Explain that we use relatives (*who, which, whose, that, where*) to introduce relative clauses.
- Explain that we use **who/that** instead of subject pronouns to talk about people; we use **which/that** to talk about objects or animals; we use **whose** instead of possessive adjectives to talk about possession and we use **where** to talk about place.
- Explain that a defining relative clause gives essential information and cannot be omitted.
- Ask Ss to read the theory and then elicit an example from the advert.

Answer Key

Examples: *Most guests who stay there*

5 Aim To practise who/that

- Explain the task and give Ss time to complete it using the phrases and the pictures, following the example.
- Check Ss' answers around the class.

Answer Key

2 A hotel receptionist is someone who/that welcomes guests.
3 A porter is someone who/that carries luggage.
4 A waiter is someone who/that serves meals.
5 A chambermaid is someone who/that cleans rooms.

6 Aim To listen for key information; to practise where

- Explain the task and ask Ss to read the columns and the example.
- Then play the recording and have students match the columns and then make sentences following the example.

Answer Key

2 a   3 d   4 e   5 c

Trafalgar Square is where they saw Nelson's Column.
The National Gallery is where they admired paintings.
The Savoy Hotel is where they had afternoon tea.
Wembley Stadium is where they watched a football match.

7 Aim To practise which/that

- Explain the task and read out the example.
- Have Ss complete the task and then elicit answers from Ss around the class.

Answer Key

2 A torch is something which/that we use to light up dark places.
3 A cool box is something which/that we use to keep food and drinks cool.
4 A bottle opener is something which/that we use to open bottles.

8 Aim To practise relatives and defining relative clauses

- Explain the task and give Ss time to complete it.
- Check Ss' answers.

Answer Key

1 who/that   3 who/that   5 whose
2 which/that   4 which/that   6 where

9 Aim To revise the definite article the

- Ask Ss to read the theory box and then elicit examples from the advert on p. 84.
- Then explain the task and give Ss time to complete it.
- Check Ss' answers around the class.

Answer Key

Examples: the Icehotel (hotel), Sweden (country), November, December, April (month)

1 –, –, the, –   5 the   9 the, –
2 the   6 –, the   10 –, –
3 –   7 the
4 –   8 the, –

10 Aim ICT To develop research skills; to prepare a quiz

- Ask Ss to work in small groups. Give them time to research online, and collect information and then prepare a quiz about various geographical features.
- Ask various groups to swap their quizzes and try and complete them or ask various Ss to share their quizzes with the class.

Suggested Answer Key

1 What is the longest river in the world? (the Nile)
2 Which is the highest mountain in Europe? (Mount Elbrus)
3 Which is the biggest ocean? (The Pacific Ocean)
4 Where is the largest canyon in the world? (the Grand Canyon in Arizona, in the USA)
5 Which is the highest waterfall in the world? (Angel Falls in Venezuela)
6 Where is the largest and the most active volcano in the world? (in Hawaii)
7 Which is the deepest lake in the world? (Lake Baikal)
8 Where is the hottest desert in the world? (in Africa, the Sahara Desert)

> **Background Information**
>
> **Sweden** is a Scandinavian country in Northern Europe. It borders Norway, Finland and is connected to Denmark by a bridge-tunnel. Its capital city is Stockholm.

10c Skills in Action

Vocabulary

1 Aim To present vocabulary for hotel services & facilities

Ask Ss to read the services and facilities. Then elicit which ones they would use at a hotel and why from various Ss around the class.

Suggested Answer Key

I would use the free Wi-Fi because I like to use the Internet on holiday.
I would use the restaurant because I would like to eat an evening meal there sometimes.
I would use the swimming pool because I like to swim on holiday and the hotel may not be near the beach.
I would use the airport shuttle service because it makes it easier to get to and from the airport when I arrive and leave.

2 Aim To listen for specific information (multiple choice)

- Ask Ss to read the questions.
- Play the recording and have Ss complete the task.
- Check Ss' answers.

Answer Key

1 B   2 B   3 C   4 A

Everyday English

3 Aim To listen and read for specific information

- Read out the questions in the rubric.
- Play the recording. Ss listen and read and answer the questions.

Answer Key

Mr and Mrs Smith will be staying in room 308.
The hotel provides free Wi-Fi, a porter, and wake-up calls.

4 Aim To role play a dialogue checking in at a hotel

- Explain the task and ask Ss to act out a similar dialogue to the one in Ex. 3 in pairs, using the prompts and the language in the box to help them.
- Write this diagram on the board for Ss to follow.

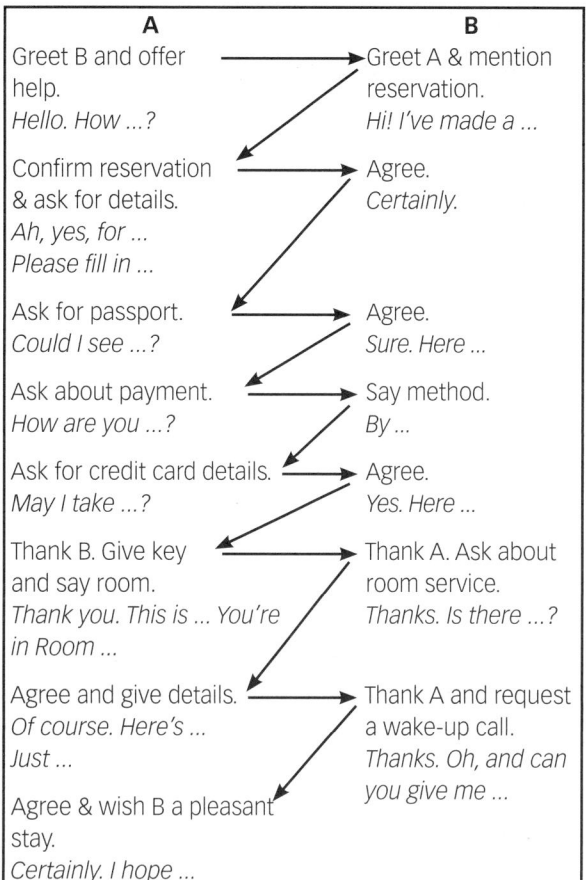

A	B
Greet B and offer help. *Hello. How …?*	Greet A & mention reservation. *Hi! I've made a …*
Confirm reservation & ask for details. *Ah, yes, for … Please fill in …*	Agree. *Certainly.*
Ask for passport. *Could I see …?*	Agree. *Sure. Here …*
Ask about payment. *How are you …?*	Say method. *By …*
Ask for credit card details. *May I take …?*	Agree. *Yes. Here …*
Thank B. Give key and say room. *Thank you. This is … You're in Room …*	Thank A. Ask about room service. *Thanks. Is there …?*
Agree and give details. *Of course. Here's … Just …*	Thank A and request a wake-up call. *Thanks. Oh, and can you give me …*
Agree & wish B a pleasant stay. *Certainly. I hope …*	

- Monitor the activity around the class and offer assistance as necessary.
- Then ask some pairs to act out their dialogues in front of the class.

Suggested Answer Key

A: Hello. How may I help you?
B: Hi! I've made a reservation for a single room. The name's Jones.
A: Ah, yes for three nights. Please fill in your name and email and sign here.
B: Certainly.
A: And could I see your passport, please?
B: Sure … here you are.
A: Thank you. How are you paying for your stay?
B: By credit card.
A: May I take your credit card details, please?
B: Yes. Here it is.
A: Thank you. This is your room key. You're in Room 426. The porter will help you with your bags.
B: Thanks. Is there room service?
A: Of course. Here's a menu. Just dial zero.
B: Thanks. Oh, and can you give me an 8:00 wake-up call, please?
A: Certainly. I hope you enjoy your stay!

10

Pronunciation

5 Aim To identify rhyming words

- Ask Ss to read the list of words and match the ones that rhyme.
- Play the recording. Ss listen and check their answers.
- Then play the recording again with pauses for Ss to repeat, chorally and/or individually.
- Check Ss' pronunciation and intonation.

Answer Key

guest – west
gym – him
city – pretty
heart – start
fun – one
yacht – hot
hotel – well

Reading & Writing

6 Aim To read for specific information (comprehension questions)

- Ask Ss to read the article and the questions and then answer them.
- Check Ss' answers.

Answer Key

1 Three days
2 Wales
3 Swimming pool, gym, restaurant, Wi-Fi
4 It was large, clean and very comfortable.
5 There was no parking and no porter.
6 She would definitely recommend it. She thinks it offers a quiet stay by the sea at a good price.

7 Aim To learn about informal style

- Read out the **Writing Tip** and explain that this information will help Ss with the writing task.
- Ask Ss to read the review again and find examples of informal style.
- Elicit examples from Ss around the class.

Answer Key

short verb forms: it's, there's, couldn't
first-person point of view: I spent, I had, it suited me, my hotel room, I had to leave, I also had to carry, I would definitely recommend
simple linking words: and, but, too,

8 Aim To expand vocabulary; to learn adjectives and their antonyms

- Ask Ss to read the two extracts and replace the words in bold with their opposites in the list.
- Tell Ss they may use their dictionaries if necessary.
- Check Ss' answers around the class.

Answer Key

A 1 enjoyable
2 quiet
3 modern
4 tasty
5 fast

B 1 unpleasant
2 rude
3 small
4 dirty
5 uncomfortable

Writing

9 Aim To write a hotel review

- Give Ss time to write their review using the advert and the plan to help them.
- Check Ss' answers.
- Alternatively, assign the task as HW and check Ss' answers in the next lesson.

Suggested Answer Key

I spent a week in June at the Beachside Hotel in Sandy Bay and I had an enjoyable stay.
It's a small friendly family hotel in a perfect location that's just 25 metres from the sea. There is free parking so you don't have to worry about your car and there is also free Wi-Fi so you can stay connected to the rest of the world. My room was large and very comfortable. Beachside Hotel's only problem? There's no lunch or dinner service. But this was not such a problem as there were plenty of restaurants next to the beach.
I highly recommend the Beachside Hotel. It is ideal for people who want a quiet getaway at a good price.

Values

Ask Ss to try to explain the saying in their mother tongue. If Ss have difficulty, explain the saying. Ask Ss to memorise this saying and check in the next lesson.
The saying means that travelling opens your mind to other ways of life and lets you learn about other places and other people.

Background Information

Wales is part of the UK. Its capital city is Cardiff.

Culture 10

Reading & Listening

1 Aim To listen and read for specific information
- Play the recording. Ss listen to and read the text and match the places to the activities.
- Check Ss' answers.

Answer Key
learn about animals – C
enjoy a short stay – E
visit old buildings – A
do winter sports – D
be near water – B

2 Aim To read a map
- Explain the task and read out the example and the useful language box for describing location.
- Ask Ss to study the map and then read the statements 1-5 and correct them following the example. Revise the compass points if necessary.
- Check Ss' answers around the class.

Answer Key
2 Mallaig isn't situated on the east coast of Scotland. It is situated on the west coast of Scotland.
3 Glasgow isn't located in the north of Scotland. It is located in the south of Scotland.
4 Edinburgh isn't situated on the west coast of Scotland. It is situated on the east coast of Scotland.
5 Mull isn't located in the centre of Scotland. It is located in the west of Scotland.

- Give Ss time to look up the meanings of the words in the **Check these words** box in the Word List.
- Play the video for Ss and elicit their comments.

Speaking & Writing

3 Aim THINK To consolidate information in a text and relate it to prior knowledge

Give Ss time to consider their answers and then ask various Ss to share their answers with the class.

Ss' own answers

4 Aim ICT To develop research skills; to create a brochure about places and types of holidays in one's country
- Explain the task and ask Ss to work in small groups.
- Give Ss time to research online and collect information about different places and types of holidays in their country and make notes and then create a brochure.
- Ask various Ss to read their brochure to the class.
- Alternatively, assign the task as HW and ask Ss to read out their brochures in the next lesson.

Suggested Answer Key

Discover Italy
Italy is full of exciting places to visit whatever kind of holiday you choose.

Rome
Historic monuments and buildings like the Colosseum, the Pantheon, the Forum and Trevi Fountain make Rome perfect for a sightseeing holiday.

Lake Como
If you enjoy sailing and celebrity spotting then you should visit Lake Como. Here you can go on a boat trip or simply walk around the lake and dine at some of the fantastic restaurants.

Grand Paradise National Park
Planning to see Italian wildlife? Then you couldn't do better than the Grand Paradise National Park. There you can have a guide take you on a tour and learn about the wildlife. You can see the alpine ibex, chamois, mountain hares, foxes and golden eagles.

Cervinia
This high-altitude resort in the Alps is perfect for skiing and snowboarding. It is famous for its long ski runs so don't forget to bring your skis with you!

Venice
This beautiful city is perfect for culture vultures. As well as the amazing architecture and cuisine, you can go to the theatre and the opera. You can also take part in the Venice Carnival if you go in February.

Review 10

Vocabulary

1 Aim To practise vocabulary from the unit
- Explain the task.
- Give Ss time to complete it.
- Check Ss' answers.

Answer Key
1 d   2 f   3 a   4 c   5 e   6 b

2 Aim To practise vocabulary from the unit
- Explain the task.
- Give Ss time to complete it.
- Check Ss' answers.

Answer Key
1 break   3 adventure
2 package   4 cruise

10 Holiday time

3 Aim To practise vocabulary from the unit
- Explain the task.
- Give Ss time to complete it.
- Check Ss' answers.

Answer Key

1 service
2 call
3 shuttle
4 pool

Grammar

4 Aim To practise the *(to)* infinitive/*-ing* form
- Explain the task.
- Give Ss time to complete it.
- Check Ss' answers.

Answer Key

1 to go
2 to eat
3 to let
4 book
5 travelling
6 swimming

5 Aim To practise relatives and defining relative clauses
- Explain the task.
- Give Ss time to complete it.
- Check Ss' answers.

Answer Key

1 This is a five-star restaurant whose chef has won many awards.
2 Maggie lives in the north of Scotland where the summers are often wet.
3 This is the tour which is on special offer this month.
4 What's the name of the guest who you spoke to just now?
5 These are the keys that Lucy was looking for.
6 This is the boy whose father works as a tour guide.

6 Aim To practise the definite article
- Explain the task.
- Give Ss time to complete it.
- Check Ss' answers.

Answer Key

1 the
2 –
3 the
4 –
5 the
6 –
7 the
8 –

Everyday English

7 Aim To match exchanges
- Explain the task.
- Give Ss time to complete it.
- Check Ss' answers.

Answer Key

1 E 2 D 3 B 4 C 5 A

Competences

Ask Ss to assess their own performance in the unit by ticking the items according to how competent they feel for each of the listed activities.

Optional activity

Work in pairs. Think of various jobs, places, objects related to holidays. Make a sentence using relatives to describe each. Your partner guesses the word.

A: It's a person who carries your luggage at a hotel.
B: Porter.

Join in the Fun! 11

Topic
In this unit, Ss will explore the topics of festival activities and types of entertainment.
11a Reading & Vocabulary   90-91
Lesson objectives: To learn vocabulary for festival activities, to listen and read for gist, to read for specific information (multiple choice), to learn prepositions and prepositional phrases, to talk about a festival, to write a festival calendar **Vocabulary:** Festival activities *(floating sky lanterns, a street parade, a local dish, a floating basket with a candle in it, a traditional dance performance)*, Nouns *(full moon, harvest, tree trunk)*; Phrases *(come alive, in full swing, give thanks, out of sight, caught in the moment)*
11b Grammar in Use   92-93
Lesson objectives: To learn reported speech (statements), to learn to change direct to reported speech, to learn personal pronouns & possessive adjectives and time expressions in reported speech, to learn reported questions
11c Skills in Action   94-95
Lesson objectives: To learn vocabulary for types of entertainment, to listen for specific information (gap fill), to act out a dialogue and practise everyday English for describing an event, to learn the pronunciation of stressed syllables, to read to identify tenses, to write an email describing an event one attended **Vocabulary:** Types of entertainment *(ice show, opera, fashion show, escape room, concert, circus)*
Culture 11   96
Lesson objectives: To listen and read for gist, to read for specific information (comprehension questions), to write about an annual cultural festival in one's country **Vocabulary:** Verb *(sample)*; Nouns *(inhabitant, bushfood, gathering)*; Adjective *(original)*; Phrase *(sandstone rock)*
Review 11   97
Lesson objectives: To test/consolidate vocabulary and grammar learnt throughout the unit; to practise everyday English

Go through the objectives box and tell Ss that these are the topics, skills and activities this unit will cover.

11a

Vocabulary

1 **Aim** **To present festival activities**
- Read out the list of festival activities and ask Ss to look at the pictures and match them.
- Check Ss' answers.

Answer Key

A floating sky lanterns
B a traditional dance performance
C a floating basket with a candle in it
D a local dish
E a street parade

Reading

2 **Aim** **To listen and read for gist**
- Read out the **Study Skills** box and tell Ss this tip will help them complete the reading task successfully.
- Ask Ss to read the title and the first sentence in each paragraph and predict what the text is about.
- Play the recording. Ss listen and read to find out.

Answer Key

The text is about a person's visit to Chiang Mai in Thailand and the festivals that took place there.

3 **Aim** **To identify the type and context of a text**

Ask Ss to look at the text and elicit what type of text it is and where one might see it from Ss around the class.

Answer Key

It is a travel article. You could see it online.

4 **Aim** **To read for specific information (multiple choice)**
- Ask Ss to read the questions and answer choices.
- Give Ss time to read the text again and then choose their answers.
- Check Ss' answers.

Answer Key

1 B   2 A   3 C   4 B

- Elicit the meanings of the words in bold from Ss around the class. They may use their dictionaries if necessary.

Suggested Answer Key

historic (adj): *important or famous in history*
thanks (pl n): *gratitude*

95

11

decorate **(v):** to make sth more attractive by adding extra items
come true **(phr):** happen in real life
release **(v):** to let go
locals **(n):** people who live in a certain area

- Give Ss time to look up the meanings of the words in the **Check these words** box in the Word List.
- Play the video for Ss and elicit their comments.

5 Aim To consolidate new vocabulary

- Ask Ss to read the verbs in the list and then give them time to complete the sentences with the correct forms of the verbs.
- Check Ss' answers.

Answer Key

1 enjoyed	4 felt	7 give
2 floated	5 come	8 make
3 light	6 celebrate	

6 Aim To consolidate vocabulary from a text

- Ask Ss to read the words in the lists. Then give them time to match them to make phrases.
- Check Ss' answers.
- Then give Ss time to use the phrases to make sentences, based on the text.
- Elicit answer from Ss around the class.

Answer Key

1 Asia	5 trunk
2 temples	6 dark
3 alive	7 in the moment
4 moon	8 parade

Suggested Answer Key

1. Thailand is in **southeast Asia**.
2. Chiang Mai has 300 **ancient temples**.
3. The city **comes alive** in November.
4. Loy Krathong takes place during a **full moon**.
5. A krathong is made from slices of a banana **tree trunk**.
6. Loy Krathong and Yi Peng celebrations take place **after dark**.
7. Samuel **was caught in the moment** watching the lanterns.
8. There is a huge **street parade** during the festival.

7 Aim To practise prepositions and prepositional phrases

- Explain the task and give Ss time to complete it.
- Tell Ss to check their answers in their dictionaries.

Answer Key

1 in	3 in	5 into
2 at	4 on	6 over

8 Aim ICT THINK To expand on the topic; to express critical thinking

Give Ss time to research online for a festival around the world they would like to go to and then elicit answers from Ss around the class with reasons.

Suggested Answer Key

I would like to go to the Edinburgh International Festival in Scotland because it's the world's largest arts festival and I love the arts.

Speaking & Writing

9 Aim To talk about festivals

Give Ss time to read the text again and make notes under the headings in their notebooks. Then ask various Ss to take the role of a tour guide and present the festivals to the class.

Suggested Answer Key

Name of festival: Loy Krathong
Place: Southeast Asia
Date: November
Reason: give thanks for the rain and the harvest and feel sorry for the wrong things they have done
Activities: make krathongs (slices of banana tree trunk decorated with leaves, flowers and a candle) and float them on the river and make a wish, traditional music, theatre and dance performances, street parade
Name of festival: Yi Peng
Place: northern Thailand
Date: November
Reason: to welcome a bright future
Activities: make or buy lanterns and release them and make a wish, traditional music, theatre and dance performances, street parade

Welcome to Chiang Mai everyone. You have come at the right time because this is a special time for the Thai people and the people of Chiang Mai. We celebrate two festivals at this time and the city comes alive.
Loy Krathong takes place all over southeast Asia in November. We celebrate it to give thanks for the rain and the harvest and feel sorry for the wrong things we have done during the year. As part of the celebrations we make krathongs. These are slices of banana tree trunk decorated with leaves, flowers and a candle. We float them on the river and make a wish. If the candle stays lit then our wish will come true.

Yi Peng is a festival that only takes place in northern Thailand but it is also in November at the same time as Loy Krathong. It is also known as the festival of lanterns and we celebrate it to welcome a bright future. We make or buy lanterns and release them into the night sky and make a wish. If it stays lit, then our wish will come true. There are lots of other activities during these festivals such as traditional music, theatre and dance performances and a huge street parade.
So, enjoy the celebrations everyone and I hope your wishes come true!

11b Grammar in Use

1 **Aim** To present reported speech (statements)

- Say then write on the board: *"I'm very tired," John said.* Explain that direct speech is the exact words someone says and it is written in quotation marks. Say then write on the board: *John said (that) he was very tired.* Explain that reported speech is the exact meaning of what someone says but not the exact words and we do not use quotation marks. Explain that we can use the word **that** to introduce the reported speech or we can omit it.
- Explain that when we report statements, we use **say** or **tell**. We use **say** in direct and reported speech without **to** when it is not followed by the person being spoken to *(e.g. Tom said "I need help."/ Tom said [that] he needed help.)* and with **to** when it is followed by the person being spoken to as well *(e.g. Tom said to me, "I need help."/ Tom said to me [that] he needed help.)*
- Ask Ss to read the theory and elicit examples from the dialogue and which verbs have been used to introduce them.

Answer Key

Examples: *She said that she would meet us outside the theatre at 7, right? (say) She told me that she was just leaving her house. (tell) She said that she really wanted to see this play. (say)*

2 **Aim** To practise using *say* and *tell*

- Explain the task and give Ss time to complete it.
- Check Ss' answers.

Answer Key

1 said	3 told	5 told
2 told	4 said	6 said

3 **Aim** To present up-to-date/out-of-date reporting

- Explain that we usually report someone's words a long time after they were said. This is called out-of-date reporting and the introductory verb is in the past simple.
- Explain that when we report someone's words a short time after they were said, the tenses can either change or stay the same in reported speech. This is called up-to-date reporting.
- Ask Ss to study the examples and then elicit answers to the questions from Ss around the class.
- Then go through the theory box and explain any points Ss are unsure of.

Answer Key

"I want to help," she says.
1 the present simple
2 says – the present simple
3 Yes, they are.
4 she
5 because it is optional

"I want to help," she said.
1 the past simple
2 said – the past simple
3 No, they aren't.
4 she
5 because it is optional

4 **Aim** To practise reported speech

- Explain the task and give Ss time to complete it.
- Check Ss' answers.

Answer Key

1 were wearing	4 had left
2 could	5 sleep
3 would meet	

5 **Aim** To practise reported speech

- Explain that the pronouns, possessive adjectives and tenses change according to the meaning *("I'm hungry," she said. = She said [that] she was hungry.)*
- Explain that certain words and time expressions change, too *(e.g. tonight = that night, today = that day, last night = the night before/the previous night, yesterday = the day before, this = that, these = those, etc.).*
- Then go through the theory box and explain any points Ss are unsure of.
- Give Ss time to complete the gaps in the sentences with the missing words/phrases.
- Check Ss' answers.

Answer Key

1 they, that day
2 she, the following
3 he, that, then

6 Aim To practise reported speech

- Explain the task and read out the example.
- Give Ss time to complete the task and then elicit answers from Ss around the class.

Answer Key

2 They said that they would meet us there the next day.
3 She said that they hadn't heard that band before.
4 James said to me that he had gone there the day before.
5 We said to Mary that we hadn't expected to see her there.

7 Aim To present reported questions

- Explain that we usually introduce reported questions with **ask** and we do not use a question mark. The verb is in the affirmative and the tenses, pronouns and time expressions change as in reported speech.
- Explain that when the direct question begins with a question word (e.g. who, where, what, why, when) then we use the same question word in the reported question, but when the direct question begins with an auxiliary verb (is, do, have, etc.) then we use **if/whether** in the reported question.
- Ask Ss to read the theory box and explain any points they are unsure of and then elicit answers to the questions.

Answer Key

We report wh-questions with subject pronoun/name/ noun + asked/wanted to know + (object pronoun/ name/noun) + question word + verb.

We report Yes/No questions with subject pronoun/ name/noun + asked/wanted to know + if/whether + subject + verb.

8 Aim To practise reported questions

- Explain the task and read out the example.
- Then give Ss time to compete the task.
- Check Ss' answers around the class.

Suggested Answer Key

2 Max asked (Andy) which bus they needed to take to get there.
3 Max asked (Andy) when the event started.
4 Max asked (Andy) if/whether there would be any famous authors there.
5 Max asked (Andy) if/whether he had been to a book fair before.
6 Max asked (Andy) if/whether he wanted to eat out afterwards.
7 Max asked (Andy) what kind of restaurant he liked.

Optional activity

Work in groups. Act out a short dialogue. The third person in the group reports it to the class.

11c Skills in Action

Vocabulary

1 Aim To present vocabulary for types of entertainment

- Ask Ss to look at the pictures A-F and then read the comments 1-6.
- Explain/elicit the meanings of any unknown words and then give Ss time to match the pictures and the comments.
- Check Ss' answers.

Answer Key

1 C   2 D   3 F   4 B   5 E   6 A

2 Aim To talk about types of entertainment

- Ask Ss to talk in pairs about one of the events in Ex. 1 and use the adjectives to describe it.
- Monitor the activity around the class and then ask some pairs to tell the class.

Suggested Answer Key

A: I had an enjoyable time at the ice show last night. It was fascinating watching the skaters glide across the rink.
B: I went to the ice show yesterday evening, too, but for me it was so boring and disappointing. I expected it to be more fun.

3 Aim To listen for specific information (gap fill)

- Ask Ss to read the gapped advert and think about the missing information.
- Play the recording. Ss listen and complete the gaps.
- Check Ss answers.

Answer Key

1 Fantasy   3 10   5 Bridge
2 Russia   4 12th

Everyday English

4 **Aim** To read for cohesion and coherence

- Explain the task and give Ss time to read the dialogue and complete the gaps with an appropriate word.
- Play the recording. Ss listen and check.

Answer Key

| 1 | time | 3 | much | 5 | it |
| 2 | Which | 4 | about | 6 | ticket |

5 **Aim** To role play a dialogue describing an event

- Explain the task and ask Ss to act out a similar dialogue to the one in Ex. 4 in pairs using the prompts and the language in the box to help them.
- Write this diagram on the board for Ss to follow.

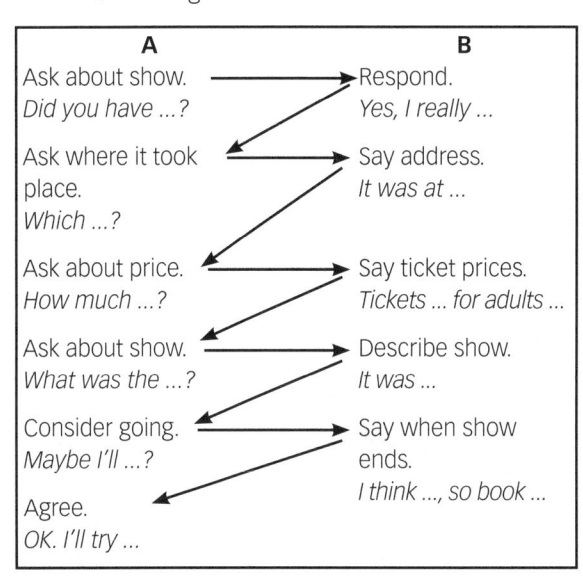

A	B
Ask about show. *Did you have ...?*	Respond. *Yes, I really ...*
Ask where it took place. *Which ...?*	Say address. *It was at ...*
Ask about price. *How much ...?*	Say ticket prices. *Tickets ... for adults ...*
Ask about show. *What was the ...?*	Describe show. *It was ...*
Consider going. *Maybe I'll ...?*	Say when show ends. *I think ..., so book ...*
Agree. *OK. I'll try ...*	

- Monitor the activity around the class and offer assistance as necessary.
- Then ask some pairs to act out their dialogues in front of the class.

Suggested Answer Key

A: *Did you have a good time at the ice show yesterday?*
B: *Yes, I really enjoyed it.*
A: *Which arena was it at?*
B: *It was at the Blue Arena on Bridge Street.*
A: *Oh yeah. How much were the tickets?*
B: *Tickets were £15 for adults and £10 for children.*
A: *I see. What was the show about?*
B: *It was a fantasy performance. You'd like it.*
A: *Maybe I'll go and see it too, then.*
B: *I think performances are about to end, so book your ticket soon.*
A: *OK, I'll try to go tomorrow.*

Pronunciation

6 **Aim** To stress syllables

- Explain the task and model the example.
- Then play the recording. Ss listen and underline the stressed syllables in the pairs of words.
- Then play the recording again with pauses for Ss to repeat, chorally and/or individually.
- Check Ss' pronunciation and intonation.

Answer Key

<u>mu</u>-sic   mu-<u>si</u>-cian
pre-<u>pare</u>   prep-a-<u>ra</u>-tion
<u>his</u>-to-ry   his-<u>to</u>-ri-an
<u>cel</u>-e-brate   cel-e-<u>bra</u>-tion

Reading & Writing

7 **Aim** To read for gist; to identify tenses

- Ask Ss to read the email and then identify the tenses the writer mostly uses.
- Check Ss' answers and elicit reasons

Answer Key

The writer uses mostly present tenses because she is writing about a recent event (present perfect) and describing a type of theatre (present simple).

8 a) **Aim** To identify opening/closing remarks

- Ask Ss to read the sentences 1-6 and identify which are opening remarks and which are closing remarks and mark them accordingly.
- Check Ss' answers.

Answer Key

1 C   2 C   3 O   4 O   5 C   6 O

b) **Aim** To expand on opening/closing remarks

- Ask Ss to identify and underline the opening and closing remarks in the email in Ex. 7 and then substitute them with appropriate alternatives from Ex. 8a.
- Check Ss' answers around the class.

Suggested Answer Key

Hope you're well! = *Thanks for your email – it was great to hear from you.*
Write back when you get the chance. = *Keep me posted about what's going on.*

11

9 a) Aim To present and identify adverbs with gradable / non-gradable adjectives

- Ask Ss to read the theory box and explain any points Ss are unsure of. Then ask them to find examples in the email in Ex. 7.
- Elicit answers from Ss around the class.

Answer Key

Examples: *really amazing, absolutely magical, very glad*

b) Aim To practise adverbs used with gradable / non-gradable adjectives

- Explain the task and give Ss time to read the text and choose the correct adverbs.
- Check Ss' answers.

Answer Key

1 absolutely
2 really
3 a bit
4 really

Writing

10 Aim To analyse a rubric

- Ask Ss to read the rubric and make notes under the headings in their notebooks.
- Ask various Ss to share their answers with the class.

Suggested Answer key

WHERE: *Palladium, Riga*
WHEN: *27th April*
WHO PERFORMED: *Rag'n'Bone Man*
DESCRIPTION: *English singer, soul and pop music, known for baritone voice, hits 'Human', 'Skin'*
FEELINGS: *amazing, great atmosphere*
RECOMMENDATION: *great music, definitely see him if you get the chance*

11 Aim To write an email describing an event

- Explain the task and give Ss time to write their email using their answers in Ex. 10 and following the plan.
- Check Ss' answers.
- Alternatively, assign the task as HW and check Ss' answers in the next lesson.

Suggested Answer Key

Hi Helen,
Thanks for your email – it was great to hear from you. You asked about the concert I attended. Well, it was absolutely amazing.
I went to see Rag'n'Bone Man at the Palladium in Riga. He's an English singer who sings soul and pop music. He's known for his baritone voice. He sang his hits 'Human' and 'Skin' and some new songs, too. I really enjoyed myself and there was a great atmosphere.

I was really glad I went. The music was amazing. If you ever get the chance to see him you should. Write back soon.
All the best,
Lidia

Background Information

Hanoi is Vietnam's capital. It's the second largest city in Vietnam. Vietnam is in Southeast Asia.

Kraków is the second largest city in Poland, a country in Europe.

Values

Ask Ss to try to explain the quotation in their mother tongue. If Ss have difficulty, explain the quotation. Ask Ss to memorise this quotation and check in the next lesson.

The saying means that everyone has drama in their lives and throughout their lives. It also means that people have a role to play in their life (e.g. mother, soldier, brother, banker, etc). We often have many different roles, sometimes at the same time, and we play these roles every day.

Culture 11

Listening & Reading

1 Aim To introduce the topic and listen and read for gist

- Ask Ss to read the words in the list. Elicit Ss' guesses as to how they are related to the Tjungu Festival.
- Play the recording. Ss listen and read and find out.

Suggested Answer Key

Ayers Rock Resort is where the festival takes place. The festival celebrates the traditions of the **Aboriginal people**. The **Inma Dance** welcomes visitors to the festival. A **didgeridoo** is a traditional musical instrument that visitors can hear at the festival. Visitors can try **Aboriginal bushfood** at the festival. They can also buy beautifully decorated **boomerangs** at the festival.

2 Aim To read for key information (comprehension questions)

- Ask Ss to read the questions and then read the text again and answer them.
- Check Ss' answers.

Answer Key

1 The first festival was in 2014.
2 The dance's purpose is to welcome people to the festival.

3 Visitors can sample Aboriginal bushfood.
4 Tjungu means 'coming together'.

- Give Ss time to look up the meanings of the words in the **Check these words** box in the Word List.
- Play the video for Ss and elicit their comments.

3 **Aim** To consolidate new vocabulary

- Give Ss time to match the words in bold in the text to their opposites in the list.
- Check Ss' answers and elicit the part of speech for each one.

Answer Key

famous (adj): unknown
oldest (adj): earliest
began (v): finished
opening (adj): last
includes (v): excludes
leave (v): come
reasonable (adj): high
together (adv): separate

Speaking & Writing

4 **Aim** THINK To expand the topic; to express an opinion

- Give Ss time to consider their answers.
- Elicit answers from Ss around the class with reasons.

Suggested Answer Key

In my country (Germany) we have a festival called the Carnival of Cultures. People should attend because it's a great way to celebrate different cultures and tradition.

5 **Aim** ICT To develop research skills; to write a short text about an annual cultural festival in your country

- Explain the task and give Ss time to make notes and then write a short text about an annual cultural festival in their country.
- Ask various Ss to read their text to the class.
- Alternatively, assign the task as HW and ask Ss to read out their texts in the next lesson.

Suggested Answer Key

name: The Carnival of Cultures
place: Berlin
date: early summer (lasts for 4 days)
reason: to celebrate the different cultures of the people who live in Berlin
activities: street festival, dancers, musicians and artists perform on stage including stilt walkers, acrobats and magicians, market stalls with food, art and crafts, huge parade at end

The Carnival of Cultures takes place in Berlin in early summer every year and lasts for 4 days. It is a huge festival to celebrate the different cultures of the people who live in Berlin. The celebrations include a street festival with dancers, musicians and artists who perform on stage. The entertainment also includes stilt walkers, acrobats and magicians. There are also market stalls with food, art and crafts. There is a huge parade at the end where people from all sorts of backgrounds come together. It is lots of fun and a great event for the whole family.

Review 11

Vocabulary

1 **Aim** To practise vocabulary from the unit

- Explain the task.
- Give Ss time to complete it.
- Check Ss' answers.

Answer Key

1 full	3 floating	5 musical
2 street	4 local	

2 **Aim** To practise prepositions/prepositional phrases

- Explain the task.
- Give Ss time to complete it.
- Check Ss' answers.

Answer Key

1 in	3 into	5 in
2 for	4 with	

3 **Aim** To practise vocabulary from the unit

- Explain the task.
- Give Ss time to complete it.
- Check Ss' answers.

Answer Key

1 escape	3 play	5 opera
2 concert	4 circus	

Grammar

4 **Aim** To practise say/tell

- Explain the task.
- Give Ss time to complete it.
- Check Ss' answers.

11 Join in the Fun!

Answer Key

1 said 3 said 5 said
2 told 4 told

5 Aim To practise reported speech

- Explain the task.
- Give Ss time to complete it.
- Check Ss' answers.

Answer Key

1 Tim said that the play had been excellent.
2 She told me that she would see me at the concert.
3 He said that we could book tickets online.
4 She said that she had turned off her smartphone.
5 They said that they were listening to music then.

6 Aim To practise reported speech

- Explain the task.
- Give Ss time to complete it.
- Check Ss' answers.

Answer Key

1 He asked if/whether Frank was coming to the cinema.
2 John asked when the exhibition started.
3 Mary asked if/whether they had attended the ballet performance.
4 Steve asked them if/whether they had ever seen an opera performance.

Everyday English

7 Aim To match exchanges

- Explain the task.
- Give Ss time to complete it.
- Check Ss' answers.

Answer Key

1 B 2 A 3 C 4 E 5 D

Competences

Ask Ss to assess their own performance in the unit by ticking the items according to how competent they feel for each of the listed activities.

Optional activity

Work in groups of four. Two act out a short dialogue. The third person reports it making three mistakes. The fourth person corrects the mistakes.

Going online! 12

Go through the objectives box and tell Ss that these are the topics, skills and activities this unit will cover.

Topic
In this unit, Ss will explore the topics of computer parts & using a smartphone.

12a Reading & Vocabulary	98-99
Lesson objectives: To learn vocabulary for computer parts, to read for gist (match headings to paragraphs), to read for specific information (sentence completion), to learn phrases with prepositions, to talk about the Internet, to write an information leaflet
Vocabulary: Computer parts (*router, screen, webcam, mouse, keyboard, speakers, scanner, flash drive, headset, USB cable, printer, hard drive, tower*)	

12b Grammar in Use	100-101
Lesson objectives: To learn reported speech (orders, instructions, commands) to learn question tags, to learn exclamations	

12c Skills in Action	102-103
Lesson objectives: To learn vocabulary for using a smartphone, to listen for key information (multiple matching), to act out a dialogue and practise everyday English for giving instructions, to learn intonation in exclamations, to read for cohesion & coherence, to write a for-and-against essay
Vocabulary: using a smartphone (*video, Wi-Fi, contacts, radio, settings, email, mobile apps, camera, messages, Internet, GPS, notepad, microphone, phone, my files, calendar, clock, mobile games, calculator, photo album*)	

Culture 12	104
Lesson objectives: To read for gist, to read for specific information (multiple matching), to talk about a place in San Francisco, to write about a museum of technology in one's country
Vocabulary: Nouns (*virtual world, hill, admission, ingenuity, stuff*)	

Review 12	105
Lesson objectives: To test/consolidate vocabulary and grammar learnt throughout the unit; to practise everyday English	

12a

Vocabulary

1 **Aim** **To present vocabulary relating to computer parts**

- Ask Ss to look at the pictures and read out the words/phrases in the list.
- Explain any unknown terms and give Ss time to complete the task.
- Check Ss' answers.

Answer Key

1 router	6 speakers	11 printer
2 screen	7 scanner	12 hard drive
3 webcam	8 USB cable	13 tower
4 mouse	9 flash drive	
5 keyboard	10 headset	

2 **Aim** **To consolidate vocabulary relating to computer parts**

- Ask Ss to read the words/phrases 1-13 and then definitions a-m and then match them.
- Check Ss' answers around the class.

Answer Key

a 13	d 1	g 2	j 8	m 9
b 6	e 4	h 5	k 11	
c 3	f 7	i 10	l 12	

Listening & Reading

3 **Aim** **To read for gist**

- Ask Ss to read the headings a-f and then give them time to read the text and match the headings to the gaps.
- Check Ss' answers.

Answer Key

2 c 3 d 4 f 5 a 6 b

4 a) **Aim** **To read for specific information (complete sentences)**

- Ask Ss to read the beginning of the sentences.
- Play the recording. Otherwise, give Ss time to read the text again and then complete the sentences.
- Check Ss' answers.

12

Answer Key

1 ... names, addresses and bank card details (and use them to steal money).
2 ... someone might know already (like your date of birth or the name of your pet).
3 ... a well-known company or organisation.
4 ... similar to the ones you use regularly.
5 ... an anti-virus program.

- Give Ss time to look up the meanings of the words in the **Check these words** box in the Word List.
- Play the video for Ss and elicit their comments.

b) **Aim** To consolidate new vocabulary in a text

Elicit the meanings of the words in bold from Ss around the class. They may use dictionaries if necessary.

Suggested Answer Key

complex (adj): difficult, complicated
familiar (adj): known
click (v): to tap, press
trick (n): a way of deceiving sb
purchase (n): sth you buy
exposed (adj): open to
records (v): to make a note of
detect (v): to notice, spot

5 **Aim** To consolidate new vocabulary

- Ask Ss to read the words in the list and then give them time to complete the phrases with them.
- Check Ss' answers. Then give Ss time to write sentences using the phrases and elicit Ss' answers around the class.

Answer Key

1 valuable	4 create	7 bank
2 access	5 pop-up	8 install
3 user's	6 enter	

Suggested Answer Key

1 The Internet is a **valuable tool**.
2/3 Hackers can **access personal information** like **user's names** and addresses.
4 They can also **create a webpage** that looks like one you often use.
5 Don't click on pop-up adverts when you're shopping online.
6 When you **enter your** name and **password** the hacker makes a note of it and uses the information to steal your money.
7 Sometimes they do this to get into your **bank account**.

8 The best way to stay safe online is to **install** an anti-virus **program**.

6 **Aim** To consolidate vocabulary from a text

- Read out the **Study Skills** box and tell Ss this is a helpful tip for learning prepositions.
- Give Ss time to read the phrases and choose the correct prepositions and then check Ss' answers.

Answer Key

1 of	3 on	5 to	7 from
2 to	4 to	6 on	

Suggested Answer Key

1 Don't use your **date of birth** for your password.
2/3 Don't **click on** a link that is not **familiar to** you.
4 Hackers can **upload** viruses **to** your computer.
5 Hackers can create a webpage **similar to** the ones you use regularly.
6 An anti-virus program can detect **a virus on** your computer and **stop your computer from** downloading others.

Speaking

7 **Aim** To personalise the topic

- Have Ss work together in pairs to discuss the question.
- Go round the class and monitor the activity.
- Ask some pairs of Ss to report each other's answers to the class.

Suggested Answer Key

A: I always create a complex password when I need one. I think that's very important. I never use my date of birth or my pet's name. I try to think of something different that nobody could guess. I'm also very careful not to click on strange messages. If there's an email on my computer and I don't recognise the sender, I don't open it.
B: Nor do I. You don't want to get a virus on your computer. That's why I've installed a new anti-virus program on mine. I'm also careful with pop-up adverts.

8 **Aim** To discuss an imaginary situation

- Read the task and give Ss time to think about their answers.
- Elicit answers from different Ss around the class.

Suggested Answer Key

I think it would be really terrible to have no Internet for a week! I'd have to go to the library to do research and carry heavy books around. I couldn't send emails *to hand in my assignments – I'd have to take them to my teacher personally. And I'd really miss not being able to watch my favourite films and listen to music. I couldn't communicate with my friends easily or send them pictures either. I'd have to phone them or send them an SMS and that is expensive. The only good thing would be I'd hang out with my friends.*

Writing

9 Aim ICT To develop research skills; to write a leaflet

- Give Ss time to research online and collect information about how to stay safe when using their social media accounts.
- Allow time for Ss to write their leaflets and give help where necessary.
- Invite one or two Ss to present their leaflets to the class.
- Alternatively, assign the task as HW and check Ss' answers in the next lesson.

Suggested Answer Key

There are a number of social media accounts that people like to use to get to know others and exchange views with them. This is great, of course, but we should also know how to stay safe when using them. Here are some useful guidelines to follow.

- **Limit information on your public profile.** *Information about your hobbies and interests is OK. Detailed information about your life could attract the wrong sort of attention.*
- **Do not tell people where you live.** *If anybody is bad out there, they won't be able to harm you if they don't know where to find you!*
- **Do not give out your phone number.** *You don't want to start getting unpleasant phone calls, so it's better to keep this information private!*
- **Avoid meeting people you get to know online.** *Most people are harmless, but some may be dangerous. So it's better to keep your online friends online and stay safe.*
- **Block anyone who seems scary or threatening.** *Use whatever tools the social media site you are using has to do this. You can also report this person to warn others.*

12b Grammar in Use

1 Aim To present reported speech (orders, instructions, commands)

- Explain that we usually use the verb **tell + sb + (not) to-infinitive** in reported commands.

- Ask Ss to read the theory and elicit examples from the chat and what were the actual words.

Answer Key

Examples: *the guy just told me not to keep too much on the hard drive – "Don't keep too much on the hard drive," said the guy to me.*
I asked him to be there when I bring it to the shop tomorrow at nine – "Be there when I bring it to the shop tomorrow at nine," said Christy to the guy.

2 Aim To practise reported speech (orders, instructions, commands)

- Explain the task and give Ss time to complete it.
- Check Ss' answers.

Answer Key

1. Mr Smith told us not to click on any unknown links.
2. He told us to use strong passwords.
3. He told us not to open strange email attachments.
4. He told us to change our password regularly.
5. He told us not to give out personal information online.
6. He told us to keep our anti-virus software up to date.

3 Aim To practise reported speech (orders, instructions, commands)

- Explain the situation and ask Ss to read the instructions. Then ask Ss to read the email and complete it using reported speech.
- Check Ss' answers.

Answer Key

1. to forward all the CVs for the computer technician position to you
2. not to make the payment to Crown Computer Supplies yet
3. to call Gordon Robinson to move my meeting with him to next Friday
4. not to book tickets for Madrid
5. to call you

4 Aim To change reported speech into direct speech

- Explain the task and give Ss time to complete it.
- Check Ss' answers.

Suggested Answer Key

"Make sure there are phone lines in each office." "Order new desktop computers for all the offices." "Finish the decorating by next week."

12

Optional activity

Work in pairs. Tell your partner what he/she should/shouldn't do while visiting a museum. He/She reports your sentences to the class.

5 **Aim** To learn about question tags

- Explain that question tags are short questions at the end of statements to confirm sth or to find out if sth is true. We form question tags with the auxiliary or modal verb of the main sentence with the correct subject pronoun.
- Explain that when the verb of the sentence is in the present simple, we form the question tag with *do/does* and the subject pronoun and when the verb of the sentence is in the past simple, we form the question tag with *did* and the subject pronoun.
- Explain that when the sentence is positive, the question tag is negative and vice versa. Explain that when the question tag contains a word with a negative meaning (never, hardly, seldom, etc), then the question tag is positive.
- Explain that when we aren't sure of the answer, we use a rising intonation in the question tag and when we are sure of the answer, we use a falling intonation in the question tag.
- Ask Ss to read the theory box and explain any points Ss are unsure of. Then elicit examples in the chat.

Answer Key

It's brand new, isn't it?
You haven't put many programs on there, have you?
I'm not wrong, am I?

6 **Aim** To practise question tags

Explain the task and give Ss time to complete it and then elicit answers from Ss around the class.

Answer Key

1 haven't you	4 does he	7 wasn't it
2 can I	5 doesn't it	8 will you
3 is it	6 aren't they	

7 a) **Aim** To practise question tags

Explain the task and give Ss time to complete it and then check their answers.

Answer Key

2 won't you	5 hasn't he
3 haven't I	6 is it
4 do you	

b) **Aim** To practise intonation in question tags

- Explain that when we aren't sure of the answer we use a rising intonation in the question tag and when we are sure of the answer we use a falling intonation in the question tag.
- Play the recording. Ss listen and tick the intonation they hear.
- Play the recording again with pauses for Ss to repeat chorally and/or individually.

Answer Key

2 ↑   3 ↓   4 ↓   5 ↑   6 ↓

8 **Aim** To practise question tags

Explain the task and ask Ss to ask and answer questions in pairs using question tags following the example. Monitor the activity around the class and then ask some pairs to ask and answer in front of the class.

Suggested Answer Key

A: You can use a computer, can't you?
B: Yes, I can.
A: You've got a tablet, haven't you?
B: No, I haven't. etc

9 **Aim** To learn exclamations

Read through the theory box and explain any points Ss are unsure of. Then elicit examples in the chat on p. 100.

Answer Key

It's so annoying!
What nonsense!

10 **Aim** To practise exclamations

Explain the task and give Ss time to complete it. Then check Ss' answers around the class.

Answer Key

1 What, How   2 What, such, so

11 **Aim** To practise exclamations

Ask Ss to read the statements and then elicit responses using exclamations from Ss around the class.

Suggested Answer Key

1 What nonsense! Of course you can!
2 How nice!
3 How annoying!
4 What a pity!
5 That's such a shame!

12c Skills in Action

Vocabulary

1 a) **Aim** To present vocabulary for using a smartphone

- Ask Ss to look at the icons. Then elicit which ones someone would tap to perform the functions in the list.
- Explain/elicit the meanings of any unknown words and then give Ss time to match the icons to the functions.
- Check Ss' answers.

Answer Key

call a friend – N
find a friend's number – C
send an email – F
send a text – I
take a photo – H
look at a photo – T
change the background photo on the phone – E
add up some numbers – S
check the time – Q
check the date – P
download a new game – G
play a game – R
go online – J
connect to a hotspot – B
find their location – K
find a file – O
make a note of something – L
watch a video – A
listen to some music – D
record their voice – M

b) **Aim** To talk about using a smartphone

Ask Ss around the class to tell the rest of the class which of the functions on a smartphone they use every day and why.

Suggested Answer Key

I use Wi-Fi every day to connect to a hotspot so I don't use my mobile data.
I use the camera every day to take pictures.
I use the clock every day to check the time.

2 **Aim** To listen for specific information (multiple matching)

- Ask Ss to read the list of gadgets.
- Play the recording. Ss listen and match the speakers to the gadgets.
- Check Ss answers.

Answer Key

1 f   2 c   3 d   4 a

Everyday English

3 **Aim** To read for sequence of events

- Explain the task and ask Ss to look at the pictures.
- Then play the recording. Ss listen and read the dialogue and put the pictures in the correct order.
- Check Ss' answers.

Answer Key

A 3   B 4   C 1   D 2

4 **Aim** To role play a dialogue giving instructions

- Explain the task and ask Ss to act out a similar dialogue to the one in Ex. 3 in pairs using the ideas in the dialogue to help them.
- Write this diagram on the board for Ss to follow.

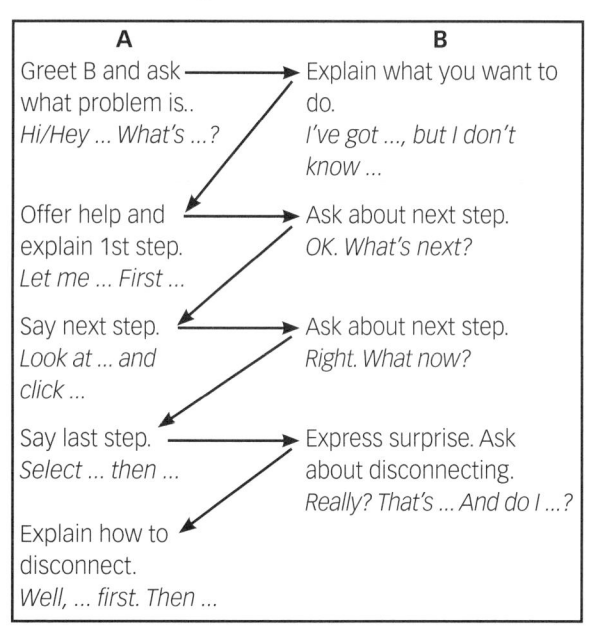

A	B
Greet B and ask what problem is.. *Hi/Hey ... What's ...?*	Explain what you want to do. *I've got ..., but I don't know ...*
Offer help and explain 1st step. *Let me ... First ...*	Ask about next step. *OK. What's next?*
Say next step. *Look at ... and click ...*	Ask about next step. *Right. What now?*
Say last step. *Select ... then ...*	Express surprise. Ask about disconnecting. *Really? That's ... And do I ...?*
Explain how to disconnect. *Well, ... first. Then ...*	

- Monitor the activity around the class and offer assistance as necessary.
- Then ask some pairs to act out their dialogues in front of the class.

Suggested Answer Key

A: Hey James. What's the matter?
B: I've got my project on this flash drive, but I don't know how to transfer the files onto my laptop.
A: Let me show you. First you insert the flash drive in the port on the side of the laptop.
B: OK. What's next?
A: Look at the window that just popped up and click on 'open folder/view files'.
B: Right. Now what?

107

A: *Select the file you want and click 'copy' and then go to 'my documents' and click 'paste'. Then the file is on your laptop.*
B: *Really? That's easy. And do I just disconnect the flash drive now?*
A: *Well, close the window first. Then click on safely remove hardware and when the computer says it's OK, pull it out.*

Intonation

5 Aim To learn intonation in exclamations

- Ask Ss to fill in the words.
- Then play the recording. Ss listen and check their answers.
- Then play the recording again with pauses for Ss to repeat, chorally and/or individually.
- Check Ss' pronunciation and intonation.

Answer Key

1 How
2 What
3 What a
4 How

Reading & Writing

6 Aim To read for cohesion and coherence

- Ask Ss to read the essay and then fill in the missing sequence words/phrases in the list.
- Check Ss' answers.

Answer Key

1 However
2 Firstly
3 What is more
4 As a result
5 On the other
6 For example
7 This is because
8 In conclusion

7 Aim To read for specific information

- Ask Ss to copy the table into their notebooks and complete it with ideas from the text.
- Check Ss' answers on the board.

Answer Key

Advantages	Justifications
you can get information easily	read newspapers, watch videos, learn about things in detail
join a social networking site	make new friends and stay in touch with old ones
Advantages	**Justifications**
it can become addictive	people spend more time in their virtual life than in their real one
online 'friends' can be dangerous	they can pretend to be someone else and steal your personal information

8 Aim To learn about topic sentences

Read out the **Study Skills box** and then elicit the topic sentences in the model essay.

Answer Key

Using the Internet offers a lot of advantages.
On the other hand, the Internet has some disadvantages.

Writing

9 Aim To prepare for a writing task; to identify ideas

- Ask Ss to read the task and then read the sentences and decide which are advantages and which are disadvantages.
- Play the recording for Ss to check their answers.

Answer Key

1 D   2 A   3 A   4 D

10 Aim To prepare for a writing task

- Ask Ss to read the sentences and match them to their functions in the list.
- Check Ss' answers around the class.

Answer Key

1 introduces points against
2 states the topic
3 introduces points for
4 sums up the topic

11 Aim To write a for-and-against essay

- Ask Ss to read the rubric in Ex. 9 again and then give them time to write their essays using their answers to Exs 9 and 10 and following the plan.
- Ask various Ss to share their answers with the class.
- Alternatively, assign the task as HW and check Ss' answers in the next lesson.

Suggested Answer Key

Thirty years ago, no one had heard of online shopping. Now it is a useful part of our everyday lives. But what about its disadvantages?

A lot of people are in favour of online shopping. It is a very convenient way to shop. This is because you can do it from the comfort of your own home at any time you want. Also, shopping on the Internet is often cheaper than in shops because it offers special discounts and shoppers can compare prices easily, too.

On the other hand, some people are against Internet shopping. Delivery of goods can take time. This means they can't use the product immediately. What is more, shoppers can't try on what they buy. As a result, they don't know if what they ordered fits them until they get it.

All in all, online shopping offers both advantages and disadvantages. I think it's a matter of personal choice which we prefer.

Values

Ask Ss to try to explain the saying in their mother tongue. If Ss have difficulty, explain the saying. Ask Ss to memorise this saying and check in the next lesson.
The saying means that if technology is used wisely, it can make people's lives easier and help us to do things better, but that if we let technology decide how we live, then it can be dangerous.

Culture 12

Listening & Reading

1 Aim **To introduce the topic and read for gist**

Ask Ss to look at the text and elicit Ss' guesses as to where you can see it and what it is about.

Suggested Answer Key

You could see this text on an Internet search engine results page. It is about technology museums in the San Francisco area.

2 Aim **To read for key information (multiple matching)**

- Ask Ss to read the questions and then read the text and answer them.
- Check Ss' answers.

Answer Key

1 A   2 C   3 B   4 C   5 A   6 D

- Give Ss time to look up the meanings of the words in the **Check these words** box in the Word List.
- Play the video for Ss and elicit their comments.
- Elicit the meanings of the highlighted words from Ss around the class. They may use dictionaries if necessary.

Suggested Answer Key

explore (v): *to search and discover about (sth)*
earliest (adj): *first*
allows (v): *to give sb a chance to do sth*
chance (n): *opportunity*
perfect (adj): *suitable*

3 Aim **To consolidate information in a text and express an opinion**

- Play the recording. Ss listen to and read the text and then discuss in pairs which of the places they would like to visit and why.

- Monitor the activity around the class and then ask some Ss to share their answers with the rest of the class.

Answer Key

A: *I would like to visit the Lawrence Hall of Science because I would like to visit the planetarium and I would like to make stuff.*
B: *That sounds good. I'd like to visit the Computer History Museum because I'd like to learn about the history of computers; I find it very interesting.*

4 Aim **ICT To develop research skills; to write a short text about a museum of technology in your country**

- Explain the task and give Ss time to research online, collect information about a museum of technology in their country and then write a short text about it.
- Ask various Ss to read their text to the class.
- Alternatively, assign the task as HW and ask Ss to read out their texts in the next lesson.

Suggested Answer Key

https://www.nemosciencemuseum.nl/en
Located on top of the River Ij car tunnel, the NEMO Science Museum in Amsterdam is a fantastic 'hands-on' science and technology museum that is very popular with both children and adults. Explore four levels and find out about DNA, electricity, the human brain, computers and the origins of life. Visitors can also watch entertaining shows and demonstrations. NEMO is open from Tuesday to Sunday, from 10:00 to 17:30. From February to September and during school holidays, NEMO is also open on Mondays.

Review 12

Vocabulary

1 Aim **To consolidate vocabulary from the unit**

- Explain the task.
- Give Ss time to complete it.
- Check Ss' answers.

Answer Key

1 webcam   3 printer   5 keyboard
2 tower   4 speaker

2 Aim **To consolidate vocabulary from the unit**

- Explain the task.
- Give Ss time to complete it.
- Check Ss' answers.

12 Going online!

Answer Key

1 send
2 downloaded
3 go
4 connect
5 Click
6 detect
7 delete
8 record

Grammar

3 Aim To practise exclamations

- Explain the task.
- Give Ss time to complete it.
- Check Ss' answers.

Answer Key

1 so
2 What a
3 such
4 How
5 such
6 What

4 Aim To practise reported speech

- Explain the task.
- Give Ss time to complete it.
- Check Ss' answers.

Answer Key

1 to log into my account first
2 not to use public Wi-Fi for company business
3 to write a comment about her picture
4 not to tell anyone our password
5 to give her the phone back

5 Aim To practise question tags

- Explain the task.
- Give Ss time to complete it.
- Check Ss' answers.

Answer Key

1 didn't he
2 have they
3 can't you
4 did we
5 are you
6 aren't we
7 will it
8 doesn't it

Everyday English

6 Aim To match exchanges

- Explain the task.
- Give Ss time to complete it.
- Check Ss' answers.

Answer Key

1 D   2 E   3 C   4 A   5 B

Competences

Ask Ss to assess their own performance in the unit by ticking the items according to how competent they feel for each of the listed activities.

Optional activity

Play in teams. Say a word related to technology. Teams, in turns, make a sentence using the word. Each correct sentence gets a point. The team with the most points wins.

Suggested list of words: *laptop, smartphone, printer, scanner, Wi-Fi, screen, GPS, contacts, tower, mouse, keyboard, password, virus, webpage, hacker*

Values: Cooperation   D

1 Aim To identify the purpose of a text

Ask Ss to guess the purpose of the text and then read through quickly to find out.

Answer Key

The purpose of the text is to inform.

2 Aim To read for key information

- Ask Ss to read the text and then give them time to match the activities to the questions.
- Check Ss' answers and then elicit explanations for the words in bold from Ss around the class.

Answer Key

1 D   2 B   3 A   4 C   5 B

Suggested Answer Key

competes (v): *to take part in a competition*
experiences (n): *sth that happens to you*
generally (adv): *usually*
survival (n): *staying alive*
tough (adj): *difficult*

- Play the video for Ss and elicit their comments.

3 Aim THINK To create a team-building activity

- Ask Ss to work in groups and think of a team-building activity including all the points listed.
- Elicit answers from Ss around the class.

Suggested Answer Key

Name: *Cooking competition*
Place: *restaurant*
Duration: *5 hours*
What the team will do: *two teams will cook two meals, together with a starter, main course and dessert, for a group of people, who will give points for the food – appearance, presentation and taste. They have to work together and share the workload and serve the food on time. The team with the most points wins.*

4 Aim To present a team-building activity

- Ask various groups to present their team-building activity to the class.
- When all the presentations have been made, have the class vote for the best idea.

Suggested Answer Key

Good morning. Team-building is important and learning to work together with other people towards a goal can help in all areas of life.

Our team-building activity involves cooking and will test who can stand the heat and the pressure of cooking for a group of people. Two teams will cook two meals, with a starter, main course and dessert, for a group of people. They have to work together and share the workload and serve the food on time. The 'customers' will award points for the food's appearance, presentation and taste. The team with the most points wins. It will be a very challenging but rewarding activity and lots of things can go wrong, but if they get it right they will feel a great sense of achievement.

What do you think? Would you like to try it? Thanks for listening.

D Public Speaking Skills

1 a) Aim To identify the topic of a public speaking task

Ask Ss to read the task. Elicit what the presentation is about *(a new piece of technology)* and where it is held *(at a technology fair)*.

b) Aim To analyse a model public speaking task; to identify opening/closing techniques

- Play the recording. Ss listen and read the model and identify the opening/closing techniques.
- Elicit answers from various Ss.

Answer Key

The writer starts his presentation by directly addressing the audience and asking them questions and ends with a statement and inviting questions.

2 Aim To introduce the use of recapping the main points

- Read out the **Study Skills** box and tell Ss that this is a helpful tip to assist them when giving a presentation.
- Give Ss time to identify the phrases the speaker has used to recap the main points in the model and identify what the key points he refers to are.
- Check Ss' answers.

Answer Key

Other than stretching – Changing into a large screen
Besides its flexibility – the mobile phone's ability to change shapes

3 Aim ICT To give a presentation

- Ask Ss to work in small groups, research online for information about a new piece of technology and make notes.
- Alternatively, Ss can think of their own piece of technology and what features it has. Help Ss with any unknown vocabulary e.g. three-dimensional holograms, internal keyboard, headgear, bendable, folded screen etc.
- Give Ss time to prepare a presentation.
- Ask various Ss to give their presentation to the class.
- Alternatively, assign the task as HW and have Ss give their presentations in the next lesson.

Suggested Answer Key

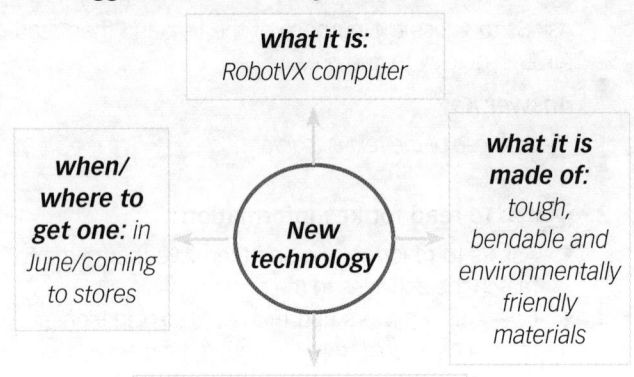

(diagram: New technology)
- **what it is:** RobotVX computer
- **what it is made of:** tough, bendable and environmentally friendly materials
- **when/where to get one:** in June/coming to stores
- **what it can do/has:** produce three dimensional holograms, has an internal keyboard and mouse, owner can transfer the computer's internal drive onto headgear, glasses, watches

Hello, everyone and thank you for joining me here at the 52nd Technology Fair. My name is John Thomas. Most of us here will agree that our lives are much better because of the computer, right? Well, thanks to the work of my organisation, your lives are going to become even better. Let me introduce to you RobotVX: the computer of the future.

With its futuristic design, this computer consists of tough, bendable and environmentally friendly materials, developed and tested in our very own research labs.

Thanks to these materials, this computer can do amazing things. Let me show you ... In front of you are three-dimensional holograms. On this one, I can communicate with people around the world. On the second hologram, I can create objects, even pieces of art. On the last hologram, I can view images of patients' body parts to get a better view of their problems. Amazing, right? But, that's not all ladies and gentlemen. Besides producing holograms, this computer has an internal keyboard and mouse. What's more, the owner can transfer the computer's internal drive onto headgear, glasses and even watches.

In June, the RobotVX will be coming to a store near you. As you saw with your very own very eyes, this product will be high in demand. This is why today only, you have the chance to pre-order this computer so that you don't miss out!

The RobotVX computer will make your lives easier and more exciting, with its holograms and unique features. I'm sure you all agree with me when I say that this computer will change your lives.

Thank you all for being here today. It would be my pleasure to answer any questions on the RobotVX computer now ...

CLIL: History A

Listening & Reading

1 **Aim** To introduce the topic through audio-visual cues

- Ask Ss to look at the pictures and play the recording.
- Ask Ss to use their imagination and answer the questions.
- Elicit answers from Ss around the class.

Suggested Answer Key

I am on a busy London street 100 years ago. I can see horses and carriages and cars moving up and down and I can hear street vendors shouting out about the things they are selling. I can smell dirt, food and smoke.

2 **Aim** To predict the content of the text and listen and read for specific information

- Elicit Ss' guesses as to which shops and jobs don't exist anymore.
- Play the recording. Ss listen and read the text and find out if their guesses were correct.

Suggested Answer Key

There are no lamplighters because we have electric lights now. There are tailors, but not on every shopping street. There are no newsboys. Cafés are more common than tearooms.

3 **Aim** To read for specific information and consolidate new vocabulary

- Ask Ss to read the statements 1-5 and then give Ss time to read the text again and mark the statements according to what they read.
- Check Ss' answers and then elicit explanations for the words in bold.
- Give Ss time to look up the meaning of the words in the **Check these words** box in the World List.

Answer Key

1 F   2 F   3 T   4 F   5 T

Suggested Answer Key

exist (v): to happen or be found
earn (v): to make money from work
freshly-baked (adj): recently cooked in an oven
measure (v): to take the measurements of sb/sth

Speaking & Writing

4 **Aim** ICT To develop research skills; To develop public speaking skills

- Ask Ss to work in small groups and research online to find out about shops and jobs 100 years ago in their country and collect information.
- Then give Ss time to prepare a presentation.
- Ask various groups of Ss to give their presentations to the class.
- Alternatively, assign the task as HW and ask Ss to give their presentations in the next lesson.

Suggested Answer Key

Good afternoon. I'm Martha James and today I'm going to talk about some of the shops and jobs that existed in my country 100 years ago.

First of all, life was very different in the country to life in the city. There was often only one shop that sold everything or a weekly market where people bought the things they needed. People grew their own food and made their own clothes. Most of the jobs were in farming, mining or fishing.

In the cities, there were lots of small family-run shops. Each one sold different goods and services and usually only one product. For example, you bought meat from the butcher's and fish from the fishmonger's but you could also buy cheese from the cheese shop, pies from the pie shop and oil from the oil shop. There was a shoe repair shop on most high streets where people took their shoes to be fixed instead of buying new ones because they were very expensive. Most high streets also had a café and a barber's shop that were just for men. Some of the jobs on the high street included the newspaper seller, the shoe shiner and different hawkers. The shoe shiner would clean people's shoes. He often had a chair for the customer and a box of brushes and cloths. The hawkers sold all sorts of small items such as matches and ribbons from a tray around their necks.

As you can see life was very different in the past. I'm certainly glad that we have supermarkets and department stores today, aren't you?

Are there any questions? ... Thanks for listening.

5 **Aim** THINK To compare shops and jobs in two different eras & countries

Elicit answers from Ss around the class as to shops and jobs 100 years ago in England and in their country.

Suggested Answer Key

Shops and jobs in England and in my country were quite similar in some ways. To start with, they both had butcher's and newsboys. The English high street had the tearoom for women, but my high street had the café for men. The English high street had the lamplighter, but my high street had the shoe shiner.

B CLIL: Food Preparation & Nutrition

Listening & Reading

1 **Aim** To listen and read for gist
   - Ask Ss to look at the label. Elicit answers to the questions.
   - Play the recording. Ss listen and read the text and find out.

   Answer Key
   You can see it on food and drink products. It shows the ingredients and nutrients. It is important to read it to find out the nutritional value of the product and the ingredients it has.

2 **Aim** To read for specific information
   - Ask Ss to read the sentences 1-5 and then give them time to read the text again and complete the task.
   - Check Ss' answers and then elicit explanations for the words in bold.

   Answer Key
   1 F   2 T   3 F   4 F   5 T

   per serving (phr): *for each portion*
   percentage (n): *an amount expressed as a part of 100*
   fool (v): *to trick*

   - Give Ss time to look up the meanings of the words in the **Check these words** box in the Word List.

Speaking & Writing

3 **Aim** THINK To talk about nutrition facts/ingredients and make an assumption
   - Ask Ss to read the label again and guess what the product is and how healthy it is.
   - Elicit answers from Ss around the class and ask Ss to give reasons.

   Suggested Answer Key
   I think the product is a chocolate and hazelnut spread because the main ingredients are sugar, vegetable oil, hazelnuts, milk powder and cocoa powder. It is not a healthy product because the main ingredients are sugar and vegetable oil (fat) which are not healthy in large amounts and the calories are quite high for a small amount.

4 **Aim** ICT THINK To develop research skills; To compare information
   - Ask Ss to work in small groups and bring clean food packaging from home with the ingredients list and nutrition facts on them and compare similar products.
   - Ask various groups to tell the class about them and answer the questions.

   Ss' own answers

CLIL: Science

Listening & Reading

1 Aim To listen and read for specific information

- Ask Ss to look at the graph and elicit what it shows. Then elicit how it relates to the greenhouse effect.
- Play the recording. Ss listen and read the text to find out the answers.
- Check the answers around the class.

Suggested Answer Key

The graph shows the percentage of carbon dioxide in the atmosphere and the average global temperature over the last 1000 years. It is related to the greenhouse effect because carbon dioxide is a greenhouse gas and as the amount of carbon dioxide increases, the Earth's temperature rises and the greenhouse effect becomes more obvious.

2 Aim To read for specific information

- Ask Ss to look at the gapped sentences and then give them time to read the text again and complete the gaps.
- Check Ss' answers.

Answer Key

1 the glass
2 Carbon dioxide
3 fossil fuels
4 global warming

- Give Ss time to look up the meanings of the words in the **Check these words** box in the Word List.

Speaking & Writing

3 Aim To consolidate new vocabulary

- Ask Ss to make sentences using the phrases in bold in the text.
- Elicit answers from Ss around the class.

Suggested Answer Key

Carbon dioxide and water vapour are the two main greenhouse gases.
When there is a lot of these gases in the atmosphere, they cause the greenhouse effect which warms the Earth.
Oil, gas and coal are all fossil fuels.
Global warming is a gradual increase in the Earth's temperature.

4 Aim ICT To develop research skills; To tell the class about our carbon footprint

- Ask Ss to research online and find out information about our carbon footprint and how we can reduce the amount of carbon we produce.
- Ask various Ss to tell the class.
- Alternatively, assign the task as HW and have Ss tell the class in the next lesson.

Suggested Answer Key

A carbon footprint is how much carbon dioxide an individual or a company produces over a period of time. To reduce our carbon footprint, we should use less energy in our homes and daily lives. We can do this by driving less and taking public transport more. We can also travel by train and other means of transport instead of flying as this has the most carbon. We can reduce how much electricity we use in our homes. We can buy fewer products which use energy to be produced and which have a lot of packaging. If we eat less meat we can reduce our carbon footprint dramatically because it takes a lot of energy to raise animals and feed them and then process them into food products.

D CLIL: Art & Design

Listening & Reading

1 **Aim** To listen and read for specific information

- Ask Ss to look at the title and the subheadings in the text. Elicit Ss guesses as to what characterises artworks from the different styles of art.
- Play the recording. Ss listen and read the texts to find out.

Answer Key

Abstract expressionist artworks are characterised by images that don't represent things from the real world.
Surrealist artworks are characterised by distorted images and things which don't usually go together.
Pop art artworks are characterised by people's everyday experiences such as supermarket products, road signs and advertisements.

2 **Aim** To read for specific information

- Ask Ss to read the sentences 1-5 and then read the text again and mark them accordingly.
- Check Ss' answers and then elicit explanations for the words in bold.

Answer Key

1 AE   2 PA   3 S   4 AE   5 S

Suggested Answer Key

claim (v): to state sth is true/a fact
drip (v): to let a liquid such as paint fall
explore (v): to search/find out about sth
melt (v): sth which turned from being a solid into a liquid
simply (adv): only/just

- Give Ss time to look up the meanings of the words in the **Check these words** box in the Word List.

Speaking & Writing

3 **Aim** **THINK** To express an opinion

Elicit answers to the question from Ss around the class with reasons.

Suggested Answer Key

I like Surrealism the most because I am interested in dreams. I like Pop art the least because I think images of supermarket products are boring.

4 **Aim** ICT **THINK** To develop research skills; To present another art movement

- Ask Ss to research online and find another art movement and collect information about it and make notes under the headings.
- Ask various Ss to present the art movement to the class using their notes.
- Alternatively, assign the task as HW and have Ss present their stories in the next lesson.

Suggested Answer Key

name: Cubism
when started: 1910
where: Paris
features: objects are analysed, broken up and reassembled in an abstracted form
famous painter/work of art: Pablo Picasso, 'Girl with a Mandolin'

Good morning, everyone. My name is Sarah Greene and today I am going to talk about one of my favourite art movements of the 20th century, Cubism.

Cubism began in Paris in 1910. Artists created paintings which showed objects or people that have been broken up and reassembled in an abstracted form often using cubes. The most famous Cubist painter was Pablo Picasso. He created paintings like 'Girl with a Mandolin'.

Are there any questions? ... Thank you for listening.

Student's Book Audioscripts

UNIT 1 – Lifestyles

1c – Exercise 3 (p. 8)

Presenter: A person's favourite colour can tell you a lot about what that person is like. With us in the studio today is Mr Chan. He's going to tell us about the colours people wear and their personalities. Welcome to our show, Mr Chan.
Mr Chan: Thank you. Let's start with the colour red. People who wear red are very brave and not afraid to face dangers in their life! In general, they're very happy people, too, and always have a smile on their face!
Presenter: But isn't pink a very happy sort of colour, too?
Mr Chan: Well, that's possible, but pink is more a sign of a kind person – the ones that show an interest in others. They're also careful types who don't like making mistakes or hurting other people's feelings.
Presenter: Some people say that blue shows a jealous personality. Do you agree?
Mr Chan: No, not at all. Blue's a very peaceful colour – people who wear it are usually very calm and rarely get angry. Blues are also reliable – when they promise to do something, you know they will!
Presenter: What about green, then? It's my favourite colour!
Mr Chan: Yes, but I must tell you that green can sometimes show a jealous character – and this makes people feel unhappy. It is a friendly colour, though – green-lovers enjoy being with lots of friends!
Presenter: I'm glad it's not all bad! (ha ha ha). We've just got time for one more colour before we stop for a break.
Mr Chan: Purple is a royal colour. People who wear it like luxury and this, unfortunately, can make them lazy at times. However, they're very clever and they have a special gift for solving problems.
Presenter: Thank you, Mr Chan. We'll be back in just five minutes …

UNIT 2 – Shop till you drop

2c – Exercise 3 (p. 16)

1 *M:* Hi, Anna! Is that blue hoodie new?
   F: No, I got it ages ago. I just don't wear it much.
   M: Didn't you get anything when you went shopping yesterday?
   F: Of course I did. I got this silk scarf.
   M: Oh, that's lovely. It'll really go with those floral denim jeans you've got.
   F: That's why I bought it!

2 *M:* These polka-dot boots are fun! What a great present for Sue!
   F: But it hardly ever rains here. She won't wear them. I'm getting Sue these pink trainers. Pink's her favourite colour.
   M: I know, Tania, but Mary got Sue trainers already. How about these flip-flops? They're pink too.

3 *F:* Are you back from the market already, Roy?
   M: Yeah. It got a bit cold, and Kate didn't have her gloves, so …
   F: Did you find the socks you wanted? The red, yellow, blue and grey checked ones?
   M: Yes, I did. And Kate got some amazing long striped ones!

UNIT 3 – Survival stories

3c – Exercise 4 (p. 24)

Speaker 1
Help! Help! Can anybody hear me? I'm trapped in the lift and I can't get out! Please! Somebody help me! I can't breathe properly!

Speaker 2
I really don't know how this happened. I locked the door before I left last night and put the key in the usual place. Now the key is where I left it, but the door is open. I don't understand it!

Speaker 3
I can't believe it! I've passed my driving test! I was sure I had failed – but I didn't, and now my parents are going to buy me a car! Isn't it exciting?

Speaker 4
I'll miss old Shep, you know. He was such a sweet dog, and so gentle with children. Ah, yes, he was my best friend. I'll never forget him …

3c – Exercise 11a (p. 25)

Narrator: A cold wind was blowing, but there was a bright blue sky that morning when Dan and Mark pushed their canoe out onto the river. "Where's the map?" asked Dan. "I didn't bring it," replied Mark. "I know this river well."
Two hours later, they stopped to have a cup of hot coffee on the river bank. They were talking about the river animals when they suddenly saw a kingfisher. "Wow!" cried Dan. "A kingfisher! Let's follow it!" They quickly got back into the canoe and started following the tiny, colourful bird.
A short while later, the bird disappeared and the two men decided to turn around. "Oh, no! A waterfall!" Dan shouted. The canoe was quickly approaching the edge and Mark and Dan didn't have the strength to stop it.
"Hold on!" yelled Mark. He knew they could not escape.
At that moment, they heard someone shout from the riverbank. "Here! Catch!" Mark quickly caught the rope that

Student's Book Audioscripts

came towards him. He looked up and saw two fishermen. It was their rope and they pulled the canoe to safety.
Two minutes later, Dan and Mark were sitting on the grassy river bank. They were tired, afraid and relieved, all at the same time. "I don't know how to thank you," Mark said to the fishermen.
"The important thing is that you're safe," one of them replied. "And besides," he added with a grin, "my friends in town will never believe me when I tell them what we caught today.

UNIT 4 – Planning ahead

4b – Exercise 4 (p. 32)

Alison: So, Robin, what are you going to do this summer?
Robin: Well, Alison, I'm going to work as a waiter. I need the money because I'm going to buy a car this summer and take driving lessons.
Alison: Oh, really? I'd love to get a car, but then I'd really like to travel around Europe, too. Maybe after I've moved house I can decide what to save up for next.
Robin: Yeah – moving house can be expensive. I'm glad I don't have to do that.
Alison: Are you going to do anything else during the summer?
Robin: Well, I'm going to study Maths. I need it if I want to do well at university. What about you, Alison?
Alison: Well, I'm volunteering at a summer camp for kids for two weeks. Then, I'm going to join a gym and get fit.
Robin: Oh, great! I'll join with you – I need to get fit, too.

4c – Exercise 2 (p. 34)

Presenter: Good morning! Today we're talking to Julia from the blog Crafty Days. Welcome, Julia.
Julia: Hello, Chris. Thanks for having me on the show.
Presenter: It's our pleasure. So tell us, what's it like to run one of the world's most successful blogs?
Julia: It's amazing, Chris, but it definitely keeps me busy! At first it was a hobby, but in the end I quit my part-time office job and now I write my blog instead. I come up with new craft ideas, make them, photograph them, create videos, write posts and newsletters, keep up my social media pages … it's hard work! And then, of course, there's my vlog.
Presenter: What's that?
Julia: A vlog is a video blog. It's a very popular way to connect with your audience these days. Did you know that 1.5 billion people watch YouTube every month? Or that people watch 100 million hours of video on Facebook every day? If you're a blogger, all those people are waiting to hear from you!
Presenter: So how do you start a vlog?
Julia: It's easy! But to make a good vlog, you need to spend a little money. People don't want to watch a low quality video where you look fuzzy and you're difficult to hear. You should buy a good camera and make sure you have a nice background with good lighting. You also want your vlog to stand out from the others online, so do something special. Don't be like everyone else – be yourself.
Presenter: Great! Have you got any other advice?
Julia: Sure. Remember that everyone starts at the beginning. I've got 100,000 subscribers now, but when I uploaded my first vlog, only 11 people watched it on the first day! The secret is to keep trying, never give up – and have fun!
Presenter: And what do people vlog about?
Julia: Anything! I vlog about crafts – my ideas and how I make them. Other people vlog about sports, their thoughts, their businesses, whatever they're interested in. I think that, if you really love something, your passion will come through and your viewers will love your vlogs.
Presenter: Well, people certainly love yours, Julia. Thank you for being with us today.
Julia: Thank you, Chris.

UNIT 5 – Food, glorious food

5c – Exercise 3 (p. 42)

1   How much is it?
2   Here you are.
3   Would you like anything to drink?
4   Anything else?
5   Can I have some ketchup on my burger, please?

UNIT 6 – Health

6c – Exercise 2 p. 50

A: Good morning everyone! Welcome to Ward 5. Let's get started. Jones, you're up.
B: Yes, Dr White. This is Rita Brown, a 54-year-old woman who was admitted yesterday with severe headaches. Painkillers had no effect and nothing showed up on the general tests, but she is scheduled for an MRI this afternoon.
A: OK. Thank you. Hang in there, Mrs Brown, we'll soon get to the bottom of it. Next, who do we have here. Dawson?
C: This is Amanda Green, 19. She came in to have her wisdom teeth taken out under general anaesthetic. The surgery will take place at 11 am, and all being well she will go home this afternoon.
A: Good. Bed three. Jackson, you can present this patient.
D: Yes, Dr White. Erm, this is Jane Smith, 34. She had minor surgery on her arm yesterday after being hit by a car.

Student's Book Audioscripts

However, her temperature is quite high – 39.5 – and she's complaining of pain.
A: Right. It sounds like an infection. I'll prescribe painkillers and antibiotics straightaway. … OK and who do we have here? Hastings?
E: This is Sarah Williams, 22. Presented with stomach pain two days ago. Tests showed a blockage which was removed yesterday. No complications so far.
A: OK. Great. And finally, Jacobs, you can present the last patient.
F: Yes. This is 25-year-old Kim Baker. She had an injury to her leg. She thought it was broken, but it turned out to be badly bruised. She also had a deep cut to her head which needed stitches.

UNIT 7 – Stick to the rules!

7b – Exercise 3a p. 58

Chris: College life is great here in Bristol, but I hate having to get up so early to catch the bus there. I need to get up at 6:30!
Ann: Poor you! I'm lucky I live on campus at York. I do have to get up on Saturday mornings, too, though. I have an extra Health and Safety lesson then.
Chris: Saturday is my day to relax. I have to spend three evenings a week at the Students' Union. I'm helping out while the president is away.
Ann: Wow! You're busy! How are you getting on with your new flatmate, by the way?
Chris: Ben? Yeah, he's great to have around. He helps me clean the flat on Sundays! We have to do the housework then – there's no other time!
Ann: Again, I'm lucky – the college cleaner takes care of my room. I'm thinking of getting a Sunday job in a café, by the way.
Chris: Really, why's that?
Ann: I need the money! For instance, even though I live on campus, lunches are not included in the fees. I have to pay extra for them.
Chris: Oh, well, I don't have to worry about that. In my college, lunches are free!

7c – Exercise 3 p. 60

Phil: How's life at the student house, Chloe?
Chloe: It's fine thanks, Phil. We each look after our own room, but we had to make some rules to share the chores in common areas.
Phil: Yes – otherwise nothing gets done! What do you do?
Chloe: I hate a dirty bathroom, so I clean ours every Saturday. Which reminds me … I mustn't forget to buy some cleaning spray!
Phil: Does Dave do any chores? I know he's a bit lazy!
Chloe: Actually, he did offer to clean the windows but we don't need to do that because a man comes once a month to clean them. He takes out the rubbish for recycling – he has to make sure everything goes in the right bin!
Phil: Dave's sister is staying there, too, isn't she?
Chloe: Penny, yes – she takes care of the dusting. She does it every week and the living room furniture always looks nice and clean!
Phil: How about the washing-up? With five of you in the house, I bet the sink's always full of dirty dishes!
Chloe: Actually, no one really has to do that job because we just put all the dishes into the dishwasher. We're not allowed to use it more than once a day, though. The landlord pays for electricity and water and he's afraid of getting huge bills.
Phil: Hmm … I can imagine. I suppose someone has to do the floors in the common areas.
Chloe: Yes, they get dirty quite quickly! Gale gets the vacuum out most days and does the carpets. Ricky sweeps the floors in the kitchen and bathroom.
Phil: Sounds like everything's under control!

UNIT 8 – Landmarks

8a – Exercise 1a p. 64

Welcome to our Extraordinary Eight podcast. This week we'll be looking at eight UNESCO World Heritage Sites, places of great importance and natural beauty. The first is Grand Canyon National Park in the USA. This canyon is 446 km long and over a kilometre deep in some places! Number two is Plitvice Lakes National Park in Croatia. It contains sixteen lakes which are connected by underground rivers. Number three is the wide green Viñales Valley in Cuba, a 132 km2 valley which is surrounded by high mountains. Fourth on our list is in Madagascar and it's the Rain forests of Atsinanana. They consist of 6 national parks. The Elephanta Caves in India come fifth on our list. These caves are located on an island near Mumbai and are full of statues carved from the rock! Sixth on the list? The Greater Blue Mountains in Australia, which was named a World Heritage Site in 2000 by UNESCO because of the large number of rare animals and plants there. Number seven – Victoria Falls in Zambia. These spectacular falls were discovered and named by Europeans in 1885, but the people living around there knew them well, and called them 'The Smoke that Thunders'. And last but not least on our Extraordinary Eight list comes the Wieliczka Salt Mine in Poland. Salt was removed from this mine for over 750 years until 2007. At 327 metres deep and 287 km long, this is the only one in the list that is man-made, but its huge size and great age earned it a place on the list. That's all for this week. Join us next week when …

Student's Book Audioscripts

8b – Exercise 6a p. 67

Teacher: Well, class, I hope you haven't forgotten you're having a quiz today. Let's see if you've studied for it! Close your books, please. First question: who was the cinematographe invented by?
S1: The Lumiére brothers.
Teacher: Correct! Can you also tell me when they invented it?
S1: Yes, sir. In, er, 1895?
Teacher: Very good! OK … who was the telephone invented by?
S2: It was invented by Alexander Graham Bell, sir, in 1876.
Teacher: That's correct! What about The *Café Concert*? Who painted it?
S3: I think it was … Paul Gaugin, sir?
Teacher: Sorry, no. It was painted by Édouard Manet in 1878. And now a tough question: who designed the Gherkin?
S4: I'm sure it was Foster and Partners, sir.
Teacher: Yes, it was. Next question: who wrote *Wuthering Heights*?
S5: It was written by Charlotte Brontë, sir. In … in 1845, I think.
Teacher: Not quite – it was written by Emily Brontë. Final question: does anyone know who *The Blue Danube* was composed by?
S6: *The Blue Danube* was composed in 1867 by Johann Strauss.
Teacher: Correct! I see most of you have studied hard. Well done, class!

8c – Exercise 2 p. 68

Thank you for calling the London Transport Museum. All our lines are busy at the moment but your query will be dealt with shortly. Or, for general information, press '1'.
The museum is open from ten in the morning to six in the evening daily. The last entry is at five fifteen.
Visitors to the museum can learn all about the history of London transport, going right back to the sedan chairs of the early eighteen-hundreds. Popular with visitors are the Victorian horse-drawn bus and London's first steam-powered underground train. Extra events include an exciting range of Hidden London tours that take you round some of the forgotten tunnels of the London Underground. For details of times and prices for these, please check our website.
Entrance to the museum costs seventeen pounds fifty for adults and is free for under-eighteens. Tickets can be booked online to save time waiting in queues. Please note that taking photographs is not allowed in the museum library.

8c – Exercise 9 p. 69

Good morning, listeners! On this week's edition of *Travel Spot*, I'd like to tell you about my recent trip to Cambodia. It was absolutely fantastic! I visited the country's star attraction – the temple city of Angkor Wat. It's located in the north near the modern town of Siem Reap. It covers an area of two square kilometres full of temples, courtyards, terraces, palaces and beautiful sculptures, all made of the same kind of stone. Everything is surrounded by an outer wall, and outside that there is a moat still with water in it.
Angkor Wat was built in the 12th century. It was used as a place of worship until the early 15th century when the Khmer civilisation was destroyed. After that, the temple buildings were slowly covered by the jungle.
In the 20th century the jungle was cut back and people could visit the ruins. Today, Angor Wat is visited by over two million people a year. When I was there, I spent three hours walking round the temples. The main one has five towers which look like lotus flowers!
If you ever go to Cambodia, you will be amazed by Angkor Wat! And don't forget to book your tickets before your visit – they shouldn't be bought at the last minute!

UNIT 9 – Live and let live

9c – Exercise 2 p. 76

1 **Man:** Do we need one by the lake?
    Woman: Oh, yes! And one in the playground. Kids are always dropping litter there.
    Man: Do we need one outside the tennis courts?
    Woman: No, there's already a bin inside.

2 **Woman:** The Falcon 3000 is your ticket to freedom. No more waiting for buses…
    Man: and you'll never want to use your car again!
    Woman: Fitter, faster and free. The Falcon 3000. Check it out!

3 **Man:** At least it's something we can do something about!
    Woman: Exactly! I mean, I can't stop loggers cutting down the forests …
    Man: … or make car companies stop making cars!
    Woman: Right! But I can come out with a pair of gloves and a bag and clear up this mess!

Student's Book Audioscripts

UNIT 10 – Holiday time

10b – Exercise 6 p. 85

Tom: I'd like to go to London for a few days. I've never been before. I know you and Sandra visited it last summer. What did you do while you were there?
Barry: We did lots of things and had an amazing time … right, Sandra?
Sandra: Yes. We went to the Piccadilly Theatre to see a wonderful modern production of *Romeo and Juliet*. I really enjoyed it.
Barry: Me too. And another great place to visit is Trafalgar Square. We took some selfies next to Nelson's Column and the lions.
Sandra: And right on Trafalgar Square is the National Gallery too. We spent a whole day in there admiring the paintings.
Tom: Yes, I know it's really worth visiting! Did you manage to have afternoon tea anywhere?
Barry: Indeed we did! We went to the Savoy Hotel. It was very luxurious!
Tom: And did you get a chance to see any sport while you were in London?
Sandra: Yes, I agreed to watch a football match with Barry at Wembley Stadium. It's the only thing I didn't really enjoy doing – but Barry loved it, of course!

10c – Exercise 2 p. 86

Penny: Oh, Robert! You're back! I wasn't expecting you for another couple of days. How was your holiday?
Robert: It was great, thanks, Penny. Two whole weeks to unwind and relax in a nice hotel near the beach. Just what I needed after all that hard work in the office last month!
Penny: So, what was the hotel like? Would you go there again?
Robert: It was very comfortable and had lots of extras. There was even a gym where you could work out. But believe it or not, there was no lift. It's a good thing they had a porter – he carried my bags up to the third floor.
Penny: Maybe they want their guests to keep fit! (ha ha) How about the weather? English summers can be a bit miserable!
Robert: No, I was very lucky. It only rained on the first day and there were one or two windy days. The rest of the time it was lovely and sunny with temperatures around twenty-three degrees.
Penny: That's good. I know you went there to do water sports, so I'm glad you had the weather for it.
Robert: Yes, the beach was ideal for kayaking and snorkelling. I saw some amazing marine life – even seahorses! I actually wanted to sign up for scuba diving lessons, but the school was closed. They don't open until late June.
Penny: Oh, that's a shame, but it sounds like you had a good time anyway!

UNIT 11 – Join in the Fun!

11c – Exercise 3 p. 94

Good afternoon, listeners. I'm Jim White, manager of the Blue Arena, and today I'm happy to announce a new ice show at our venue from next week. Following the success of the ice show we organised last year, 'Fairytales on Ice', this year, we have a show with a similar theme called 'Fantasy on Ice'. The performers are a group of dancers from Russia and this is the second stop on their world tour following a series of shows in Germany. Critics loved the show there, so you shouldn't miss this great opportunity! Tickets cost just £15 for adults, while kids and disabled people pay £10. You can also buy a high-quality DVD of a previous performance of the show for £5. The show will run from the 5th to the 12th of March. Following that date, on 18th March, the arena will close for two weeks for some building work. If you haven't visited us before, the arena is located in Bridge Street in the centre of the city. This is a pedestrian street, so visitors should park in the arena's own car park in Kent Street nearby. For more information, please phone us on 01-124135. We can't wait to see you!

UNIT 12 – Going online!

12c – Exercise 2 p. 102

Speaker 1
I know it sounds funny, but I don't have my own laptop or desktop or anything. But I do a lot of travelling and a lot of work in hotels and airports and Internet cafés. So for me it's ideal, because I can just get on the nearest computer, plug it in and access all my files on the spot. No time wasted!

Speaker 2
It's been great for me, because I spend a lot of time online, and there's nothing worse than being bent over a computer all day. This way I can sit in an armchair or even lie on the couch and do it, and because the screen is quite a bit bigger than a smartphone's, it's not too hard on the eyes.

Speaker 3
I didn't think I could learn how to use a new piece of technology so easily! My old mobile phone took me ages. But because I touch the screen with my finger, and make calls or send messages that way, it's always very clear what I have to do!

Speaker 4
I know everyone talks about being mobile these days, and gadgets that make our lives easier and so on. But at the moment, I'm doing an online graphics course and working for an Internet company, and I don't have time to leave my desk at home most of the time! I want a powerful machine that will never let me down, and I don't care if I can't carry it around.

Student's Book Audioscripts

12c – Exercise 9 p. 103

Presenter: Welcome to Chat Room, the programme where you get a chance to air your opinions. Send us your comments, by email or voice mail, and let us know what you think. On last week's show, Fritz in Germany raised the question of online shopping. This was Fritz's comment …

Fritz: Online shopping was unheard of fifty years ago. Now it is a useful part of our everyday lives. But what about the disadvantages of this way of shopping?

Presenter: We received a lot of replies, quite a few in favour of online shopping. Here's one from Kim in Thailand.

Kim: I think going online can be a very convenient way to shop! You can shop from the comfort of your own home, any time you want and that saves a lot of time. I think that's great!

Presenter: And Julia from Italy had this to say …

Julia: Online shopping isn't just more convenient, it's often cheaper than in shops! You can often find bargains and discounts that you don't find anywhere else and it's a good way to compare prices, too.

Presenter: On the other hand, some people were strongly against Internet shopping. This is Margaret from Wales …

Margaret: I'm not a great fan of shopping this way. I find that the delivery of goods takes time. I'm a teacher. If I order a book online, that means I need it straightaway, but things usually take one to three weeks to be delivered. Not good enough for me, I'm afraid!

Presenter: Someone called Ken – no address given – mentioned another negative point.

Ken: Don't laugh, but my problem is I can't try on what I buy. You need to wait to see if the product matches the description. A piece of clothing that looks great online is different in real life or the material is not what you expected.

Presenter: Good point, Ken. So we can see that online shopping offers both advantages and disadvantages. I suppose really it's just a matter of personal choice …

Formative Evaluation Chart

Name of game/activity: ....
Aim of game/activity: ....
Unit: .... Course: ....

Students' names:	Mark and comments
1	
2	
3	
4	
5	
6	
7	
8	
9	
10	
11	
12	
13	
14	
15	
16	
17	
18	
19	
20	
21	
22	
23	
24	
25	

Cumulative Evaluation

Student's Self Assessment Forms

CODE			
**** Excellent	*** Very Good	** OK	* Not Very Good

Student's Self Assessment Form — UNIT 1

Go through Unit 1 and find examples of the following. Use the code to evaluate yourself.

- use words/phrases related to daily routines & free-time activities; people's appearance & character
  ....
- understand texts related to daily routines
  ....
- understand short descriptions with visual support
  ....
- read for specific information – get an idea of the content of simple informational material & short simple descriptions about people
  ....
- listen to and understand dialogues related to character
  ....
- greet & introduce yourself/others
  ....
- describe people's appearance & character
  ....
- interview a person about a typical day in his/her life
  ....
- identify homophones
  ....

Go through the corrected writing tasks. Use the code to evaluate yourself.

- write a short text comparing typical days
  ....
- write an email about a holiday
  ....
- link words/groups of words with basic connectors (and, with)
  ....
- write a blog entry about a favourite person
  ....

CODE			
**** **Excellent**	*** **Very Good**	** **OK**	* **Not Very Good**

Student's Self Assessment Form   UNIT 2

Go through Unit 2 and find examples of the following. Use the code to evaluate yourself.

- use words/phrases related to shops & services; clothes
- understand information in texts about shops
- listen to dialogues and identify objects
- ask for things & respond – describe objects
- describe lost property – compare markets
- identify words with silent letters

Go through the corrected writing tasks. Use the code to evaluate yourself.

- write an email about a weekend break
- use adjectives
- brainstorm for ideas
- write a short text about a market

CODE			
**** Excellent	*** Very Good	** OK	* Not Very Good

Student's Self Assessment Form — UNIT 3

Go through Unit 3 and find examples of the following. Use the code to evaluate yourself.

- use words/phrases related to weather phenomena, feelings & sounds
- read for specific information – understand short texts related to survival
- understand narration
- identify sounds – listen and identify
- understand everyday expressions and ask people for information about renting a house
- give a witness statement
- identify meaning based on stressed words

Go through the corrected writing tasks. Use the code to evaluate yourself.

- write a blog entry
- set the scene in a story
- use adverbs & adjectives in narrations
- write a story

CODE			
**** **Excellent**	*** **Very Good**	** **OK**	* **Not Very Good**

Student's Self Assessment Form UNIT 4

Go through Unit 4 and find examples of the following. Use the code to evaluate yourself.

- understand & use words/phrases related to jobs & job qualities
  ....
- understand short texts about jobs
  ....
- express preferences giving reasons
  ....
- have a job interview
  ....
- listen to and understand a dialogue about a job
  ....
- pronounce '/l/'
  ....

Go through the corrected writing tasks. Use the code to evaluate yourself.

- write an entry about a future job in a forum
  ....
- write an email applying for a job
  ....
- write a short text about a typical part-time job for students
  ....

CODE			
**** Excellent	*** Very Good	** OK	* Not Very Good

Student's Self Assessment Form — UNIT 5

Go through Unit 5 and find examples of the following. Use the code to evaluate yourself.

- understand words/phrases related to food & drinks; fast food dishes
- express preferences
- understand texts about food
- listen to everyday conversations and complete exchanges
- make offers/requests
- decide on a shopping list
- order a takeaway
- understand texts about sweets
- pronounce *like – 'd like*

Go through the corrected writing tasks. Use the code to evaluate yourself.

- design a menu
- write an online review about a restaurant
- recommend a restaurant
- write a short text about a sweet

128 © Express Publishing PHOTOCOPIABLE

CODE			
**** Excellent	*** Very Good	** OK	* Not Very Good

Student's Self Assessment Form   UNIT 6

Go through Unit 6 and find examples of the following. Use the code to evaluate yourself.	
• understand words/phrases related to illnesses & remedies; parts of the body and injuries	
• express concern & give advice	
• understand short texts related to illnesses	
• listen to and identify people & their problems	
• shop for clothes	
• pronounce words with /ɪd/	

Go through the corrected writing tasks. Use the code to evaluate yourself.	
• write a forum post giving advice	
• write an email about a health issue	
• proofread a piece of writing	
• write a short text about a health service	

Student's Self Assessment Form

UNIT 7

Go through Unit 7 and find examples of the following. Use the code to evaluate yourself.

- understand words/phrases related to rules & regulations; chores
  ....
- understand texts related to rules
  ....
- ask for/give permission – express agreement
  ....
- listen to and match people to chores
  ....
- ask about/explain rules
  ....
- pronounce *can – can't*
  ....

Go through the corrected writing tasks. Use the code to evaluate yourself.

- write a leaflet with rules
  ....
- write an advert about a flat for rent
  ....
- group information
  ....

Student's Self Assessment Form — UNIT 8

Go through Unit 8 and find examples of the following. Use the code to evaluate yourself.

- understand words/phrases related to landmarks & materials
- understand information/advertising texts about landmarks & tourist attractions
- understand texts with visual support about man-made landmarks
- ask for/give information
- listen & understand a recorded message about a tourist attraction
- listen and identify people
- use correct intonation in passive questions

Go through the corrected writing tasks. Use the code to evaluate yourself.

- write a blog entry about a visit to a landmark
- write an article about a landmark
- use appropriate tenses in descriptions of places
- write titles
- prepare a poster about landmarks

Student's Self Assessment Form

UNIT 9

Go through Unit 9 and find examples of the following. Use the code to evaluate yourself.

- understand words/phrases related to endangered animals & their body parts; green activities
  ....
- understand texts about endangered animals
  ....
- make speculations
  ....
- make suggestions – agree/disagree
  ....
- listen to and identify information based on visual prompts
  ....
- identify feelings
  ....

Go through the corrected writing tasks. Use the code to evaluate yourself.

- write a tweet about an endangered animal
  ....
- write an article providing solutions to problems
  ....
- support solutions with results
  ....
- make notes to present a festival
  ....

Student's Self Assessment Form

UNIT 10

Go through Unit 10 and find examples of the following. Use the code to evaluate yourself.

- understand words/phrases related to types of holidays & weather; hotel services & facilities
  ....
- understand texts related to holidays
  ....
- listen to and understand events in a narration
  ....
- check in at a hotel
  ....
- identify rhyming words
  ....
- describe location
  ....

Go through the corrected writing tasks. Use the code to evaluate yourself.

- write a weather forecast
  ....
- write a hotel review
  ....
- use adjectives
  ....
- use informal style
  ....
- create a brochure
  ....

Student's Self Assessment Form

UNIT 11

Go through Unit 11 and find examples of the following. Use the code to evaluate yourself.	
• understand words/phrases related to festivals; types of entertainment	
• understand texts related to festivals	
• present a festival	
• listen to an advert and identify missing information	
• describe an event	
• identify stressed syllables	

Go through the corrected writing tasks. Use the code to evaluate yourself.	
• write an email about an event you attended	
• use adverbs with gradable/non gradable adjectives	
• write a short text about an annual cultural event	

Student's Self Assessment Form

UNIT 12

Go through Unit 12 and find examples of the following. Use the code to evaluate yourself.	
• understand words/phrases related to computer parts; smartphones	
• understand an informational article about safety online	
• understand texts about places of interest	
• listen and match speakers to devices	
• give instructions	
• express feelings using exclamations	

Go through the corrected writing tasks. Use the code to evaluate yourself.	
• write a short information leaflet	
• write a for-and-against essay	
• use topic sentences to start main body paragraphs	
• support main ideas	
• write a search engine entry about a museum	

Progress Report Cards

Progress Report Card

.... (name) can: **Unit 1**

	very well	OK	not very well
use words/phrases related to daily routines & free-time activities; people's appearance & character			
understand texts related to daily routines			
understand short descriptions with visual support			
read for specific information – get an idea of the content of simple informational material & short simple descriptions about people			
listen to and understand dialogues related to character			
greet & introduce yourself/others			
describe people's appearance & character			
interview a person about a typical day in his/her life			
identify homophones			
write a short text comparing typical days			
write an email about a holiday			
link words/groups of words with basic connectors (and, with)			
write a blog entry about a favourite person			

Progress Report Card

.... (name) can: **Unit 2**

	very well	OK	not very well
use words/phrases related to shops & services; clothes			
understand information in texts about shops			
listen to dialogues and identify objects			
ask for things & respond – describe objects			
describe lost property – compare markets			
identify words with silent letters			
write an email about a weekend break			
use adjectives			
brainstorm for ideas			
write a short text about a market			

Progress Report Card

.... (name) can: **Unit 3**

	very well	OK	not very well
use words/phrases related to weather phenomena, feelings & sounds			
read for specific information – understand short texts related to survival			
understand narration			
identify sounds – listen and identify			
understand everyday expressions and ask people for information about renting a house			
give a witness statement			
identify meaning based on stressed words			
write a blog entry			
set the scene in a story			
use adverbs & adjectives in narrations			
write a story			

Progress Report Card

.... (name) can: **Unit 4**

	very well	OK	not very well
understand & use words/phrases related to jobs & job qualities			
understand short texts about jobs			
express preferences giving reasons			
have a job interview			
listen to and understand a dialogue about a job			
pronounce /l/			
write an entry about a future job in a forum			
write an email applying for a job			
write a short text about a typical part-time job for students			

Progress Report Card

.... (name) can:			Unit 5
	very well	OK	not very well
understand words/phrases related to food & drinks; fast food dishes			
express preferences			
understand texts about food			
listen to everyday conversations and complete exchanges			
make offers/requests			
decide on a shopping list			
order a takeaway			
understand texts about sweets			
pronounce *like* – *'d like*			
design a menu			
write an online review about a restaurant			
recommend a restaurant			
write a short text about a sweet			

Progress Report Card

.... (name) can:			Unit 6
	very well	OK	not very well
understand words/phrases related to illnesses & remedies; parts of the body and injuries			
express concern & give advice			
understand short texts related to illnesses			
listen to and identify people & their problems			
shop for clothes			
pronounce words with /ɪd/			
write a forum post giving advice			
write an email about a health issue			
proofread a piece of writing			
write a short text about a health service			

Progress Report Card

.... (name) can: **Unit 7**

	very well	OK	not very well
understand words/phrases related to rules & regulations; chores			
understand texts related to rules			
ask for/give permission – express agreement			
listen to and match people to chores			
ask about/explain rules			
pronounce *can – can't*			
write a leaflet with rules			
write an advert about a flat for rent			
group information			

Progress Report Card

.... (name) can: **Unit 8**

	very well	OK	not very well
understand words/phrases related to landmarks & materials			
understand information/advertising texts about landmarks & tourist attractions			
understand texts with visual support about man-made landmarks			
ask for/give information			
listen & understand a recorded message about a tourist attraction			
listen and identify people			
use correct intonation in passive questions			
write a blog entry about a visit to a landmark			
write an article about a landmark			
use appropriate tenses in descriptions of places			
write titles			
prepare a poster about landmarks			

Progress Report Card

.... (name) can:			Unit 9
	very well	OK	not very well
understand words/phrases related to endangered animals & their body parts; green activities			
understand texts about endangered animals			
make speculations			
make suggestions – agree/disagree			
listen to and identify information based on visual prompts			
identify feelings			
write a tweet about an endangered animal			
write an article providing solutions to problems			
support solutions with results			
make notes to present a festival			

Progress Report Card

.... (name) can:			Unit 10
	very well	OK	not very well
understand words/phrases related to types of holidays & weather; hotel services & facilities			
understand texts related to holidays			
listen to and understand events in a narration			
check in at a hotel			
identify rhyming words			
describe location			
write a weather forecast			
write a hotel review			
use adjectives			
use informal style			
create a brochure			

Progress Report Card

.... (name) can: **Unit 11**

	very well	OK	not very well
understand words/phrases related to festivals; types of entertainment			
understand texts related to festivals			
present a festival			
listen to an advert and identify missing information			
describe an event			
identify stressed syllables			
write an email about an event you attended			
use adverbs with gradable/non gradable adjectives			
write a short text about an annual cultural event			

Progress Report Card

.... (name) can: **Unit 12**

	very well	OK	not very well
understand words/phrases related to computer parts; smartphones			
understand an informational article about safety online			
understand texts about places of interest			
listen and match speakers to devices			
give instructions			
express feelings using exclamations			
write a short information leaflet			
write a for-and-against essay			
use topic sentences to start main body paragraphs			
support main ideas			
write a search engine entry about a museum			

Workbook Key

Unit 1

1a – Vocabulary

1 1 E   3 G   5 H   7 D   9 A
      2 J   4 B   6 I   8 F   10 C

2 1 play video games   4 wash the dishes
      2 have dinner   5 listen to music
      3 read a newspaper   6 ride a bicycle

3 1 going   4 listening
      2 playing, watching   5 washing
      3 having

4 1 Shaving, running   3 put, go
      2 crew, space, equipment   4 typical

5 1 day   5 break   9 going
      2 newspaper 6 news   10 meeting
      3 sitting   7 music   11 housework
      4 projects   8 admire

1b – Grammar

1 1 b   2 b   3 a   4 a

2 1 walks the dog, is working out at the gym
      2 washes the car, is meeting with friends

3 1 Is Tom sleeping, is reading
      2 doesn't like, prefers
      3 Do you fancy, hate
      4 Is she talking, is chatting

4 1 usually   2 always   3 ever   4 never

5 1 I do   3 Neither do I
      2 I don't   4 So do I

6 1 Do you remember   7 always
      2 'm staying   8 having
      3 live   9 eating
      4 'm having   10 'm taking
      5 enjoying   11 'm also visiting
      6 So do I   12 'm coming

1c Vocabulary

1 1 D   2 F   3 E   4 B   5 C   6 A

2 **Suggested answer**
      2 Peter is in his late seventies with short, white hair and wrinkles.
      3 Mike is middle-aged. He has got short, black hair and a beard and a moustache.
      4 Sara is in her early forties with short, wavy, black hair.

3 1 friendly   3 careful   5 brave
      2 jealous   4 calm

Everyday English

4 1 c   2 a   3 d   4 b

5 1 a   2 b   3 a

6 1 Great to see you
      2 Nice to meet you, too
      3 who's that over there
      4 I'd like to meet her
      5 Nice to meet you
      6 Are you here for shopping

Reading

7 1 F   2 T   3 F

8 1 C   2 C

9 1 The Butlers have got **three** children.
      2 Gerard **sometimes** eats fried food.
      3 He **likes** water skiing.

Unit 2

2a – Vocabulary

1 1 baker's   5 bookshop
      2 hair & beauty salon 6 antique shop
      3 jeweller's   7 department store
      4 post office   8 bank

2 1 post office   4 florist's
      2 travel agent's   5 chemist's
      3 department store

3 1 loaf   3 happen   5 about
      2 aisle   4 afraid   6 like

4 1 took   4 handed
      2 employs   5 security
      3 missed

5 1 department   5 opportunity   9 ordinary
      2 customers   6 haircut   10 sales
      3 jeweller's   7 beauty
      4 necklaces   8 markets

142

Workbook Key

2b – Grammar

1
1. was
2. received
3. went
4. learnt
5. had
6. grew
7. wanted
8. got
9. visited
10. sold

2
1. use
2. used
3. used to
4. didn't use to

3
1. didn't have
2. loved
3. travelled
4. didn't receive
5. forgot

4
1. Was, wasn't
2. Did Pam buy, did
3. Did they own, didn't, had
4. Did James learn, did

5
1. expensive, big, black
2. small, square, blue
3. light, brown, leather
4. lovely, red, velvet

6
1. heavier
2. cheaper
3. impressive, more comfortable
4. the most crowded
5. the best
6. big, fewer

7
1. was
2. Did you enjoy
3. saw
4. played
5. liked
6. looked
7. wore
8. beautiful
9. used
10. broke down
11. worst
12. gave

2c Vocabulary

1
1. plain
2. floral
3. leather
4. denim
5. checked
6. striped
7. linen

2
1. scarves
2. skirts
3. jacket
4. trousers

3 Jane is wearing a plain white linen coat, **grey** trousers and brown **leather** boots. She's got a **striped** scarf round her neck and she is holding a plain black and brown **leather** handbag.

Everyday English

4
1. c
2. a
3. b
4. d

5
1. a
2. b
3. a

6
1. How can I help you?
2. What does it look like?
3. What's it got in it?
4. Where and when did you lose it exactly?
5. Is this it?

Reading

7
A. Where to find it
B. How it changed
C. The best time to go

8
1. T
2. F
3. DS
4. T

9
1. largest antique market
2. like any other (market) in the area
3. selling unwanted household items
4. anything you desire (from clothes, household items and food to second-hand goods and antiques).

Unit 3

3a – Vocabulary

1
1. flood
2. tsunami
3. blizzard
4. tornado
5. hurricane
6. lightning

2
1. tsunami
2. flood
3. hurricane
4. lightning

3
1. Suddenly, pouring
2. shining, brightly
3. lucky, heavily
4. lightning, easily

4
1. picked
2. gets
3. hit
4. threw

5 a)
1. d
2. g
3. f
4. b
5. a
6. e
7. c

b)
1. stormy weather
2. dry land
3. giant wave
4. satellite phone

6
1. rough
2. board
3. waves
4. rolled
5. hard
6. heavy
7. falling
8. land
9. achievements

3b – Grammar

1
1. was making
2. Was Tom playing
3. was waiting
4. was Nicole doing
5. weren't shopping

2
1. last night
2. At 10 o'clock
3. yesterday afternoon
4. all
5. This time

143

Workbook Key

3 2 Were the girls swimming? No, they weren't. They were watching TV.
3 Was Naomi shopping? No, she wasn't. She was talking on the phone.
4 Were they sleeping? No, they weren't. They were eating.

4 1 when it started to rain.
2 while we were watching TV.
3 while her brother was setting the table.
4 when the lights went out.

5 1 were watching 4 was waiting
2 heard 5 went
3 Were you working

6 1 It was snowing heavily when the climbers reached the camp.
2 It stopped raining so the children went out to play.
3 The thieves stole the painting while the guard wasn't looking.
4 Sami screamed when she saw a snake in her tent.
5 The sun was shining when we left for the beach.

7 1 burnt/burned, while, was cooking
2 was lying, when, heard
3 were walking, when, started
4 was singing, while, was playing
5 was sleeping, when, woke

3c
Vocabulary

1 1 puzzled 4 relieved 7 sad
2 frightened 5 anxious 8 thrilled
3 proud 6 angry

2 1 screeching 4 barking 5 wailing
2 blowing 5 falling 6 knocking

Everyday English

3 1 c 2 d 3 a 4 b

4 1 a 2 b 3 a

5 1 Where were you at the time of the burglary?
2 What were you doing?
3 What happened exactly?
4 Did you see his face?
5 I'm glad I could help.

Reading

6 1 DS 2 T 3 DS 4 F

7 A 6 C 1 E 7 G 5
B 8 D 4 F 3 H 2

8 1 (the) *Endeavour*. 3 1772.
2 New Holland. 4 maps.

Skills Practice (Units 1–3)
Reading

1 1 C 2 A 3 D 4 B

2 1 T 2 T 3 F 4 F 5 DS

3 1 department stores
2 old port of London
3 bought their trendy clothes
4 the Royal Opera House

Everyday English

4 1 d 3 e 5 g 7 a
2 h 4 b 6 c 8 f

5 1 a 2 b 3 b 4 b 5 a 6 a

6 1 E 3 B 5 H 7 F
2 D 4 C 6 A

Listening

7 1 Routine 5 go shopping for clothes
2 bath 6 5:00
3 emails 7 husband
4 department stores 8 a film

8 1 C 2 F 3 G 4 D 5 A

9 1 C 2 B 3 A 4 C 5 B 6 B

Writing

10 Name: Kit Harington
Job: actor
Age: 32
Appearance: of medium height
long, curly, dark hair
moustache
friendly smile
Character: caring, sociable
Interests: reading, travelling, the theatre

Workbook Key

11 Hi Emily!
You asked me to tell you about my favourite celebrity. He's the actor **Kit Harington** and he's in his early **30s**. Kit is **of medium height** with **long, curly, dark hair**. He's also got a beard and a **moustache**.
When it comes to character, Kit is **caring** and **sociable**. He loves going to parties and supporting charities.
Kit enjoys **reading** and **travelling**. As an actor, he is also interested in **the theatre**.
I think Kit Harington is a really special person because of his **friendly smile**.
Who's your favourite celebrity? Write back soon.
Charlotte.

12 1 drive in the countryside on a sunny day
2 start raining
3 tree hit by lightning & car crashes into tree
4 get out of car safely
5 emergency services arrive
6 take the car away & give us a lift

Suggested answer
A Drive in a Storm
One day last summer, my family and I were driving in the countryside. It was a sunny day and we couldn't expect what happened later.

After a while, the sky became dark and it started raining. Then we heard a loud crack. A tree near us was hit by lightning.

The tree fell onto the street and our car crashed into it! It was badly damaged but luckily we got out of the car safely. We were shocked.

We waited patiently until the emergency services arrived. They took the car away and kindly gave us a lift home. When we reached home, we thanked them. We all felt very lucky.

Revision (Units 1-3)

Vocabulary

1 B	6 C	11 A	16 C	21 C
2 A	7 A	12 C	17 B	22 B
3 C	8 C	13 B	18 B	23 C
4 B	9 B	14 B	19 C	24 A
5 C	10 C	15 A	20 A	25 B

Grammar

1 A	6 C	11 A	16 A	21 B
2 C	7 C	12 C	17 B	22 B
3 A	8 B	13 C	18 A	23 C
4 B	9 B	14 B	19 B	24 B
5 C	10 A	15 C	20 C	25 C

Unit 4

4a – Vocabulary

1
1 developer 3 guide 5 planner
2 trainer 4 tester 6 designer

2 1 e   2 c   3 a   4 b   5 f   6 d

3 1 firefighter
2 public relations specialist
3 lifeguard
4 event planner
5 stuntman
6 social media editor

4 1 for   2 with   3 for   4 of   5 at

5 1 suits 3 do 5 follow
2 has 4 take 6 treat

6 1 study 5 make 9 course
2 work 6 editor 10 start
3 designer 7 job
4 skills 8 planner

4b – Grammar

1 1 's going to 4 won't
2 will 5 is going to
3 'm going to 6 will

2 1 are you going, won't be
2 are you going to do, am going to visit
3 isn't joining, will see
4 are you attending, starts

3 2 I am travelling to London on Monday.
3 look out! You're going to fall down.
4 Are you going to apply for university next year?
5 I think I will go horse-riding but I hope it won't rain.

4 2 a   3 e   4 b   5 c

5 1 will/'ll do 3 wakes up 5 doesn't set
2 don't have 4 will/'ll feel 6 are/'re not

6 b When Mark graduates, he'll travel to New York.
c When Gary graduates, he'll get a job.
d When I graduate, I'll get my own flat.
e When they graduate, they'll start their own business.
f When Kim graduates, she'll become a fashion designer.

145

Workbook Key

4c
Vocabulary

1 1 brave   3 imaginative
   2 caring   4 hard-working

2 a) brave, patient, imaginative, caring, careful, sociable

```
w x b r a v e k j h g l s
c h i k l b v z a p o c o
a g h v p a t i e n t a c
r p o i u y t r e w n r i
i m a g i n a t i v e e a
n f g j m x c y q l p f b
g a l s k d j f h t b u l
m a y d a o r x i p g l e
```

b) 1 careful
   2 imaginative
   3 sociable
   4 patient

Everyday English

3 1 d   2 a   3 b   4 c

4 3, 6, 1, 8, 2, 5, 7, 4

5 1 Have a seat, please.
   2 What can you tell me about yourself, Ms Mayers?
   3 I'm very creative and imaginative.
   4 Do you live near the school?
   5 That's not a problem.

Reading

6 1 F   2 T   3 T   4 DS

7 1 B   2 A   3 B   4 A   5 B

8 1 A   2 C

Unit 5

5a – Vocabulary

1 1 buffalo wings   7 doughnuts
   2 jacket potato   8 fish and chips
   3 cheesecake   9 carrot juice
   4 spaghetti Bolognese 10 fruit salad
   5 mussels   11 wholemeal bread
   6 bread rolls   12 watermelon

2 1 pizza   3 fruit salad   5 made
   2 mayonnaise   4 yoghurt

3 1 snack   3 stocked   5 cupboard
   2 bar   4 ingredients

4 1 A   2 B   3 C   4 A   5 B

5 1 junk   5 doughnuts   9 poached
   2 wings   6 produce   10 mashed
   3 chips   7 juice   11 bar
   4 snack   8 salad

5b – Grammar

1 1 some – U   5 some – U   9 an – C
   2 an – C   6 a – C   10 some – U
   3 an – C   7 some – C   11 a – C
   4 a – C   8 a – C   12 some – C

2 A 1 much   3 a few   5 many
     2 a little 4 some

   B 1 a   2 some   3 any   4 glass

3 2 some – **a**   7 some – **any**
   3 some – **any**   8 few – **little**
   4 some – **a**   9 many – **any/much**
   5 little – **few**   10 any – **some**
   6 much – **many**

4 1 everything   3 anywhere
   2 Everybody   4 no one

5 1 anywhere, nowhere
   2 Someone/Somebody, something
   3 anything, everything

6 1 don't drink   3 becomes
   2 eat   4 are

7 2 If/When you heat ice, it melts.
   3 If/When you don't put milk in the fridge, it goes bad.
   4 If/When you press this switch, the lights comes on.

5c
Vocabulary

1 1 garlic   3 rings   5 brownies
   2 pie   4 milkshake   6 chicken

2 1 polite   3 noisy   5 varied
   2 slow   4 delicious   6 high

Workbook Key

3
1. dessert
2. course
3. sparkling
4. thumbs
5. side
6. worth

Everyday English

4 1 b 2 a 3 d 4 c

5 1 a 2 a 3 b

6
1. What can I get you?
2. Would you like some chips with it?
3. Anything else?
4. Anything to drink?
5. Is that to eat in or take away?
6. How much is it?
7. Here you are.
8. Here's your change.

Reading

7 **Food:** delicious, tasty, menu rather disappointing for vegetarians
Prices: quite reasonable
Service: staff friendly and helpful, service fast
Atmosphere: relaxing: comfortable seating, lovely furnishings, live piano music
Suggestions: make a few changes to the menu: wider selection of vegetarian dishes

8 1 F 2 F 3 DS 4 T 5 T

9
1. The Blue Moon is in York.
2. It serves salad, pasta and meat dishes.
3. The service was fast and excellent.
4. The comfortable seating, lovely furnishings and live piano music made the atmosphere relaxing.
5. The writer suggests changes to the menu because there weren't many vegetarian dishes.

Unit 6

6a – Vocabulary

1
1. earache
2. stomach ache
3. temperature
4. sore throat
5. cold
6. cough
7. headache
8. toothache

2
1. prescription
2. remedy, ache
3. sick
4. pain
5. diseases

3
2. She sounds like she's got the flu.
3. Janet looks exhausted.
4. It tastes like chicken. What kind of meat is it?
5. This blanket feels really warm.
6. This milk smells awful. It's gone bad.

4 1 down 2 for 3 of 4 in 5 from

5
1. ill
2. suffer
3. treat
4. sore
5. Soak
6. works
7. take
8. remedy

6b – Grammar

1
1. hasn't slept
2. has been
3. Have they moved
4. has broken
5. haven't tried
6. Have you ridden

2 1 gone 2 been 3 gone 4 been

3
1. just
2. since
3. for
4. yet
5. already

4 1 a 2 b 3 a

5
1. 've hurt
2. did it happen
3. fell
4. hurt
5. Have you seen
6. went
7. haven't broken
8. have never injured

6
1. Have you been sleeping
2. has been waiting
3. hasn't been studying
4. has she been working
5. have been living
6. hasn't been feeling

7
1. has been performing
2. moved
3. has made
4. has played
5. has been trying
6. has been painting

6c Vocabulary

1
1. wrist
2. ankle
3. finger
4. hand
5. foot
6. head

2
1. finger
2. wrist
3. ankle
4. leg
5. chest
6. hand
7. head

3
2. He's bumped his head.
3. He's sprained his ankle.
4. She's cut her finger.

Everyday English

4 1 d 2 c 3 a 4 b

5 1 b 2 a 3 a

147

Workbook Key

6
1. What seems to be the problem?
2. I've got a terrible stomach ache.
3. What did it start?
4. It sounds like food poisoning.
5. I'm going to give you a prescription.
6. I will, doctor.

Reading

7
1. bush medicine
2. lemon grass
3. skin infections
4. eucalyptus leaves
5. witchetty grubs

8 1 T   2 F   3 DS   4 DS   5 T

9 Suggested answers
1. over 40,000 years
2. in the 1920s
3. mouthwashes and cough sweets
4. treat toothache

Skills Practice (Units 4-6)

Reading

1 C

2 1 F   2 T   3 F   4 F

3 1 B   2 A   3 A   4 A

Everyday English

4
1 f   3 g   5 c   7 d
2 b   4 a   6 e

5
1 a   3 b   5 b   7 a
2 a   4 a   6 b   8 a

6 1 E   2 B   3 A   4 C   5 H   6 G

Listening

7 1 E   2 D   3 F   4 A   5 C

8 1 C   2 C   3 C   4 A   5 B

9 1 C   2 C   3 B   4 B   5 B

Writing

10
1. 18 years old
2. a student at York University
3. Food Science
4. summer
5. waitress
6. serving
7. tidying up
8. communication skills
9. hard-working
10. 236262523
11. Jane Levinson

11 Suggested answer

Hi **Diana**,
How's things? I haven't been well recently. **I've had the flu**. I think I got worse when **I got wet in the rain**.
The next day, **I had a bad cough and a high temperature**. I went to the doctor's on **Monday** and told her **my symptoms**. She wrote me a prescription for **some aspirin and cough medicine**. She also **told me to get plenty of rest**.
Now, **I'm feeling a bit better but I don't think I'll be back to college until next week**. Have you ever **had a bad attack of the flu**?
Write soon.
Dave

12 Suggested answer

Luigi's
A Great Dinner Date!
This smart Italian restaurant at 24 Denton Street, York is the perfect place for a tasty Italian dinner. I went there on Friday evening, the 23rd of August, and the place was full!
The varied menu included lots of pasta and pizza dishes. I decided to skip the starter to make room for the main course. I chose the spaghetti carbonara and it was delicious. The staff were very helpful and explained all the dishes on the menu. The prices were very reasonable.
On the other hand, the desserts were a bit disappointing, as the choices were very limited. The atmosphere was rather noisy, too, and the music was annoying because it was too loud at times.
All in all, however, Luigi's is an elegant place to eat and definitely worth a visit.

Revision (Units 4-6)

Vocabulary

1 C	6 C	11 B	16 B	21 B
2 B	7 B	12 C	17 A	22 B
3 C	8 C	13 B	18 A	23 C
4 B	9 B	14 C	19 B	24 B
5 A	10 A	15 A	20 C	25 A

Workbook Key

Grammar

1	B	6	C	11	C	16	C	21	B
2	C	7	A	12	B	17	C	22	A
3	C	8	B	13	A	18	A	23	C
4	A	9	C	14	A	19	A	24	C
5	A	10	C	15	B	20	B	25	B

Unit 7

7a – Vocabulary

1
1 recycle 3 play 5 loud
2 Keep 4 pick up 6 light

2 1 d 2 e 3 a 4 b 5 c 6 f

3
1 stick 4 provided
2 respect, disturb 5 supply
3 clean

4 1 of 2 from 3 in 4 In 5 to 6 at

5
1 A 3 B 5 C 7 C
2 C 4 C 6 C 8 B

7b – Grammar

1
2 Jane has to/needs to do the ironing.
3 Jane and Brad have to/need to tidy their rooms.
4 Brad doesn't have to/need to do the washing-up.
5 Jane doesn't have to/need to give the dog a bath.
6 Brad has to/needs to wash the car.

2
1 must 3 mustn't 5 shouldn't
2 have to 4 must 6 have to

3
1 d – mustn't 3 a – could 5 c – might
2 e – have to 4 b – may

4
2 A: Can he cross the street here?
  B: No, he can't cross the street here, but he is allowed to cross at the pedestrian crossing.
3 A: Can I drive in the city centre?
  B: No, you can't drive in the city centre, but you are allowed to ride your/a bike.

5 1 A 2 B 3 B 4 B

6
2 You should/ought to save all your files on your computer.
3 Can we enter this room?
4 We weren't able to/couldn't send emails while we were on holiday.
5 It may/might/could rain later.
6 You mustn't drop litter on the streets.
7 We must recycle what we can.
8 You shouldn't light fires near trees and plants.

7c Vocabulary

1 1 d 2 f 3 e 4 a 5 b 6 c

2
1 vacuum the carpets 3 take out the rubbish
2 dust the furniture 4 do the laundry

3
1 Clean 3 clean, dust 5 cleans
2 do 4 does 6 sweep

Everyday English

4 1 b 2 d 3 a 4 c

5 1 a 2 b 3 a

6
1 welcome 6 quiet 11 provided
2 check 7 Right 12 available
3 latest 8 street 13 Enjoy
4 keys 9 main
5 rules 10 problem

Reading

7
1 the Pacific Ocean.
2 Wolf Island, Darwin Island and Santa Cruz.
3 January and June.
4 a flag.

8 1 F 2 T 3 DS 4 T

9
1 There is no perfect time to go scuba diving. It is great all year round.
2 Around the Galapagos Islands, you can turtles, sharks, dolphins, sea lions, reef fish and much more.
3 During the wet season, the temperature is 20-25°C.
4 You shouldn't panic when you see a shark because they can smell fear.

Unit 8

8a – Vocabulary

1
1 falls 3 valley
2 cave 4 canyon

2
1 in 3 out 5 by
2 from 4 on 6 to

Workbook Key

3
1 sight
2 chambers
3 lake
4 crystals
5 ceilings

4
1 carved
2 digging
3 decorated
4 legend
5 servants
6 attraction
7 surface
8 crystals

5
1 famous
2 ancient
3 beautiful
4 huge
5 underground
6 interesting
7 amazed

8b – Grammar

1 a)
1 *Macbeth* was written between 1603 and 1607 by Shakespeare.
2 A festival is being held next month.
3 The telephone was invented by Alexander Graham Bell.
4 Guided tours will be offered by the company.
5 Her ring hasn't been found yet.

b) Suggested answers
1 People admire the Eiffel Tower for its unusual design.
2 Ray has decorated the room.
3 Elaine will give some money to charity.
4 People know the Atacama Desert as the driest desert in the world.

2
1 will be opened
2 be hired
3 is offered
4 must be worn
5 be contacted

3
1 The Acropolis is visited by a lot of tourists every year.
2 English and French are spoken in Canada.
3 The Royal Albert Hall is/was named after the husband of Queen Victoria.
4 Pollution has damaged the monument over the years.

4
1 was built
2 be opened to
3 has been closed
4 was painted by

5
1 is located
2 is believed
3 was completed
4 was built
5 is made
6 was used
7 can be visited

8c Vocabulary

1
1 stone
2 brick
3 steel
4 concrete
5 marble
6 clay

2
1 steel
2 marble
3 wood
4 stone

3
1 is made of glass
2 is made of steel
3 is made of wood
4 is made of stone

Everyday English

4 1 b   2 c   3 d   4 a

5 1 a   2 b   3 b

6
1 feel
2 anything
3 Could
4 Certainly
5 When
6 century
7 more
8 take
9 forbidden
10 help

Reading

7
1 Uluru National Park/Australia (450 km from Alice Springs in Australia)
2 1985.
3 the Anangu Aborigines.
4 'The centre of the Earth'
5 small caves (which contain fascinating carvings and drawings).

8 1 F   2 T   3 DS   4 F   5 DS

9
1 Uluru was first seen in 1873.
2 It was discovered by William Gosse.
3 Uluru was first called Ayers Rock.
4 Visitors can see a fantastic view of the countryside.

Unit 9

9a – Vocabulary

1
1 whiskers
2 horns
3 tusk
4 webbed feet
5 paw
6 hoof

2 1 in d   2 in c   3 on a   4 on b   5 in e

3
1 lion
2 bird
3 bat
4 peacock
5 kitten
6 mouse
7 bee
8 dog

4
1 fur
2 species
3 treetops
4 deforestation
5 dropped
6 endangered
7 action
8 protection

9b – Grammar

1
1 hadn't left
2 Had Sam called
3 had cooked
4 had caught
5 had already fallen
6 had watered

Workbook Key

2
1. Had Mary already fed, got, had also put
2. was, went out, was, took
3. Had they finished, returned, had also fixed

3
1. By the time we arrived at the harbour, the boat had already left.
2. She had just gone to sleep when her brother came round to see her.
3. Pam and Tom didn't go to the concert before they had finished their work.
4. Lucy called for a taxi after she had packed her suitcase.

4
If Bill had enough money, he would buy a car.
If Bill had enough money, he would go on a cruise.
If Bill had enough money, he would build a swimming pool.

5
1. used, wouldn't be
2. weren't, would feel
3. recycled, would cut
4. were, would be
5. stopped, wouldn't disappear

6
2. If people didn't leave rubbish on beaches, they wouldn't be dirty.
3. If we took care of our planet, it wouldn't be in danger.
4. If I didn't have a car, I would cycle to work.
5. If factories didn't pour chemicals into rivers, they wouldn't be polluted.
6. If people didn't waste water, there wouldn't be serious water shortages in many parts of the world.

7
1. myself
2. ourselves
3. yourselves
4. yourself
5. herself

9c
Vocabulary

1 1 d   2 c   3 a   4 e   5 b

2
1. bagfuls of rubbish
2. solar panel
3. public transport
4. air pollution

3
1. A pollution
2. B space
3. A transport
4. A rubbish
5. B air
6. A greenery

Everyday English

4 1 d   2 b   3 a   4 c

5 1 b   2 a   3 b

6
1. discuss
2. encourage
3. public
4. point
5. about
6. idea
7. get
8. Why
9. agree
10. nobody

Reading

7 1 T   2 DS   3 F   4 F

8 Suggested answers
1. four months
2. workshops and seminars
3. the friendly atmosphere

9 1 A   2 C   3 C

Skills Practice (Units 7-9)
Reading

1
1. What They Look Like
2. Then and Now
3. What to Look For
4. Why important

2
1. their thick powerful tails
2. the (otter) population started to go up again
3. send in photos or videos
4. fish

3
1. Chemicals from factories caused the pollution of the otter's habitat.
2. By the 1980s they had almost disappeared.
3. It helps Protect Our Otters to check the size and health of otter populations.
4. If otters can't find clean food in rivers, they have to search for other food on land.

Everyday English

4 1 b   2 e   3 d   4 h   5 f   6 a   7 c   8 g

5 1 b   2 b   3 b   4 a   5 b   6 a   7 a   8 b

6 1 B   2 D   3 E   4 A   5 C

Listening

7 1 A   2 B   3 B   4 A   5 C   6 B

8
1. 10/ten
2. Crown
3. tours
4. September
5. 22.70
6. House

9 1 D   2 F   3 E   4 C   5 A

Workbook Key

Writing

10
1. mountain
2. 4/four
3. mini-market
4. rubbish
5. clean
6. 15/fifteen

11 Suggested answer

The Tower of London is a historic castle in central London. It has a long history which goes back to the early 11th century.

The main attractions for visitors are seeing the Crown Jewels, visiting the White Tower and going on one of the Beefeaters' guided tours.

Sometimes special events are held at the Tower, where you can watch cooks preparing medieval meals or see knights dressed up in shining armour!

This place is highly recommended for anyone who likes history. The Beefeaters tell their visitors wonderful stories about the Tower and the many uses it had in the past. If you go to London, it's a must-see!

12 a) Causes
2. chemical soaps & shampoos
3. plastic plates & cups

Effects
2. pollute soil & rivers
3. create litter

Solutions
2. use eco-friendly toiletries
3. bring reusable eating utensils

Results
2. cleaner environment
3. don't need to recycle them

b) Suggested answer

Camping is a good way to enjoy nature, but campers don't always respect the environment. Instead of keeping the campsite clean and green, they often leave it polluted.

One problem is litter. For example, plastic plates and cups are often left lying around. Another problem is the pollution of soil and rivers. This is because people use chemical soaps and shampoos when they use the showers, and these chemicals find their way into the environment.

The solution is to eat and drink from reusable utensils. If people did that, they wouldn't need to recycle them. Using eco-friendly toiletries would also mean a cleaner environment.

If all campers took these simple steps, campsites would be a lot greener.

Revision (Units 7-9)

Vocabulary

1 C	6 B	11 B	16 C	21 A
2 A	7 C	12 A	17 A	22 B
3 C	8 A	13 B	18 A	23 A
4 B	9 A	14 A	19 C	24 C
5 A	10 B	15 B	20 B	25 C

Grammar

1 B	6 C	11 C	16 C	21 C
2 A	7 C	12 A	17 B	22 B
3 C	8 A	13 C	18 C	23 A
4 A	9 B	14 C	19 C	24 C
5 C	10 A	15 B	20 B	25 C

Unit 10

10a – Vocabulary

1
1. City break
2. Cruise
3. Adventure
4. Package

2
1. interesting
2. relaxing
3. expensive
4. close
5. sights

3
1. five-star, cuisine
2. down
3. guide
4. warm, crystal
5. tropical
6. sandy
7. deal

4
1. g
2. h
3. f
4. a
5. c
6. b
7. e
8. d

5 1 in 2 from 3 on 4 on 5 on 6 in

6
1. huge
2. best
3. fine
4. thick
5. showers
6. bright
7. sunshine
8. relaxing
9. care
10. strolling
11. dining
12. delicious
13. expensive
14. budget
15. fortnight

10b – Grammar

1 1 c 2 e 3 a 4 b 5 d

2
1. –
2. –
3. –, the
4. the
5. –
6. –
7. the
8. –, –

3
1. to write
2. writing
3. visiting
4. to visit
5. to ask
6. asking

4
1. travelling
2. to fly
3. talking
4. to let
5. try
6. meeting
7. to go
8. camping

Workbook Key

5
1. which
2. whose
3. who
4. where
5. who
6. which

6
1. whose wife works
2. the boy who's
3. that my dad
4. which my brother worked in
5. where many families

7
1. where
2. who
3. which
4. which
5. who
6. where
7. which
8. who

10c
Vocabulary

1
1. gym
2. laundry
3. swimming pool
4. room service
5. wake-up call
6. restaurant

2
1. room service
2. gym
3. Wi-Fi
4. swimming pool

3
1. shuttle
2. café
3. beauty salon
4. parking
5. porter
6. laundry

Everyday English

4
1. c
2. d
3. a
4. b

5 Put in following order: 8, 1, 3, 4, 2, 5, 6, 7

6
1. reservation
2. under
3. fill
4. sign
5. passport
6. paying
7. details
8. right
9. password
10. dial
11. enjoy

Reading

7
1. (north) Iceland
2. purple, red, pink, orange and blue
3. the southwest of Iceland
4. healing powers
5. south Iceland
6. mountains, forests, active volcanoes and rivers

8
1. BL
2. NL
3. SNP
4. BL

9
1. Another name for the Northern Lights is the aurora borealis.
2. You can go on a boat trip to see the Northern Lights.
3. The Blue Lagoon is surrounded by black lava and dark green moss.
4. The temperature of the water in the Blue Lagoon is 39°C.
5. You can have a trekking holiday at Skaftafell National Park.

Unit 11

11a – Vocabulary

1
1. d
2. e
3. c
4. f
5. a
6. b

2
1. local dish
2. street parade
3. sky lanterns
4. ancient temples
5. dance performance
6. full moon

3
1. moon
2. sight
3. swing
4. celebrates
5. released
6. dark

4
1. into
2. in
3. over
4. at

5
1. give
2. come
3. caught
4. fire
5. welcome

6
1. A
2. C
3. B
4. C
5. A
6. B
7. A
8. A

11b – Grammar

1
1. said
2. said
3. told
4. said
5. told

2
2. He told us (that) he had been in New York recently.
3. They said (that) they had just arrived at the street parade.
4. She said (that) she was trying local dishes.
5. Martin said (to me) (that) he would come and visit me in a couple of weeks.
6. They told us (that) we could set off fireworks after dark.

3
2. The boy asked his mother if/whether he could go and play in the park then.
3. The teacher asked her students if/whether they had ever been to Britain.
4. Jill asked the shop assistant how much that candle cost.
5. My friend asked me if/whether I thought it would rain the next/following day.
6. Jillian asked Tom what the name of the street was.

4
2. you enjoy your visit
3. did you like best about the parade
4. there anything you didn't like
5. you visit the festival again
6. you recommend the festival to your friends

Workbook Key

5
1. I told him
2. why he had done, he hadn't done
3. me if/whether I, I told her
4. Mike asked Joanne, she said
5. whether I had seen, I told her

6
1. (that) he had forgotten to do
2. asked me/us if I/we liked
3. does the dog food cost
4. asked when they would
5. can't help you
6. told us (that) she had

11c
Vocabulary

1
1. concert
2. opera
3. ice show
4. circus
5. escape room
6. fashion show

2
1. escape room
2. fashion show
3. concert
4. circus

3
1. acrobats, disappointing
2. show, boring
3. move, fascinating
4. live, awesome

Everyday English

4 1 b 2 a 3 d 4 c

5 1 a 2 b 3 a

6
1. yourself
2. loved
3. arena
4. much
5. tickets
6. free
7. stunning
8. maybe
9. end
10. try

Reading

7 1 F 2 T 3 DS 4 F

8
1. Park City, Utah, USA
2. promote quality films / find films that inspire, move and thrill viewers
3. $20 / twenty dollars
4. warm clothes

9 1 A 2 C 3 B

Unit 12

12a – Vocabulary

1
1. keyboard
2. headset
3. mouse
4. USB
5. speakers
6. printer
7. router
8. flash drive
9. tower
10. screen
11. webcam
12. scanner

2
1. print
2. webcam
3. speakers
4. flash drive
5. screen
6. router

3 1 to 2 of 3 to 4 on 5 from 6 to

4
1. create
2. detect
3. access
4. link
5. bank account

5
1. attachment
2. anti-virus
3. access
4. download
5. adverts
6. purchase
7. hacker
8. access
9. detected
10. complex

12b – Grammar

1
2. He told her to wait for her computer to upload the webpage.
3. He told her to click on the print symbol to go to the print options page.
4. He told her to decide which part of the webpage she wanted to print.
5. He told her to enter the page number she wanted to print and click 'Print'.

2
2. Mrs Penny told them not to bring any books into the classroom.
3. Mrs Penny told them to raise their hands if they had any questions.
4. Mrs Penny told them to write their names clearly at the top of the sheet.
5. Mrs Penny told them to use a pencil, not a pen.
6. Mrs Penny told them to write neatly.
7. Mrs Penny told them not to look at anyone else's sheet.
8. Mrs Penny told them to stop writing at five o'clock.

3
1. Switch off the tower.
2. Stop talking.
3. Don't be late for work again.
4. Show us your driver's licence.
5. Don't print the documents.
6. Download the files.

4
1. wasn't
2. do
3. What
4. so
5. How
6. will
7. doesn't
8. so

Workbook Key

5
1. What a
2. such a
3. so
4. so
5. such an
6. How

6
1. doesn't she
2. How
3. so
4. were they
5. so
6. such an
7. isn't it
8. so
9. What

12c
Vocabulary

1
1. GPS
2. Calendar
3. Calculator
4. Email
5. Camera
6. Wi-Fi

2
1. Contacts
2. Mobile apps
3. Messages
4. My files

3
1. f
2. e
3. g
4. a
5. c
6. b
7. h
8. d

Everyday English

4 1 a   2 c   3 b

5 Put dialogue in following order: 3, 2, 6, 4, 1, 5, 7

6
1. matter
2. transfer
3. know
4. show
5. What's
6. click
7. copy
8. Really
9. first
10. Once

Reading

7 1 B   2 C   3 A   4 D

8 1 B   2 D   3 A   4 C

9 1 F   2 T   3 DS   4 T   5 DS

Skills Practice (Units 10-12)

Reading

1 B

2
1. Minneapolis, Minnesota in 2012
2. a huge sports event
3. cat costumes
4. the Golden Kitty Award
5. enjoyable

3 1 B   2 A   3 A   4 B

Everyday English

4
1. c
2. b
3. a
4. d
5. e
6. h
7. f
8. g

5
1. b   3 b   5 b   7 a
2. a   4 a   6 b   8 b

6 1 H   2 G   3 C   4 F   5 B   6 D

Listening

7
Speaker 1   b
Speaker 2   f
Speaker 3   e
Speaker 4   d

8
1. Rose
2. classical (music)
3. Austria
4. 12 / twelve
5. Hill

9 1 B   2 C   3 B   4 C   5 C

Writing

10 **Suggested answer**

Last month, I spent three days at **the Spring Plaza Hotel** in **Malibu**. This hotel has some problems, but overall it's good.

It is a **large, modern** hotel with **120 rooms**. It's got lots of **excellent** facilities, too, like **a fully-equipped gym and an indoor swimming pool**. Also, the hotel's **rooftop restaurant offers a beautiful view and delicious vegetarian dishes**.

My hotel room was **clean and spacious**.

However, it was located **in the city centre**, so **I was not close to the beach and had to get a taxi there**. Also, the **Wi-Fi in my room** didn't work. That meant that **I had to go to the lobby**.

In spite of these small problems, I'd definitely **recommend this hotel**. It's the perfect choice for **families**.

11 **Suggested answer**

Hi **Kate**,

Thanks for your email; it was great to hear from you. I'm writing to tell you about a great event I attended yesterday here in **London**.

It was a **music concert**. It was held at **the Rose Concert Hall in Hill Road in north London** and it started at **7 pm**. The performers were **the Danube Quartet from Austria. They are currently on tour around Europe**. They played **classical music**. I really enjoyed their **performance and I'm glad I booked in advance**. The whole event was **successful**! Throughout the performance, I felt **amazed by how talented they were**. If you ever get the chance, **go and see them**.

Write back soon.
Lucy

Workbook Key

12 1 enjoy a different climate
2 pick up phrases, learn about a country's history
3 expensive

Suggested answer

Every year, millions of people go on holidays aboard. Is this a good thing or not?

There are a number of advantages to holidaying abroad. Firstly, you can experience a different climate. For example, you can escape the rainy weather at home. Also, you can learn about the country you visit. For instance, you can pick up some of the local phrases and learn about the country's history.

However, there are a number of disadvantages, too. To begin with, holidaying aboard can be expensive. This is because flights, accommodation and food can be costly. Secondly, you can face cultural problems. As a result, you can get into trouble when you do not follow local customs.

Overall, while holidaying abroad can be costly and can involve cultural problems, I believe it is still worth doing. You always experience and learn something new.

Revision (Units 10-12)

Vocabulary

1 C	6 B	11 A	16 A	21 A
2 B	7 B	12 C	17 B	22 A
3 C	8 A	13 B	18 A	23 B
4 A	9 B	14 C	19 B	24 C
5 B	10 C	15 B	20 C	25 C

Grammar

1 C	6 C	11 C	16 C	21 A
2 C	7 B	12 C	17 C	22 A
3 B	8 A	13 A	18 B	23 B
4 A	9 C	14 C	19 B	24 C
5 B	10 C	15 B	20 C	25 B

Workbook Audioscripts

Skills Practice A

Exercise 7 p. 18

Presenter: With us in Shopping Around this week is personal shopper Gayle Moneypenny. She buys clothes for people who don't have time to do it themselves! Gayle, what's your daily routine like?
Gayle: Hello, and thank you for having me on the show. Well, I like an early start. I get up at seven-thirty and have a bath. I find it more relaxing than a shower! After breakfast, at nine o'clock, it's time to check my emails. I might send a few messages to clients as well. By 10 am, I'm down in the shopping mall looking around department stores for ideas. I find the high street shops don't have much variety. I take photos of the outfits I think my clients might like. At eleven thirty, I meet clients to discuss the clothes they want me to buy for them. I don't usually see more than two or three clients a day. At around one-thirty, I stop for lunch. Usually it's something light, like a sandwich or a salad. I spend the afternoon shopping for the clothes my clients have chosen. They usually send someone round to my house later to collect them. I like to be home by five o'clock to help my son with his homework. We're usually finished by six-thirty. Then, at seven o'clock, my husband and I cook dinner together. At eight o'clock the family usually settles down together to watch a nice film on TV. We don't bother watching the news as we read it online in the morning. I usually go to bed at around 11 pm – I prefer not to stay up late on weeknights!
Presenter: That's great! Now, Gayle, can you tell us how you deal with clients who …

Exercise 8 p. 18

Mum: I'm glad your first term at college went well, Jim. Have you made many new friends there?
Jim: Of course! Take a look at this group photo of the First Year students.
Mum: How nice! Who's that boy in the back row with the wavy fair hair?
Jim: That's Brendan. He's doing the Biology course, like me. And that's his sister Mary next to him.
Mum: The girl with the freckles?
Jim: No, that's Olga. Mary is the tall slim one on the other side of Brendan.
Mum: Oh yes, she looks just like a model! What about this boy in the first row? Who's he?
Jim: You mean the well-built guy with dark hair. His name is Steve. He's on the college football team. Believe it or not, he used to be chubby once. It shows what training can do!
Mum: Mmm … he looks very athletic. So … who's your closest friend here?
Jim: Maurice. We study and hang out together. That's him in the middle row at the end.
Mum: Oh yes, I can see him there – with the moustache.....
Jim: No, Mum, that's the lecturer! Maurice is the boy with the pale complexion.
Mum: Well, anyway dear, they all seem like very nice college mates!

Exercise 9 p. 18

1 **A:** Hi Samantha! That's a nice jacket.
   B: Thanks. It was a present together with this silk scarf. I thought they were a bit boring, so I bought this floral skirt to go with them.
   A: It's very pretty.
   B: It's great, isn't it? I wear it all the time!

2 **A:** Wow, Phoebe, I heard the weather was pretty crazy while you were away on holiday.
   B: Yes, that part of the world can get hurricanes and floods, but strange to say, we got stuck in a blizzard!

3 **A:** How did basketball practice go, Bob?
   B: Great thanks, Tim. The coach says we've definitely improved. I did something silly coming back on the train, though.
   A: What's that?
   B: I left my basketball under the seat. It wouldn't fit in my bag with my trainers and basketball shirt.
   A: Oh no!

4 **A:** Why has Imelda stopped playing video games?
   B: She wanted to do something more active, so she's started playing tennis. She actually prefers ice skating but there's no rink in her area.

5 **A:** Did you go shopping in the new mall last Saturday, Harry?
   B: Just for an hour or two in the morning. I had to wash the car in the afternoon.
   A: I thought Mark usually does that.
   B: He does, but on Saturday he was studying for his exams all day, so I did it instead.

6 **A:** Hello Frank. What's that you've got there?
   B: It's my violin. I have a lesson every Tuesday from six o'clock till seven. I'm just going in to class.
   A: OK. When it's over, why don't you come round to my house? There's a good film on at eight.
   B: Sounds good!

Workbook Audioscripts

Skills Practice B

Exercise 7 p. 36

A: Hi Becky. Have you found a part-time job for the summer yet?

B: Oh, hi Fred. Yes, I have! I read an advertisement on the Web for a tour guide in the local museum. So, I applied and I got the position. I've been working there for five days now, and I really like it!

A: That's great! I've got good news, too! I've found a part-time job as a video games tester! As you know, I love gaming, so it's a dream job for me, even though I don't get a big wage.

B: Did your brother Greg help you find that job? He works as a software developer, doesn't he?

A: Yes, that's exactly what happened. He works for a company which makes computer games, so he asked his boss to give me a job for the summer. Greg wants to change his career, though. He's not very happy there.

B: Really? Does he want to become a doctor like your older sister Anna?

A: No, that job's way too stressful for Greg! I'm not sure what he wants to do, to be honest.

B: Maybe he should become a social media editor. My cousin Laura does that and she absolutely loves it. And you don't need any special qualifications, I think. You just need to have experience surfing the Net.

A: OK, I'll mention it to him. Anyway, I'd better go, Becky. See you later.

B: OK, bye Fred!

Exercise 8 p. 36

A: Now, I'm happy to welcome Stephen Malley to the show. Stephen's a hospital chef and he's here to tell us about his job. Stephen, did you always want to be a chef?

B: Not at all. At university, I studied web design, and after I graduated I worked as an app developer. I didn't like it, though. Then, my best friend, who's a nurse, told me about a job in the kitchen of the hospital where he works.

A: What were your duties when you started working there?

B: First, I just washed-up in the kitchen, and now and then I served patients their meals. I did that for two years, and completed a cooking course in the evenings. After a while, I became a qualified chef.

A: I see. And what are the differences between a hospital chef and a chef in a restaurant?

B: Well, it might be less interesting, but being a hospital chef is far more relaxed. We plan patients' meals a day before we serve them, and we have the same number of patients each day. That's a lot less stress than in a busy restaurant!

A: There must be some challenges to your job, though, right?

B: Yes, of course. We don't work with patients directly, so we don't need to be sociable and chat to them like the nurses do. And we don't need to be imaginative with the meals we prepare because they all follow the diet the doctor has prescribed for them. But we do have to be very careful that patients only eat the food they are allowed to.

A: I see. So, I guess you avoid giving patients desserts, right?

B: No, every patient gets a dessert if they want one. We serve a delicious cheesecake sometimes! And patients who can't eat sugar often get a tasty fruit salad. We never serve ice cream, though, even though patients often request it.

A: OK, we'll ask Stephen more questions after the break. ....

Exercise 9 p. 36

1. **A:** Hello, Pam. What brings you here? I hope you don't have another stomach ache.
   B: No, Doctor Johnson, it's not that. I've got a really bad cough.
   A: OK, well you don't have a temperature, so it's probably nothing serious. Let me take a closer look …

2. **A:** Hi Brian. I saw a job advertisement for lifeguards at the local pool. You were looking for a part-time summer job, weren't you?
   B: Thanks, Lisa, but I've already found something. My uncle's a gardener, so I'm going to help him out.
   A: I'll be a tour guide, but your job sounds like more fun.

3. **A:** What do you want to eat, Rachael? I'm going to get a pizza. They're really nice in this restaurant.
   B: Hmm, I think I'll have the fish and chips.
   A: Oh, wait a second. They have spaghetti Bolognese, too. That's your favourite dish, isn't it?
   B: It is, but I don't feel like it today.

4. **A:** Alan, what happened to your hand? I think we need to go to the hospital straight away!
   B: No, Mum, it's not serious. I just burnt it while I was taking a pizza out of the oven.
   A: Well, you're not going to football practice with your hand like that. Let's go to the chemist's to get some cream and a bandage at least.
   B: OK, Mum. I suppose that's a good idea.

Workbook Audioscripts

5 A: Where are you meeting your friend this afternoon, Brian? Are you going to try the new café on Kent Road?
B: No, I feel like something to eat, so we will probably go to a fast food restaurant.
A: Brian, you eat too much junk food. Why don't you go to that nice restaurant that opened on Mill Street instead?
B: No way! It costs a fortune! If I went there, I wouldn't have any money left!

Skills Practice C

Exercise 7 p. 54

1 A: Hi Tom! How about going for a bike ride this afternoon, say about two o'clock? … No, wait – I've got to wash up after lunch for my mum. I always do the plates on Saturdays. Let's say two thirty?
B: I'll be sweeping the floors then. That's my weekly chore. At least it's better than cleaning the windows – my older brother does that! Can we make it 3 pm?
A: Yes, OK.

2 A: It says in this guidebook that the Tower of London once had a zoo with exotic animals. I didn't know that.
B: Neither did I. I thought it had a bakery where the Fire of London started back in 1666.
A: No, that was in Pudding Lane. But they used to make all of England's money there right up until 1812. There's a coin exhibition there now.

3 A: I'm going to the supermarket, Amy. Do you want me to get you anything?
B: Well, I do need some greengroceries, but I prefer to shop at the market. They've got fresh garden produce there.

4 A: Right, I've got the tickets. You should finish that ice cream – you can't bring that into the museum!
B: OK. What about the camera? Can I take photos?
A: I asked at the ticket office and they said there's no problem. Oh, but we have to put Fido's lead on. Dogs can't come in without one!

5 A: Hey Avril! What was that holiday cottage that you rented like?
B: It was fabulous! Right by the beach looking out to sea. And it was so clean! The landlady had dusted all the furniture and even cleaned the oven. I didn't have to do a thing – I just vacuumed the carpets quickly for her before we left!

6 A: I think I'll enter the go-green competition at college. You have to design a poster about ways to help the environment and there's a prize of £500!
B: If I won that much money, I'd buy a new tablet to replace my old one.
A: I wouldn't. I'd buy a bicycle so I could cycle to college. It's more eco-friendly than driving my car, like I do now!

Exercise 8 p. 54

Thank you for calling the Tourist Information Centre. For information on the Tower of London, press One.

The Tower of London is a historic castle in central London. It has a long history which goes back to the early 11th century. It is open to visitors from nine in the morning to five thirty in the evening, Tuesday to Saturday. On Sundays and Mondays, the opening time is one hour later, at ten o'clock. The most popular things to see are the Crown Jewels collection and the White Tower with its displays of ancient armour and weapons. The guided Beefeater tours are also highly recommended. As well as the regular attractions, the Tower has some special events coming up later this year. Opening in the month of August is Go Medieval at the Tower. In this event you can watch how medieval cooks prepared meals and see knights in shining armour in action! The Tower of London Festival takes place the following month, September. This stylish celebration of food and drink is held in the Tower's famous moat. Entrance to the Tower costs £24.80 for adults and £11.50 for children. Or you can book online for just £22.70. Please note that photography is allowed in most parts of the Tower, apart from the Jewel House and the Chapel of St John.
For further details, please visit the Tower of London website.

Exercise 9 p. 54

George: I've got some campsite brochures, Milly. Let's choose one to stay at. This one called Green Valley accepts pets so we won't have to hire a dog sitter.
Milly: OK, George, but I fancy being near the sea. Golden Beach looks nice.
George: Yes, but you can only stay there for fourteen days. We want somewhere for three weeks.
Milly: True. How about Silver Brook, then? It's not expensive!
George: But there's a big fee for using their Wi-Fi – I'm not paying that! We could try Blue Hills. It's looks like it's got excellent facilities.
Milly: Mmm … but it says here that campers have to use the communal kitchen to cook. They're not allowed to cook anywhere outside.
George: Too bad. I don't mind sharing facilities, but I fancy cooking a meal on a campfire some nights, too.

Workbook Audioscripts

Milly: Oh, look at this brochure, George! Daisy Meadow! There's the campfire you want. Doesn't it look lovely?
George: It does. We can hire a caravan and your sister can visit us for a few days. What time do you have to check in?
Milly: No earlier than 4 pm, I'm afraid. They inspect the site after the others campers leave.
George: That's OK. It's a long drive, so it'll give us plenty of time to get there. What do you say?
Milly: OK, Daisy Meadow it is!

Exercise 7 p. 72

Speaker 1
I live in the countryside, so when I go on holiday, I like to experience the exact opposite! I usually go on short holidays to urban areas around Europe. I love going on adventures down busy shopping streets, visiting museums and experiencing the heart of the country where I'm visiting!

Speaker 2
It's a strange experience living on a boat for two weeks, but that's exactly what I do each time I go on holiday! It's great to visit different ports in different cities, all on the same trip. And there's plenty of time to relax when we're travelling between destinations.

Speaker 3
For me, holidays are just about sun and sand! My friends say I should do something more adventurous like camping, but I like nothing more than sunbathing and going for a swim now and then.

Speaker 4
I have quite a stressful job, so when I go on holidays, I try to do as little as possible. I'm not interested in sightseeing around cities or doing water sports by the beach – I just want to relax by the hotel pool! And my travel agent always has everything ready for me – flights, accommodation and meals – all included in one fee.

Exercise 8 p. 72

Good afternoon, everyone. My name is Olive Little and I'm the manager of the Rose Concert Hall in London. Today, I'm delighted to tell you about an upcoming series of concerts at our venue. Last month, we had a very successful series of jazz concerts from various international musicians, and this month we're going to bring you the best in classical music! First off, we're very proud to welcome the Danube Quartet – a group of four talented musicians from Austria. They are currently on tour around Europe, and before visiting us they will stop off in Paris. Admission for this unique event is just £12 for adults, while disabled people enter for free. A CD of the group's music will also be on sale for just £10. The group will perform for one week from the 4th to the 10th of March – beginning each evening at 7 pm. You can buy tickets from our ticket office on Long Road in the city centre, or from the concert hall itself in Hill Road in the north of London. Please book in advance to avoid disappointment. There is an underground car park at the venue which visitors can use for a small charge. For more information, please visit our website: www.rch_london.co.uk. We look forward to seeing you!

Exercise 9 p. 72

Lucy: Hi Sarah. My family has decided to go on holiday to Blackpool in July. Do you fancy coming along? I know you've got a summer camp in June, so you'll be free then, won't you?
Sarah: Thanks, Lucy, but I've already got holiday plans. I'm going with my family to Italy in August.
Lucy: Oh, that's a pity. You always go on holiday abroad, don't you?
Sarah: Well, once or twice we had a holiday in England, but it's true … we usually go abroad. Not very often, though … mostly just once every two years. We really enjoy experiencing a different climate. It's great to escape the rain here and go somewhere nice and sunny. It allows us to do activities like water sports which we rarely do in England.
Lucy: I know what you mean. Last summer, we went on a hiking holiday in Cheshire, but because of the rain, we spent most of the time playing board games!
Sarah: Exactly. Also, I find that you learn a lot when you holiday abroad. For example, on our last holiday in Spain, I picked up a few phrases, and learned about the country's history – even though I didn't visit any museums or read any guide books.
Lucy: Good point, but don't you think that holidaying abroad is expensive – especially the aeroplane tickets?
Sarah: Actually, in Spain our biggest cost was our hotel rooms – and food and flights weren't cheap either. So, you're absolutely right.
Lucy: Also, I guess people face cultural problems when they holiday abroad.
Sarah: You're right. It's very easy to get in trouble with locals when you didn't follow the local customs.
Lucy: Well, if I were you, I'd give a holiday in England a try. If you're lucky with the weather, it can be a great experience.
Sarah: Hmm, well, not this year, but maybe in the future!

Grammar Book Key

Unit 1

1
1. them
2. Ann and Ian's, ours
3. my, his
4. us, she
5. your, Jenny's
6. He

2
1. Is
2. aren't, 're/are
3. Are, am
4. isn't
5. 'm/am not

3
2. A: Has Carl got a beard?
   B: No, Carl hasn't got a beard. He's got a moustache.
3. A: Has Samantha got blue eyes?
   B: No, Samantha hasn't got blue eyes. She's got brown eyes.
4. A: Have Jane and Tim got a computer?
   B: No, Jane and Tim haven't got a computer. They've got a TV.
5. A: Has Joe got wrinkles?
   B: No, Joe hasn't got wrinkles. He's got freckles.
6. A: Have you got long hair?
   B: No, I haven't got long hair. I've got short hair.
7. A: Has Lucy got a typewriter?
   B: No, Lucy hasn't got a typewriter. She's got a computer.

4
2. A typist can type letters.
3. A whale can't read.
4. An artist can paint pictures.
5. A sheep can't fly.
6. A chef can cook delicious dishes.

5 (Suggested Answers)

I can dance but I can't sing.
I can ride a bike but I can't drive a car.
I can speak English but I can't play the guitar.

6

-s	dives, drinks, types, writes, stays, says
-es	teaches, fixes, misses, crashes
-ies	tries, flies, fries, cries

7
2. John hasn't got brown eyes.
3. Is Bob a mechanic?
4. He enjoys reading books in his free time.
5. Are there many festivals in your country?
6. I usually don't work on Saturdays.

8
1. comes
2. lives
3. gets
4. snows
5. love
6. learn
7. ride
8. spend
9. is
10. enjoys

9
2. A: Are they working in the garden?
   B: No, they aren't. They're walking on the beach.
3. A: Are they washing the car?
   B: No, they aren't. They're riding their bikes.
4. A: Is he listening to music?
   B: No, he isn't. He's reading a newspaper.

10
2. are eating
3. am not cleaning, am playing
4. is riding
5. am not going, am staying
6. is watering
7. are washing
8. are having

11
2. A: What does Tracey do?
   B: She's a painter.
   A: Where does she live?
   B: She lives on a farm.
   A: Is she painting right now?
   B: No, she's taking pictures.

3. A: What do you do?
   B: We are teachers.
   A: Where do you live?
   B: We live in a house.
   A: Are you teaching right now?
   B: No, we're riding our bicycles.

12
1. 'm writing
2. are staying
3. 'm sitting
4. 'm drinking
5. 's walking
6. 's collecting
7. is
8. 're spending
9. 're going
10. 're leaving
11. make
12. 're
13. love
14. don't want

13
2. a
3. b
4. a
5. b
6. b
7. a
8. b
9. b
10. b

14
1. C
2. A
3. B
4. B
5. C
6. A
7. B
8. C
9. A
10. B
11. A
12. B

15
2. Mary often meets her friends at a café.
3. I'm never late for school.
4. They sometimes make their beds in the morning.
5. He often goes to the cinema on Friday nights.
6. I always brush my teeth before going to bed.
7. Carla rarely cooks dinner on Sundays.
8. I never leave for work before 8 o'clock.

16
1. Paul seldom wakes up early.
2. We occasionally go on picnics in the summer.
3. Do you practise the violin every day?

Grammar Book Key

4 Bob is hardly ever home in the morning.
5 I rarely read comic books.
6 They often drive to the seashore at the weekend.

17 (Suggested Answers)
2 My family usually watches TV
3 I rarely get up early
4 I often go swimming
5 I always do my homework
6 My brother eats breakfast

18
3 So do I.
4 Neither/Nor does Fred.
5 Neither/Nor do I.
6 So do we.
7 Neither/Nor does Bob.
8 So does Pierre.
9 Neither/Nor do I.
10 So does Tim.

Unit 2

1
work – work**ed**: watched, opened, visited
liv**e** – liv**ed**: welcomed, closed, moved
pla**y** – pla**yed**: enjoyed, employed, stayed
tr**y** – tr**ied**: tidied, studied, cried
sto**p** – sto**pped**: preferred, dropped, planned
trave**l** – trave**lled**: controlled, cancelled, labelled
irregular: sat, took, made

2
1 flew
2 did he stay
3 offered
4 chose
5 did he go
6 needed
7 did he return
8 came

3
1 Did you see, found, didn't buy, cost
2 were, met
3 called, was
4 received
5 did you do, finished, travelled
6 sent, wrote
7 Did they go, watched
8 Did you finish, gave, didn't like

4
1 didn't come
2 went
3 was
4 caught
5 missed
6 told
7 had

5
1 Did you stay
2 visited
3 Did you enjoy
4 did you do
5 tried
6 helped
7 did you spend
8 were
9 didn't have
10 played
11 did you do
12 listened
13 read
14 Did you go
15 finished
16 had
17 surfed
18 saw
19 came
20 started
21 fell

6 a)
2 Jerry used to live with his parents then. Now, he has his own house.
3 Jerry used to take the bus to university then. Now, he drives to work in his car.
4 Jerry used to wear jeans and pullovers then. Now, he wears suits.
5 Jerry used to shop at discount stores then. Now, he shops at expensive stores.

b)
2 No, Jerry didn't use to live in his own house ten years ago. He used to live with his parents.
3 No, Jerry didn't use to wear suits ten years ago. He used to wear jeans and pullovers.

7
1 A: Did Sally use to wear glasses?
   B: Yes, she did.
2 A: Did Sally use to have a cat?
   B: No, she didn't.
3 A: Did Sally use to have/play with dolls?
   B: Yes, she did.
4 A: Did Sally use to have/ride a bicycle?
   B: Yes she did.
5 A: Did Sally use to have/use a computer?
   B: No, she didn't.

8 (Suggested Answers)
When I was ten years old, I used to ride my bike, I used to read comic books, I used to play football, I used to study French and I used to play video games.
When I was six years old, I didn't use to listen to music, I didn't use to have a computer, I didn't use to play basketball, I didn't use to go horse riding and I didn't use to eat spinach.

9
2 a big, blue, cotton towel
3 a pair of nice, Italian, leather shoes
4 a tall, heavy, silver candlestick
5 a cute, little, yellow, plastic duck
6 a beautiful, round, white and golden, china plate

10 (Suggested Answers)
I have got a big, square, light blue, woollen blanket on my bed.
I sometimes wear a black, leather jacket.
I have got a big, pink and yellow, canvas schoolbag.
I sometimes wear a beautiful, long, purple, cotton dress.
I have got a pretty, round, wooden jewellery box in my room.

Grammar Book Key

11
1. expensive, brown, leather
2. red, silk
3. small, round, metal lock
4. precious, old
5. little, square, wooden
6. small, green, Chinese-style

12
2. tall
3. more polluted
4. worst
5. less modern
6. famous
7. healthier
8. most beautiful
9. more comfortable
10. farther/further
11. cheaper
12. thinner

13
2. dirtier
3. the shortest
4. better
5. the most expensive
6. colder
7. the weakest

14
1. shorter than
2. clever
3. the fastest
4. heavier
5. the best
6. more, than
7. valuable
8. cheaper than
9. newer than
10. better than
11. the most
12. more beautiful than

15
1. quieter
2. noisy
3. interesting
4. more boring
5. more peaceful
6. healthier
7. less
8. safer

16
3. not as/so intelligent as dolphins
4. as hot as Greece in the summer
5. not as/so fast as going by plane
6. not as/so exciting as playing basketball
7. as kind as his brother

Unit 3

1
1. loudly
2. hard
3. heavily
4. carefully
5. violently
6. early
7. freshly
8. incredibly
9. easily
10. well

2
1. perfect
2. sweetly
3. smartly
4. quickly
5. beautiful
6. finally
7. pretty
8. generous
9. terrible
10. great
11. quietly
12. carefully
13. fluent
14. polite
15. easy

3
2. relieved
3. brightly
4. exciting
5. terrified
6. kindly
7. awful
8. excited
9. cheerfully
10. extremely

4
1. was driving, was listening
2. were gathering, was blowing
3. was having
4. wasn't paying, was talking

5
2. A: Was Jack practising the guitar at noon?
   B: Yes, he was. He was learning a new song.
3. A: Was she doing chores at 10 o' clock on Sunday morning?
   B: Yes, she was. She was doing the ironing.
4. A: Were they sleeping at midnight last night?
   B: No, they weren't. They were watching a DVD.

6
2. were playing, when, started
3. met, while, was walking
4. As, was exercising, felt
5. While, was making, was setting

7
1. woke up
2. dressed
3. left
4. was driving
5. noticed
6. was standing
7. were
8. stopped
9. was waiting
10. realised
11. made

8
1. was raining
2. were you doing
3. wasn't sleeping, called, was reading
4. was fixing, was watering
5. were trying, started
6. was feeding, heard
7. lost, fell, was riding
8. were you and Don arguing, saw
9. opened, saw
10. came, was talking
11. was making, was reading
12. went, had
13. dropped, smashed
14. wasn't working

Revision A (Units 1-3)

1
1. They
2. us
3. Stella's, yours
4. he
5. My, me

2
1. aren't
2. are
3. is
4. are
5. have
6. haven't
7. has
8. hasn't
9. can
10. can't
11. isn't

3
1. don't go
2. does
3. Do James and Lily live
4. doesn't eat
5. does Peter work
6. worries

Grammar Book Key

4 2 He **occasionally** plays video games in the evenings.
3 She is **never** rude to others.
4 They **rarely** travel abroad.
5 Do they **often** go fishing in the summer?
6 The children are **always** in bed by 9.

5 1 are you watching, spend
2 Is Martha coming, has
3 is staying, never leaves
4 do you get up, start

6 2 So   4 doesn't   6 do
3 Neither/Nor   5 does

7 1 went   5 paid   9 chose
2 gave   6 took   10 had
3 collected   7 changed   11 left
4 put   8 opened   12 brought

8 2 I didn't use to work at the post office.
3 My parents used to own a bookshop.
4 The local greengrocer's didn't use to sell organic vegetables.

9 1 was snowing, was blowing, woke up
2 was jogging, broke
3 didn't sell
4 travelled
5 was talking, were taking
6 was studying

10 1 faster   4 hotter
2 heaviest   5 the most destructive
3 highest, tall   6 more extreme

11 1 heavily, terrible   4 total, hard
2 rudely, polite   5 amazing, cheap
3 well, annoying

12 2 ~~are playing~~   play
3 ~~Are you needing~~   Do you need
4 ~~was falling~~   fell
5 ~~hasn't~~   haven't
6 ~~than~~   as
7 ~~blue, small, nice~~ nice, small, blue
8 ~~goes~~   is going

Unit 4

1 1 'll/will
2 'll/will, won't, 'll/will
3 'll/will, 'll/will, 'll/will, won't
4 'll/will, will, Will

2 2 I'll turn on the heating.
3 I'll make you a sandwich
4 She's going to travel to Italy.
5 It's going to run out of ink soon.
6 I'll turn off the music.
7 I'll take you to the doctor.

3 2 A: Is Nancy going to bring her swimming costume?
   B: Yes, she is.
   A: Is John going to bring his swimming costume?
   B: No, he isn't. He is going to bring his hiking boots.
3 A: Is Nancy going to go with her friends?
   B: Yes, she is.
   A: Is John going to go with his friends?
   B: No, he isn't. He is going to go with his family.
4 A: Is Nancy going to stay at a hotel?
   B: Yes, she is.
   A: IS John going to stay at a hotel?
   B: No, he isn't. He is going to go camping.

4 2 is going to kick   5 are going to cut
3 is going to play   6 is going to eat
4 is going to wash

5 2 'll   4 's going to
3 're going to   5 's going to

6 1 is coming   4 is flying
2 'll put on   5 leaves
3 Will you drive   6 is having

7 2 d   3 e   4 a   5 b
2 A: What will you do if you go to Paris?
   B: If I go to Paris, I'll visit the Eiffel Tower.
3 A: What will you do if you finish your homework?
   B: If I finish my homework, I'll watch TV.
4 A: What will you do if you don't feel well?
   B: If I don't feel well, I'll see a doctor.
5 A: What will you do if you earn a lot of money?
   B: If I earn a lot of money, I'll travel the world.

8 1 repairs, will/'ll go
2 visit, will/'ll play
3 bake, will/'ll bring
4 calls, will/'ll tell
5 doesn't cook, will/'ll order
6 will not/won't have, gets
7 will/'ll burn, are not/aren't
8 doesn't finish, will/'ll do
9 graduates, will/'ll travel

Grammar Book Key

9
1. When, get
2. If, will/'ll become
3. If, will not/won't pass
4. When, will/'ll start
5. will/'ll call, unless
6. When, will/'ll check
7. When, will buy
8. when, wakes up
9. Unless, arrives
10. will/'ll catch, if

10
2. won't have, until, won't be
3. before, leave
4. 'll make, after, wash
5. 'll do, before, go
6. Will you visit, while, 're
7. 'll water, when, finish
8. barks, as soon as, sees

Unit 5

1
1. some
2. any, any
3. some
4. any, some
5. some
6. any, some
7. some

2
1. some
2. any
3. much
4. a little
5. some
6. few
7. many
8. many
9. any
10. few
11. any
12. some
13. a little

3
2 – f Do you want any sugar in your coffee?
A little. Just half a teaspoonful.
3 – d Would you like mustard in your hamburger?
A little. Can I have ketchup as well?
4 – g How much money have you got?
A little. So let's not go anywhere very expensive.
5 – a Can you stay a bit longer?
A little. Then I'll have to leave and catch the bus.
6 – c Did you find any dresses you liked?
A few. But none of them were my size.
7 – e Have we got any milk left?
A little. I'll go to the shop and buy some more.
8 – h Are there any apples in the fridge?
A few. But not enough to make a pie.

4
3. some, How many do we need?
4. little, How much have we got?
5. a few, How many do we need?
6. any, How many will you buy?
7. some, How much have we got?
8. a little, How much do we need?
9. much, How much have we got?
10. any, How many will you buy?

5
1. a lot of, a few
2. many, a few
3. a little, much
4. few
5. little

6
1. bottle
2. jar
3. cup
4. box
5. bar
6. bag
7. carton
8. glass
9. slice
10. bowl

1. bowl
2. slice
3. box
4. bar
5. bag
6. bottle/glass
7. carton
8. glass/bottle
9. cup
10. jar

7 2 f   3 a   4 b   5 g   6 c   7 d

8
1. anybody
2. something
3. some
4. anything
5. any
6. No one
7. no
8. anywhere
9. Everything
10. somewhere
11. something
12. somewhere
13. everything
14. anyone

9
2. Someone/Somebody
3. no
4. every
5. anything
6. nowhere
7. anyone/anybody
8. somewhere
9. nothing
10. Some
11. Everyone/Everybody
12. no one/nobody
13. anywhere
14. some
15. any

10
1. C   2. B   3. B   4. C   5. C   6. A   7. C   8. A   9. C   10. C   11. C   12. B   13. A   14. A   15. B

Unit 6

1 2 e   3 a   4 d   5 c

2
2. A: The food is burning. Have you turned off the oven?
B: No, I haven't.
3. A: The flowers are dry. Has Ann watered them?
B: Yes, she has.
4. A: The kitchen floor is dirty. Has Scott mopped it?
B: No, he hasn't.
5. A: The baby is crying. Has Carol fed her?
B: Yes, she has.
6. A: There isn't any milk. Have Chris and Tim done the shopping?
B: No, they haven't.
7. A: Mary is on the phone. Have you told her the good news?
B: Yes, I have.

Grammar Book Key

    8 A: The fridge isn't working. Has Sam called a repairman?
        B: Yes, he/she has.
    9 A: Our guests are here. Has Bill set the table?
        B: Yes, he has.

3
1. have gone
2. have gone
3. have already been
4. have been
5. has gone
6. has been
7. have never been
8. has gone

4
2. since
3. for
4. since
5. for
6. since
7. for
8. since
9. for
10. since

5
1. since
2. for
3. since
4. for
5. for
6. since

6
1. yet
2. for
3. already
4. just
5. since
6. yet
7. already
8. for
9. since
10. just
11. already
12. for

7
1. 's just left
2. 've been playing
3. 's been doing
4. haven't spoken
5. 's been exercising
6. 's been working
7. 've been living
8. haven't finished

8
2. Sandra has been painting the picture for a month.
3. Tom has been waiting for his flight for two hours/since 8:00.
4. James and Amy have been playing with their friends for an hour.
5. The Moores have been travelling for four hours/since 7:00.
6. Roger has been playing the piano for two hours.

9
2. A: How long has Frank been working as a chef?
   B: He has been working as a chef for two months.
3. A: How long has Julie been making her own clothes?
   B: She has been making her own clothes for four years.
4. A: How long have you been reading that book?
   B: I have been reading this book since Monday.
5. A: How long has Andrew been sleeping?
   B: He has been sleeping for three hours.
6. A: How long have Helen and Carla been cooking for the party?
   B: They have been cooking for the party since 10 am.
7. A: How long has Sue been decorating the living room?
   B: She has been decorating the living room for two hours.
8. A: How long has Bob been fixing the dishwasher?
   B: He has been fixing the dishwasher since this morning.

10
1. has been practising
2. Has Jimmy been taking
3. has Jenny been writing
4. hasn't been sleeping
5. has been driving
6. Have Peter and Paul been watching
7. has been raining
8. haven't been waiting

11
2. A: Why is Grace happy?
   B: Grace is happy because she has graduated from university.
3. A: Why is Nancy tired?
   B: Nancy is tired because she has been shopping all day.
4. A: Why are Frank and Lisa excited?
   B: Frank and Lisa are excited because they have booked tickets for Hawaii.
5. A: Why is Flora smiling?
   B: Flora is smiling because she has won first prize.
6. A: Why is Andy in pain?
   B: Andy is in pain because he has broken his leg.

12
1. Have you ever been, spent
2. Did you see, haven't seen
3. Has Fred ever visited, went
4. ate, have eaten
5. Has Mum spoken, called
6. Has Michael bought, hasn't saved up
7. Have you bought, haven't found
8. Has Sara come, called, said

13
1. graduated
2. has never worked
3. decided
4. found
5. has been writing
6. has published
7. has received
8. became
9. has been working

Revision B (Units 1-6)

1
1. aren't
2. cannot
3. Have, their
4. nor
5. her
6. is

2
1. usually dresses, 's wearing
2. don't believe, 're talking
3. lives, 's spending

Grammar Book Key

4 departs, 're still packing
5 'm meeting, don't know
6 goes, 's staying

3
2 f was cooking, was listening
3 c finished, found
4 a was playing, was watching
5 b were swimming, were sunbathing, got
6 e was sleeping, woke

4
2 ✓ Did you use to travel
3 (no change possible)
4 ✓ didn't use to eat

5
1 little, round, plastic
2 new, blue, silk
3 antique, heavy, crystal
4 nice, long, purple

6
1 more
2 the tastiest
3 easy
4 more expensive
5 the most exciting

7
1 B 3 C 5 A 7 A
2 A 4 B 6 C

8
1 snows
2 don't water
3 will burn
4 are
5 turns
6 won't go

9
1 much
2 some
3 a lot of
4 a little
5 some
6 any

10
2 anything
3 someone/somebody
4 any
5 everything
6 every
7 no
8 anywhere
9 something

11
1 has not taken
2 has been walking
3 has been trying
4 has cut
5 started
6 met
7 have travelled

12
1 ours
2 bar
3 has gone to
4 easily
5 is sleeping
6 few

Unit 7

1
2 You should bring a beach umbrella or find a spot on the beach where there is shade.
3 You should wear a hat as well as sunglasses.
4 You shouldn't stay out in the sun from 11:00 to 3:00, when the sun is very strong.
5 You shouldn't go swimming immediately after eating.
6 You shouldn't swim far away from the shore.

2
1 should   5 shouldn't   9 shouldn't
2 should   6 shouldn't 10 should
3 shouldn't   7 should
4 should   8 should

3
2 e   3 a   4 b   5 c

A: Have some of the local currency with you.
B: Why?
A: You might not find banks open when you arrive.

A: Reserve a hotel room before you leave.
B: Why?
A: You could have trouble finding a place to stay.

A: Don't take any valuables with you.
B: Why?
A: Someone might steal them or you might lose them.

A: Always carry your passport with you.
B: Why?
A: You may have to prove your identity.

4
1 have to   4 must
2 didn't have to   5 had to
3 don't have to   6 mustn't

5

Waiters ...	must	mustn't	don't have to
know all the dishes on the menu	✓		
be slow with the customer's order		✓	
be very tall			✓
forget what the customer ordered		✓	
make sure the customer is satisfied	✓		
be good cooks			✓

Waiters must know all the dishes on the menu.
Waiters mustn't be slow with the customer's order.
Waiters don't have to be very tall.
Waiters mustn't forget what the customer ordered.
Waiters must make sure the customer is satisfied.
Waiters don't have to be good cooks.

6
3 You mustn't smoke in public places. It's against the law.
4 Sara must study hard. She has a test tomorrow.
5 We don't need to go to bed early. It's Sunday tomorrow.
6 You mustn't talk to strangers. It isn't safe.
7 You mustn't eat fatty foods. They're unhealthy.

Grammar Book Key

7
1. can't
2. Am I allowed to
3. could
4. was finally able to
5. Can
6. couldn't
7. could
8. wasn't able to

8 1 C 2 C 3 A 4 B 5 C 6 A

9
2. Put
3. Be
4. Bring
5. Don't talk
6. Don't bite
7. Try
8. Don't cry

Unit 8

1
2. will
3. is
4. has
5. was
6. will
7. was
8. should

2
1. with
2. with
3. by
4. by
5. by
6. with

3
2. The keys couldn't be found anywhere.
3. A fantastic party was arranged by George and Sarah.
4. The dog is walked twice a day.
5. Public transport is often used by young people.
6. The new menswear line was launched by Cherry Lane.
7. My wedding dress might be designed by Claire.
8. The children will be entertained by the clown.

4
1. be delivered
2. was built
3. was given
4. will be put
5. is held
6. was written
7. will be torn down
8. is done

5
2. The house will be cleaned next weekend.
3. The fence was painted last Tuesday.
4. The invitations were sent yesterday.
5. The painting will be displayed in an exhibition next month.
6. These old toys could be given to a charity.
7. The rubbish has to be taken out daily.
8. The washing-up is done by Joseph every night.

6
2. the store will be closed
3. Volunteers are needed
4. Speed is checked by radar
5. English teachers are wanted

7
2. d Penicillin was discovered by Sir Alexander Fleming.
3. g Rockets will be used by people to travel further in space in the future.
4. h Buildings are designed by architects.
5. f Millions of people were entertained by Charlie Chaplin.
6. a Chips can be fried in a frying pan.
7. e Endangered species must be saved.
8. b Eggs are laid by hens.

8
2. No. The window may be left as it is.
3. Yes. A fireplace was built last week.
4. No. A new sofa will be bought next month.
5. No. A mirror was hung over the fireplace.
6. Yes. The shelves were put up yesterday.
7. The carpets were laid two days ago.
8. No. The air conditioning will be installed next Tuesday.

9
1. was named
2. are connected
3. was designed
4. was completed
5. was made
6. was added
7. was built
8. was placed
9. be seen

10
1. was seriously damaged
2. was hit
3. were injured
4. are still trapped
5. be struck
6. will be given
7. will be collected

11
1. The hotel was booked two months ago.
2. Two hundred guests are expected.
3. The menu was designed by a top chef.
4. Vegetarian options are included.
5. Flowers will be delivered on Saturday morning.
6. A professional DJ might be hired for the music.

12
2. must be worn
3. are treated
4. shouldn't be kept
5. will be visited
6. was baked
7. was stolen
8. is made

Unit 9

1
1. had broken into
2. hadn't finished
3. had written
4. had ended
5. hadn't seen
6. Had the kids gone
7. had heard
8. had planned
9. had lost
10. had already started

2 **Suggested answers**

By the time I was seven, I had started school, too.
By the time Michael was seven, he hadn't travelled by train.
By the time I was seven, I had travelled by train lots of times.

Grammar Book Key

By the time Michael was seven, he had learned how to read.
By the time I was seven, I had also learned how to read.
By the time Michael was seven, he hadn't used a computer.
By the time I was seven, I hadn't used a computer either.

3 2 By the time Ivan was 12 years old, he had learned to speak English.
3 Tim had lived in London before he moved to Paris.
4 Mum had cooked dinner by the time I came home from school.
5 She went to work as soon as she had had breakfast.
6 After Susan had tried on lots of dresses, she decided to buy the green one.
7 Jason had failed his driving test three times before he finally got his licence.
8 After Wendy had finished the washing-up, she played chess.

4 2 had rained   7 had snowed
3 had forgotten   8 hadn't slept
4 had borrowed   9 had watched
5 had walked   10 had won
6 hadn't cleaned

5 2 A: Had Fay fed the dog?
    B: Yes, she had.
3 A: Had Fay paid the electricity bill?
    B: No, she hadn't.
4 A: Had Fay visited her grandparents?
    B: Yes, she had.
5 A: Had Fay cleaned her room?
    B: No, she hadn't.
6 A: Had Fay done the ironing?
    B: Yes, she had.
7 A: Had Fay been to the greengrocer's?
    B: No, she hadn't.

6 1 did you do   11 was driving
2 went   12 ran
3 stayed   13 happened
4 were having   14 turned
5 stole   15 had already climbed
6 Did they catch   16 ran into
7 had driven   17 was driving
8 arrived   18 saw
9 crashed   19 Did you give
10 did you manage

7 1 d   2 e   3 a   4 b   5 c

8 2 paid, had arrived/arrived
3 was walking, rang
4 had made, arrived
5 was watering/watered, came

9 1 came, realised, had forgotten
2 wanted, got, noticed, hadn't put
3 went, had watched
4 started, had graduated
5 had just mopped, spilt/spilled

10 1 arrived   5 had eaten
2 had finished   6 was having
3 was sweeping   7 was slicing
4 had brushed   8 heard

11 2 would buy   8 would miss
3 studied   9 would become
4 bought   10 wouldn't order
5 tried   11 recycled
6 would/could get 12 would/could eat
7 were

12 2 she would go roller-blading
3 he would buy a laptop
4 she would grow her own vegetables
5 he would go skiing
6 he would cycle to the office
7 she would go shopping
8 he would adopt a dog

13 2 h   4 i   6 e   8 c   10 d
3 a   5 b   7 j   9 g

14 If I studied Medicine, I would become a doctor.
If I became a doctor, I would work for Doctors Without Borders.
If I worked for Doctors Without Borders, I would travel around the world.
If I travelled around the world, I would treat sick people from different parts of the world.

15 2 If I were you, I would go to bed early.
3 If I were you, I would get a job.
4 If I were you, I would make a sandwich.
5 If I were you, I would join a gym.
6 If I were you, I would take French lessons.
7 If I were you, I wouldn't eat it.
8 If I were you, I would go for a walk.

16 (Suggested answers)
1 I would do better in my exams.
2 I would buy a pizza.

Grammar Book Key

    3 I would buy a car.
    4 I would see a doctor.
    5 I would go swimming every day.
    6 I would take them a gift.
    7 I would move to Spain.
    8 I would be very happy.

17
1 yourselves   5 herself
2 ourselves   6 itself
3 himself   7 myself
4 themselves   8 yourself

18
1 herself   5 ourselves
2 yourselves   6 himself
3 itself   7 themselves
4 yourself   8 myself

Revision C (Units 1-9)

1
1 b   3 b   5 a   7 b
2 a   4 a   6 b

2
1 C   3 C   5 A   7 C
2 A   4 B   6 B   8 B

3
1 more impressive   4 oldest
2 more   5 biggest
3 tall   6 most mysterious

4
1 many, lots of, anyone
2 some, a little
3 somewhere, any
4 very little, much
5 anything, everything

5
2 don't have to leave early
3 might stop soon
4 mustn't talk during the exam
5 should start exercising

6
1 was running   4 did you get up
2 had never been   5 were watching
3 hadn't/had not finished   6 had already served

7
1 ourselves   4 herself
2 myself   5 themselves
3 himself   6 yourself

8
1 would you do   6 would find
2 were   7 wouldn't say
3 had   8 knew
4 would join   9 did
5 organised   10 wouldn't be

9
1 Will you do   3 put
2 didn't have   4 finish

10
1 The cinema tickets were booked by Sally.
2 Flowers have been cut from our garden.
3 Perhaps a playground will be built in the park.
4 The ironing is done by Betty every Sunday.
5 Your old newspapers should be recycled.
6 The Jetsons haven't been invited to the party yet.

11
2 ~~will get~~   gets
3 ~~leave~~   are leaving
4 ~~if~~   when
5 ~~must~~ or ~~yesterday~~   had to or today/tomorrow
6 ~~loaf~~ or ~~cake~~   piece/slice or bread
7 ~~gone~~   been
8 ~~Not~~   Don't
9 ~~was completing~~   had completed
10 ~~saw~~   see
11 ~~had waited~~   have been waiting
12 ~~step~~   are going to step

Unit 10

1
1 too   4 too   7 enough
2 enough   5 too   8 enough
3 enough   6 enough

2
3 too difficult   5 too small
4 fast enough   6 enough money

3
2 c   4 a   6 h   8 d
3 g   5 b   7 f

4
1 teacher   3 photographer   5 carpenter
2 doctor   4 painter   6 tailor

2 A doctor is someone who takes care of sick people.
3 A photographer is someone who takes photographs.
4 A painter is someone who paints pictures.
5 A carpenter is someone who makes things from wood.
6 A tailor is someone who makes clothes.

5
2 a   4 h   6 g   8 c
3 d   5 f   7 b

2 An umbrella is something which shelters you from the rain.
3 A fire extinguisher is something which you put out fires with.
4 A spoon is something which you eat your soup with.
5 A fan is something which keeps you cool.

Grammar Book Key

6. A tape measure is something which you measure things with.
7. A pair of scissors is something which you cut things with.
8. A hanger is something which you hang clothes on.

6
1. which
2. who
3. which
4. where
5. where
6. who

7
2. which/that
3. which/that
4. whose
5. who/that
6. who/that
7. which/that
8. whose
9. which/that
10. who/that

8
2. d, whose
3. a, which/that
4. c, who/that
5. f, where
6. e, whose

9
1. B
2. B
3. C
4. A
5. C
6. B
7. A
8. A

10
2. e
3. d
4. f
5. a
6. c

11
1. who
2. where
3. whose
4. who
5. who
6. which

12
2. That's the boy whose sister moved abroad.
3. This is the dress which/that I bought yesterday.
4. That's the gym which/that has a swimming pool.
5. Tom is the boy whose mum is our English teacher.
6. This is the shop where I buy my clothes.

13
1. to give
2. listening
3. seeing
4. do
5. to buy
6. helping
7. park
8. to lend
9. reading
10. to go

14
2. d
3. i
4. a
5. h
6. j
7. b
8. e
9. f
10. g

15
1. to ask
2. to book
3. to have
4. go
5. to eat
6. paying
7. telling
8. to enjoy
9. to celebrate
10. know

16
1. to feed
2. cooking
3. buying
4. to admire
5. to water
6. to take
7. to pack
8. meeting

17
2. Andrew enjoys flying kites.
3. My father can't stand snorkelling.
4. Carol doesn't mind making her bed.
5. Most people hate visiting the dentist.
6. Pamela doesn't like doing the housework.
7. She loves solving Maths problems.
8. I like eating chocolate.

18
1. going, doing
2. trying, breaking
3. to keep, to take
4. feeling, to have
5. to say, waiting

19
1. to write
2. meeting
3. laugh
4. to get
5. to be
6. know
7. come
8. hearing

20 (Suggested answers)
1. the, —, —, —
2. The, —, —
3. —, the, the
4. —, —, the
5. the, —
6. —, the
7. the

21
1. —
2. —
3. the
4. the
5. —
6. —
7. the

Unit 11

1
1. said
2. told
3. say
4. said
5. said
6. told
7. said
8. told
9. said
10. told
11. said
12. said
13. said

2
2. his, him
3. she, me/us, her
4. she, her
5. they, their
6. his, him

3
2. She said (that) she had lived in Montreal for ten years.
3. Dad said (that) we were leaving in June.
4. Annie said (that) she had forgotten to take the dog for a walk.
5. Ben said (that) he was going to work till late that night.
6. He said (that) he always woke up early on Mondays.
7. She said (that) the Browns were looking for a new house.
8. He said to Carol (that) they had bought a flat two months before.
9. He said to Sam (that) he would paint the garage the following week.
10. He said to Julie (that) he couldn't go to the gym with her.

4
2. He said (that) penguins can't fly. Tenses do not change – general truth.
3. She said (that) they were watching a film on TV then/at the time.
4. He says (that) it will be sunny tomorrow. Tenses do not change – the introductory verb is in the present simple.

171

Grammar Book Key

  5 He said (that) they had served dinner by 9:00. Tenses do not change – the main verb is in the past perfect.
  6 The teacher said (that) mammals feed their babies on milk. Tenses do not change – general truth.

5
  2 My mother asked what I wanted for lunch.
  3 Harry asked me if/whether I would take him to the beach on Saturday.
  4 Brad asked me if/whether I had seen his dog.
  5 My father asked us where we were going.
  6 Ian asked Mary how tall she was.
  7 Eve asked if/whether I had bought any bread.
  8 He asked Kate if she was going to go out.

6
  1 how many people he had invited
  2 what time the party would begin
  3 who was doing the cooking
  4 if/whether there was going to be a DJ
  5 if/whether he had ordered a birthday cake

7
  2 what time the accident had taken place
  3 who had called the police
  4 if/whether anyone had been hurt
  5 how many cars had been involved

8
  1 why the princess was laughing
  2 he had forgotten (that) they had a meeting that day
  3 if/whether she was OK
  4 (that) she would be there around 11:00
  5 what he had written
  6 (that) they had won the race

9
  1 had graduated
  2 I was not
  3 would visit them
  4 she had never been
  5 was fixing the car
  6 are very intelligent
  7 if I liked
  8 had invited him

10
  2 ~~said~~ told/said to
  3 ~~was the supermarket~~ the supermarket was
  4 ~~told to~~ said to/told
  5 ~~said us~~ told us/said to us
  6 ~~last week~~ the week before
  7 ~~did he want~~ he wanted
  8 ~~told~~ said/told us

Unit 12

1
  2 to pass her a bowl
  3 to get her some eggs from the fridge
  4 to roll out the mixture
  5 to place it into the baking tin and then put it in the oven
  6 not to forget to close the oven door
  7 to tidy the kitchen

2
  2 Mr Cross asked his dogsitter not to give the dog any sweets.
  3 Mr Cross asked his dogsitter to take the dog for a walk three times a day.
  4 Mr Cross asked his dogsitter not to let the dog bark all the time.
  5 Mr Cross asked his dogsitter to keep the dog's bowl full of water.
  6 Mr Cross asked his dogsitter to feed the dog twice a day.

3
  1 What a
  2 How
  3 such a
  4 such an
  5 How
  6 so
  7 How
  8 such
  9 such
  10 What an
  11 so
  12 What

4
  1 such a
  2 How
  3 How
  4 so
  5 such
  6 What

5
  2 How gracefully they dance!
  3 She is so busy!
  4 What a nice haircut she has!
  5 This is such an adorable kitten!

6
  1 aren't you
  2 does he
  3 did you
  4 does she
  5 hasn't she
  6 won't you
  7 have you
  8 hasn't she
  9 can't I
  10 isn't she
  11 will you
  12 don't you
  13 isn't it
  14 isn't there
  15 aren't I

7
  1 shall we
  2 have you
  3 didn't he
  4 do you
  5 isn't she
  6 aren't we
  7 aren't there
  8 aren't I
  9 hadn't they
  10 did you
  11 is she
  12 haven't you
  13 will/won't you
  14 will it
  15 can she
  16 don't they

8
  2 is it, it isn't
  3 have you, I haven't
  4 aren't you, I am
  5 haven't we, you/we have
  6 has she, she hasn't
  7 is she, she isn't
  8 doesn't she, she does
  9 wasn't he, he was
  10 has he, he hasn't

Grammar Book Key

11 can't she, she can
12 won't she, she will
13 isn't it, it is
14 didn't they, they did
15 are there, there aren't

9
1 isn't she (↘)
2 has she (↘)
3 isn't it (↗)
4 don't you (↘)
5 isn't he (↘)
6 were you (↗)
7 hadn't she (↘)
8 has he (↗)
9 didn't they (↗)
10 can't she (↘)
11 aren't I (↘)
12 are you (↗)
13 did she (↗)
14 isn't it (↘)
15 hasn't she (↗)

10 (Suggested answers)
A: You're going to the gym later, aren't you?
B: Yes, I am.
A: You have got blue eyes, haven't you?
B: No, I haven't.
A: You can't speak Spanish, can you?
B: Yes, I can.
A: You live near a park, don't you?
B: Yes, I do.
A: You've been to Spain, haven't you?
B: No, I haven't.

Revision D (Units 1-12)

1
1 've been staying
2 love
3 'm writing
4 'm enjoying
5 've been sightseeing
6 'm going
7 Have you received

2
1 hadn't slept
2 was talking
3 had already done
4 did you buy
5 had

3
1 Is Judy coming, 'll call
2 're going to be late, leaves
3 'm going to look
4 'll fail

4
1 adventurous
2 more relaxing
3 the best
4 the most enjoyable
5 quieter
6 cheaper
7 the greatest

5
1 wouldn't buy
2 follow
3 didn't have
4 'll be
5 'll visit

6 1 C 2 C 3 B 4 C 5 A 6 B

7
1 could
2 don't have to
3 are allowed to
4 can
5 must
6 mustn't
7 shouldn't
8 need

8
1 Millions of trees are cut down by loggers every year.
2 The Guggenheim Museum was designed by the architect Frank Lloyd Wright.
3 A new section will be added to the local art gallery.
4 The campsite must be kept clean (by everyone).
5 A new web designer has been hired by the company.

9
1 The dodo was a kind of bird which/that disappeared centuries ago.
2 Adam is my neighbour who/that looks after my dog when I'm away.
3 Frangelico's is an Italian restaurant where you can have great pizza.
4 J.K. Rowling is an author whose books are popular.
5 I know a shop where we can find nice clothes.

10
1 light
2 starting
3 hiking
4 leave
5 to live
6 being
7 breaking
8 to buy

11
1 Ann said to Tom (that) she had bought him a present the day before/the previous day.
2 She told me (that) they were spending that weekend at their summer house.
3 Ben asked me what Kim's new address was.
4 Kate asked George if/whether he had ever been to the opera.
5 The teacher told the noisy student to leave the room immediately.
6 He asked me to help him set up his email account.

12
2 ~~myself~~ — herself
3 ~~happily~~ — happy
4 ~~enough~~ — too
5 ~~USA~~ — the USA
6 ~~will close~~ — close
7 ~~gone~~ — been
8 ~~do~~ — will/won't
9 ~~so~~ — nor/neither
10 ~~How~~ — What a

Progress Tests Key

Progress Test A (Units 1-3)

1	C	6	C	11	B	16	A
2	B	7	A	12	A	17	B
3	A	8	A	13	C	18	B
4	A	9	B	14	B	19	C
5	A	10	A	15	C	20	A

Progress Test B (Units 4-6)

1	C	6	C	11	A	16	C
2	A	7	B	12	C	17	B
3	B	8	C	13	B	18	B
4	A	9	A	14	C	19	C
5	B	10	A	15	B	20	A

Progress Test C (Units 1-6)

1	B	6	B	11	A	16	C
2	C	7	B	12	B	17	C
3	B	8	A	13	C	18	A
4	A	9	C	14	B	19	B
5	A	10	C	15	C	20	C

Progress Test D (Units 7-9)

1	C	6	B	11	C	16	A
2	B	7	B	12	A	17	A
3	C	8	B	13	C	18	B
4	B	9	A	14	A	19	C
5	A	10	B	15	C	20	B

Progress Test E (Units 10-12)

1	A	6	C	11	C	16	C
2	B	7	C	12	A	17	A
3	B	8	C	13	A	18	B
4	A	9	B	14	B	19	B
5	B	10	A	15	A	20	A

Progress Test F (Units 1-12)

1	A	6	A	11	A	16	A
2	C	7	B	12	B	17	A
3	B	8	A	13	C	18	B
4	C	9	A	14	A	19	C
5	B	10	C	15	B	20	A